1978

Coleridge the Moralist

Coleridge the Moralist

Laurence S. Lockridge

CORNELL UNIVERSITY PRESS

Ithaca and London

Cornell University Press gratefully acknowledges a grant from the Andrew W. Mellon Foundation that aided in bringing this book to publication.

First published 1977 by Cornell University Press.
Published in the United Kingdom by Cornell University Press Ltd., 2-4 Brook Street, London W1Y 1AA.

International Standard Book Number 0-8014-1065-7
Library of Congress Catalog Card Number 77-3120

Printed in the United States of America
by York Composition Co., Inc.

Librarians: Library of Congress cataloging information appears on the last page of the book.

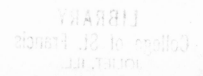

To Susan

Contents

Acknowledgments

Without the help of many people, this work would have all the coherence of Coleridge's Gutch Memorandum Notebook. Jerome Buckley has been most generous in his support, scholarly and personal; his uncommon willingness to encourage and advise has made this book possible. I am grateful to Kathleen Coburn for her help in my research at the British Library and at the Victoria University Library, Toronto, and for her permission to read Volume Three of the *Notebooks* prior to its publication. David Perkins introduced me to Coleridge studies in a provocative seminar, to which Walter Jackson Bate was an occasional contributor. Henry Auster, Donald Davie, Thomas R. Edwards, Paul Fussell, Michael Goldman, and Richard Haven read the manuscript and offered useful suggestions at crucial moments. Thomas McFarland, who also read it, kindly consulted with me on the Opus Maximum manuscript. I am only one of many to have profited from the good assistance of Marilyn Gaull, who has done so much to promote Romantics studies. Martin Mueller has been generous with his Greek, Latin, and German erudition. Kenneth Lewes gave the manuscript a close and sensitive reading and made many challenging criticisms. I am pleased to acknowledge the contribution of Barbra Apfelbaum, whose fine critical eye and gracious support were indispensable.

I wish to thank the Danforth Foundation and the Rutgers Research Council for financial assistance, and to acknowledge the cooperation of trustees and librarians at the British Library, Victoria University Library, the Henry W. and Albert A. Berg Collection of the New York Public Library, the Archibald Stevens Alexander Library of Rutgers University, the Houghton and Widener libraries of Harvard University, the Lilly Library of Indiana University, and the Henry E. Huntington Library.

I wish to extend special thanks to Russell Noyes, who has watched over my progress as a Romantics scholar and whose warmth and accomplishment are a lasting inspiration.

The greatest assistance has come from Susan Fox, whose intelligence as poet, teacher, and scholar I have discovered anew at every moment in writing this book. Her acute and sympathetic counsel has kept me at the task and has held at bay such Coleridgean vices as indolence, dread, and shifting from one side of the footpath to the other. She gave me the presumption to undertake it, the will to bring it to completion.

L.S.L.

New York, New York

Abbreviations Used in Notes

AR   *Aids to Reflection*. London: Taylor and Hessey, 1825.

BL   *Biographia Literaria*. Edited by John Shawcross. 2 vols. London: Oxford University Press, 1907.

CL   *Collected Letters of Samuel Taylor Coleridge*. Edited by Earl Leslie Griggs. 6 vols. Oxford: Clarendon Press, 1956–1971.

EOT   *Essays on His Own Times*. Edited by Sara Coleridge. 3 vols. London: William Pickering, 1850.

F   *The Friend*. Edited by Barbara E. Rooke. 2 vols. Princeton: Princeton University Press, 1969.

IS   *Inquiring Spirit*. Edited by Kathleen Coburn. London: Routledge & Kegan Paul, 1951.

N   *The Notebooks of Samuel Taylor Coleridge*. Edited by Kathleen Coburn. Bollingen Series 50. 3 vols. New York: Pantheon, 1957, 1961; Princeton: Princeton University Press, 1973.

OM   Opus Maximum MS. Victoria University Library. Toronto.

PL   *The Philosophical Lectures of Samuel Taylor Coleridge*. Edited by Kathleen Coburn. London: Pilot Press, 1949.

Grateful acknowledgment is made for the use of copyright material from these and other works. Mr. A. H. B. Coleridge of Devonshire has granted permission to quote from unpublished Coleridge manuscript material at the British Library, Victoria University Library, Toronto, and the New York Public Library. Permission to quote from the Opus Maximum manuscript, the 1799 College Commemoration Sermon, and other unpublished materials has been granted by Victoria University Library; from the as yet unpublished Coleridge notebooks by the British Library; and from MS Notebook 29 and MS Notebook Q, by the Henry W. and Albert A. Berg Collection, the New York Public Library, and the Astor, Lenox, and Tilden Foundations. Permission to reprint quotations from the following works has been granted by Princeton University Press and by Routledge & Kegan Paul: *The Notebooks of Samuel Taylor Coleridge*, ed. Kathleen Coburn (Bollingen Series L, Volume 1 © 1957 by Bollingen Foundation, Volume 2 © 1961 by Bollingen Foundation, Volume 3 © 1973 by Princeton University Press); *The Collected Works of Samuel Taylor Coleridge*, Kathleen Coburn, General Editor; Bart Winer, Associate Editor: Volume 1, *Lectures 1795: On Politics and Religion*, ed. Lewis Patton and Peter Mann (© 1971 by Routledge & Kegan Paul Ltd.), Volume 2, *The Watchman*, ed. Lewis Patton (© 1970 by Routledge & Kegan Paul Ltd.), Volume 4, *The Friend*, ed. Barbara E. Rooke (© 1969 by Routledge & Kegan Paul Ltd.), Volume 6, *Lay Sermons*, ed. R. J. White (© 1972 by Routledge & Kegan Paul Ltd.). Permission to reprint quotations from the following works has been granted by Oxford University Press: *The Complete Poetical Works of Samuel Taylor Coleridge*, ed. Ernest Hartley Coleridge (2 volumes, 1912); William Wordsworth, *The Prelude*, ed. Ernest de Selincourt (1933); *Collected Letters of Samuel Taylor Coleridge*, ed. Earl Leslie Griggs (6 volumes, 1956, 1959, 1971).

Coleridge the Moralist

Introduction

This book is a construction and analysis of Coleridge's moral thought as it revealed itself in his life, theories, and poetry. Coleridge himself initiated many of the moral judgments that were passed on him during his lifetime and have persisted to this day. Wordsworth wrote in 1809 that Coleridge was suffering from "a derangement in his intellectual and moral constitution—In fact he has no voluntary power of mind whatsoever, nor is he capable of acting under any *constraint* of duty or moral obligation."[1] Whether or not the diagnosis was correct, it was close to Coleridge's advertising of his own problem, as when he complained that duty acted on him as a "narcotic" and not as a "stimulant." Hazlitt picked up a familiar refrain in 1816 when he wrote of Coleridge, "All that he does or thinks is involuntary; even his perversity and self-will are so. They are nothing but a necessity of yielding to the slightest motive. Everlasting inconsequen-

1. *The Letters of William and Dorothy Wordsworth: The Middle Years,* ed. Ernest de Selincourt, rev. Mary Moorman, 2d ed., II (Oxford: Clarendon Press, 1969), 352.

tiality marks all that he does."[2] Coleridge himself had said it better in 1802 when he wrote to Godwin: "I am a Starling self-incaged, & always in the Moult, & my whole Note is, Tomorrow, & tomorrow, & tomorrow. The same causes, that have robbed me to so great a degree of the self-impelling self-directing Principle, have deprived me too of the due powers of Resistances to Impulses from without. If I might so say, I am, as an *acting* man, a creature of mere Impact."[3] That Coleridge was so often judged in such terms resulted, in part, from his own insistent and vocal self-criticism, from his own moral formulations.

He was dismayed when his critics took him so literally. Had he not preempted criticism by having the first word? Should they not have known better than to oversimplify his case, and in so moralistic a spirit? Matthew Arnold declared, as if there could be no dispute, that Coleridge "had no morals."[4] This would have seemed to Coleridge a naive equation of moral struggle with lack of morals. He was certainly not a paragon, but he thought those who tried to be, such as his problematic friend Robert Southey, were likely to be vapid and mean-spirited. Far from lacking a moral sense, he thought he had one too highly refined, one which, challenged by his opium addiction and other lapses, left him paralyzed and guilt-ridden. His celebrated lack of will was more precisely a failure to execute the schemes of a prodigious will. Was it not his ambition to write the massive "Organum verè Organum" on the Logos?

2. Unsigned review, *Examiner*, 8 Sept. 1816, in *Coleridge: The Critical Heritage*, ed. J. R. de J. Jackson (New York: Barnes & Noble, 1970), p. 251. The editor comments that the review seems to have been based on a prospectus of *The Statesman's Manual* (1816) and was published prior to that work.

3. *CL*, II, 782.

4. *Lectures and Essays in Criticism*, in *Complete Prose Works of Matthew Arnold*, ed. R. H. Super, III (Ann Arbor: University of Michigan Press, 1962), 189.

The man with no morals has left a large body of writing that treats both personally and theoretically the paradoxes of moral struggle. These writings have never been discussed, except in passing, in any book on Coleridge.[5] They are scattered throughout the corpus to an even greater degree, perhaps, than his writings on other subjects. They will show he was one of the great British moralists; though I will not argue the matter, I suspect that in many ways he may have been the greatest. The material I have collected is simply different in kind from that of any other British moralist. It offers an uncommon density of argument and imaginative application of theory to moral situation, a richness of language, an awareness of the close relationship of morality and psychology, and a sensitivity to moral ambiguity and evil, which more than compensate for his failure ever to consolidate his thinking in any single, immediately coherent document.

Coleridge's personality has not yet received the attention paid Byron's. His was every bit as subversive in its time, however, and it is Coleridge's personality more than Byron's that anticipated what were to become the concerns of twentieth-century letters. When he said that he had always been "preyed on by some Dread" and when he gave theoretical primacy to moral awareness over all other forms of consciousness, he

5. John H. Muirhead devotes a chapter to Coleridge's moral thought in *Coleridge as Philosopher* (London: George Allen & Unwin, 1930), pp. 136–161. Basil Willey ends his book, *The English Moralists* (London: Chatto & Windus, 1964), with a chapter on Coleridge. Gian N. G. Orsini discusses the relationship of Coleridge's moral thought to German sources, particularly Kant, in *Coleridge and German Idealism* (Carbonville and Edwardsville: Southern Illinois University Press, 1969), pp. 149–159. Elio Chinol treats the subject in *Il Pensiero di S. T. Coleridge* (Venice: Neri Pozza, 1953), pp. 99–122. Two books with bearing on the topic, Anthony John Harding's *Coleridge and the Idea of Love* (London: Cambridge University Press, 1974) and Michael G. Cooke's *The Romantic Will* (New Haven: Yale University Press, 1976), appeared too recently to be instrumental in my argument. The notes to this volume can only begin to specify my indebtedness to the many other Coleridge scholars who have, at times, dealt with moral issues.

was making explicit the components of a now all-too-familiar malaise. The guilt, mental paralysis, and sense of emptiness he complained of are now often taken to be proof of one's abiding moral sensitivity, and we may see moral struggle where an earlier age saw obtuseness or lack of will.

There is ironically a danger that we will now find Coleridge too accessible. If one removes the manifest "bump of reverence" that Owen Barfield reminds us of in *What Coleridge Thought* (1971), Coleridge can be made to fit too easily the contours of our self-image.[6] But there were limits to how far he would go in fashioning a new sensibility. Though I will emphasize those elements that seem prophetic of modern concerns, I will not ignore his habitual withdrawal into orthodoxy. The Coleridgean drama embraced both the resolve to stay on an alien perimeter and the tendency to withdraw into structures of church, state, and social role. To be true to the subject, one must keep in mind that the same person who wrote *The Ancient Mariner* also wrote that high-minded and dreary sermon, *The Statesman's Manual, or The Bible the Best Guide to Political Skill and Foresight* (1816).

The contrasting works most important to this study, however, are *The Ancient Mariner* and "Frost at Midnight." He wrote the latter poem in early 1798, near the end of the time he was composing *The Ancient Mariner*, and the simple question I pose is how the same mind could have conceived both poems. *The Ancient Mariner* seems to be telling us something about human depravity, "Frost at Midnight" something about good will and love, and both seem eminently "Coleridgean." Coleridge thought his capacity for love persisted even when he found no worthy objects for it; and yet we know that his nightmare world was a vision of his own interior as demonic and alien. Theoretical formulation of the link between the two poems and between these two views of himself is found in his moral discussions.

6. *What Coleridge Thought* (Middletown, Conn.: Wesleyan University Press, 1971), pp. 10–11.

These discussions grew out of the corrosive psychological self-analysis that Coleridge helped to bring into vogue. It is easy to say that he missed more about himself than he discovered; but he knew that he did not wish to know the complete truth about himself, and in a coded notebook entry he went so far as to say he would not undertake to know what on some level he already *knew:* "Thought becomes a thing when it acts" on one's full consciousness, and "therefore I dread to tell my whole & true case," because to do so would make it "a substantial reality/I want it to remain a thought in which I may be deceived whole [?wholly]."[7] In another entry, on the false relief of laudanum, he describes

the knowlege, and the fear, and the remorse, and the wilful turning away of the eye to dreams imperfect, that float like broken foam on the sense of reality, and only distract not hide it, these are the wretched & sole Comforts, or rather these are the hard prices, by which the Armistice is accompanied & paid for. O who shall deliver me from the Body of this Death? Meanwhile the habit of inward Brooding daily makes it harder to confess the Thing, I am, to any one—least of all to those, whom I most love & who most love me—.[8]

Coleridge recognized that the self cannot see itself in absolute perspective. He spoke of the "slippery and protean nature of all self-inquisition."[9] Self-consciousness became an "eddy without progression," an incapacitating though worthy affliction that reminded him that he was a poet and prevented him

7. *N*, II, 3045. Coleridge occasionally resorted to cryptogram in his notebooks when confiding something personally painful or compromising. See *N*, II, Appendix C.

8. *N*, II, 3078. Coleridge's punctuation is followed throughout. He thinks of punctuation "not as logical Symbols, but rather as dramatic *directions* representing the process of Thinking & Speaking conjointly—" (*N*, III, 3504). With this in mind, I have preserved most dashes and slashes occurring at the end of quotations, but, for the sake of fluidity, have not employed end ellipses.

9. *CL*, V, 182.

from writing poetry. More basic than the fear the self was defrauded when it looked inward was the fear there was no self to examine. He thought of himself as a huge vegetable full of "pith," not a tree of solid wood; he looked at his son, Hartley, and saw a "moral *Idiocy*" that signified no self at all.

The extraordinary paradoxes of the man have perhaps still not been adequately appreciated. We find a thinker whose most fundamental idea was organic unity, yet who seemed incapable of systematic exposition. He must have been able to detect the lack of continuity. He could see what a mish-mash Chapter X of the *Biographia Literaria* (1817) was, and he called it "a chapter of digression and anecdotes, as an interlude preceding that on the nature and genesis of the imagination or plastic power—." One can guess the apologetic title was conceived after the composition. The organization, or lack of it, does not differ in kind from that found in most of his prose. There was some kind of regressive dialectic at work in him; he became more and more the thing he did not wish to be. The more he described the whole personality, the more he experienced dissociation; the more he knew that he ought to do something, the less he felt so inclined. The more he dreamt of a grand synthesis, the more he scattered his reflections in notebooks, letters, marginalia. It was as if he reminded himself of his own powers by crippling them.

Thomas Carlyle's most brilliant of Victorian portraits, the one of Coleridge in *The Life of John Sterling* (1851), tells us of a man both crippled and foolish.

The good man, he was now getting old, towards sixty perhaps; and gave you the idea of a life that had been full of sufferings; a life heavy-laden, half-vanquished, still swimming painfully in seas of manifold physical and other bewilderment. Brow and head were round, and of massive weight, but the face was flabby and irresolute. The deep eyes, of a light hazel, were as full of sorrow as of inspiration; confused pain looked mildly from them, as in a kind of mild astonishment. The whole figure and air, good and amiable otherwise, might be called flabby and irresolute; expressive of weakness under possibility of strength.[10]

He had been a suffering but self-indulgent man, Carlyle argues, who had lacked the daring to pass beyond alienation to "the new firm lands of Faith beyond," and who had become arrested in an unholy alliance of Kantian categories and the English Church. The portrait is so inspired that its ridicule nearly convinces. One might protest that even the Sage of Highgate must have been a windbag and humbug at times, and that in being so he provided the deft Carlyle with excellent raw material. But the acuity of the portrait is that it reaches into Coleridge's worst fear about himself—his fear he was a fraud, a coward, an indolent, unloved, physically repulsive oddity.

The main thrust of Carlyle's attack is that Coleridge had an "eye to discern the divineness of the Heaven's splendours and lightnings, the insatiable wish to revel in their godlike radiances and brilliances; but no heart to front the scathing terrors of them, which is the first condition of your conquering an abiding place there."[11] Coleridge himself spoke frequently of his "cowardice of moral Pain," which meshes with Carlyle's comment that "harsh pain, danger, necessity, slavish harnessed toil, were of all things abhorrent to him." Whether or not he had the courage to seek them out, however, he was confronted with "scathing terrors" that did not promise an empyrean on the other side of apocalypse; they were hellish through and through. He would have been the first to admit the Everlasting Yea was beyond his powers. He construed his problem in terms similar to those of Carlyle's portrait. The object of living, in moral and not supernatural terms, was the evolution of the self through and beyond

10. *Coleridge the Talker*, ed. Richard Armour and Raymond Howes (Ithaca: Cornell University Press, 1940), p. 114.
11. Ibid., p. 120.

alienation. It was an evolution he could better describe than manifest. Faced with terror and profound alienation, he knew he had not found an "abiding place" anywhere. Carlyle's portrait errs in underestimating the genuine torment of the man, for which there is more than ample evidence, and in overestimating the personal blindness. Erring mostly in degree, it still has the accuracy of caricature. Here too, Coleridge himself was acutely aware of the frustrating inadequacy of one's "representative image," the self one presents to others. His uneasy public stance always indicated a clumsiness in disposing of that image, as he tried not to lend himself to caricature.

As moralist, Coleridge sought to describe what it is that the real self, and not merely its representative, may become. The self was a prisoner waiting to be led out; it was also a willing prisoner, which would sabotage its own release. The question of freedom was most fundamental, and I will take it up in Chapter 1. Coleridge felt himself hemmed in by a society of accusers who judged him by his foolish gestures, and not by any intuition of his interior self. The interior self cooperated, though, by being its own accuser and jailer. Coleridge has left us a close and affecting analysis of these mind-forged manacles that is extraordinary in its modernity.

This imprisonment entailed for him a lifelong search for a principle of freedom. He postulated that below the reaches of human consciousness was the abysmal will, which was the ground of the self's individuality and freedom, and also, horribly, of its evil. Coleridge's "indolence" seemed almost commendable in that it was a check on the evil potential, but it was also a parody of real moral endeavor and its own worst punishment. The free act entailed, after all, a moral risk that had to be embraced.

More accessible to human consciousness were imagination and feeling, two powers of self that, in their promise of enriched consciousness, adumbrated the human or moral potential. Coleridge's emphasis in moral concerns lay here—and his giving up on imagination and feeling was always symptomatic of his giving up on moral solutions. He hoped in theory and in his life to develop and preserve the integrity of the conscious, feeling, imagining self. This development required a full commitment to nature, the phenomenal world, the stage on which the human drama would be enacted. The mysterious will forever below the range of human consciousness was the threat to the moral life that had somehow to be accommodated at the same time that it provided the motive power of all human action.

Coleridge questioned whether the release of the self would come through obedience to duty. As we will see in Chapter 2, he found in Kant an impressive moral formula, but he did not temperamentally or even theoretically approve of it. What he called Kant's "giant's hand" appeared to operate a "Procrustean bed" and to ignore, even threaten, the psychological health that Coleridge thought so essential to any moral formulation. The conscience, as rational inquisitor, could remind one so much of human fallibility that its purpose could be subverted. Even worse, one who took the dictates of conscience too literally could himself become the Procrustes, the "conscientious persecutor." This emphasis on duty became for Coleridge a false and destructive one and ironically tended only to confirm his imprisonment.

In Chapter 3 I will show that he explored another procedure for freeing the self, a procedure that emphasized not constraints put upon us but our inherent powers. The true moral task was the "nurture and evolution of humanity." I will piece together his significant writings on "self-realization," the best available word for it and one that he himself probably introduced into the language. He described the evolution of the inherent powers of the self from childhood to adulthood. What was required was the active and, in a Coleridgean sense, organic appropriation of ideas, actions, environment. The education (or as he was fond of saying, the "educing") of the self had as its goal a self-government best witnessed in the person with "method." Yet love, the most intense exercise of feeling and imagination, was the necessary complement of self-government; the greatest development of the sense of self came ironically through yielding that self to another. One would have no sense of self until one had defined one's relation to other selves; this sense of relatedness was conscience developed beyond its narrow punitive function.

In Chapter 4 my approach is more historical. Hobbes, the Cambridge Platonists, Shaftesbury, Joseph Butler, Hartley, Paley, Bentham, and Godwin were read by Coleridge extensively and, as usual, unsystematically. I will place him in the British moral tradition and define his unique contribution to it. He rejected morality based on sensibility as self-indulgent and lacking in moral imagination, but he also criticized those rationalists who, like Godwin, exaggerated the power of reason alone to guide the conduct of life. His self-realization theory combined with his view of the will's depravity constituted what I call "Romantic humanism," an unconventional and indeed unstable formulation of the humanist perspective. It was unconventional because, unlike the British humanist tradition, it did not minimize human depravity; instead it took the evil potential itself as the source of energy by means of which liberal and humane consciousness was activated. It was unstable because these powers of consciousness remained vulnerable to the inscrutable and evil will above which they were suspended.

The enlarged human potential that was the basis of Coleridge's humanism made the rival British traditions of hedonism, egoism, and utilitarianism seem reductive and falsely confident. His critique of the rival tradition was extensive and has not yet been adequately explored. I will suggest, among other things, what he learned from his enemies. He himself achieved something of the reconciliation of "Coleridgean" and "Benthamite" perspectives that John Stuart Mill thought was missing in nineteenth-century thought.

In Chapter 5 I will develop the argument in the Opus Maximum manuscript concerning the nature and justification of moral judgments. Coleridge thought them to be neither the assertions based on "facts" of the empiricists nor the analytic truths of the rationalists. A moral judgment could not be proved; rather it was a "postulate of humanity," which could certainly be denied but not without compromising humanity itself. I argue that Coleridge himself found it difficult, both in theory and practice, to affirm consistently these postulates of humanity. His philosophy of religion implied the "collapse of the ethical." His politics often reasserted the primacy of prudence over morality, in ways that compromised his stance as moral critic of the times. And his plagiarisms were his most telling demonstration of moral collapse, here into the living contradiction of bad faith.

Coleridge's critique of British ethics in the Opus Maximum manuscript was often equal in thoroughness and acumen to the kind of analysis one finds in the traditional line of British moral philosophers, past and present. But his moral writings tended elsewhere to be more literary, personal, and tentative than those of the moral philosophers. Though much of the material I present will be of interest to a historian of moral philosophy, I think of Coleridge not as a "moral philosopher" but as a "moralist," who addressed himself passionately and informally to moral problems.

My method of presentation is thematic and structural, not chronological, except where chronology seems necessary to make a developmental point. Often I will silently link passages written several years apart. Coleridge thought Godwin, though he disagreed with him in substance, had demonstrated the "most important of all important Truths, that Morality might be built up on it's own foundation, like a Castle built *from* the rock & *on* the rock."[12] I will attempt to build this structure using the fragments that Coleridge left in such disorder. The fragments suggest their own interrelationships. Though I will locate him in the larger context of British and Continental moralism, past and present, my main interest is the continuities and paradoxes of his own vision as he confronted the daily terror of Life-in-Death.

Hazlitt wrote that the *Biographia Literaria* was "an elaborate account of what he has undertaken to do, because no one else has been able to do it—and an *assumption* that he has done it, because he has undertaken it. If the will were to go for the deed, and to be confident were to be wise, he would indeed be the prince of philosophers."[13] Anyone who has worked with Coleridge is aware of the problems. Nobody really *reads* him in any normal sense of the word; instead one sifts through the brilliant wreckage and salvages bits and pieces. The challenge to the scholar is, in the first place, to find the material. This alone can take years since much of it even today is unpublished and spread out in many libraries.[14] Then too, Coleridge would explore any idea by multiple extensions, analogies, queries, seeming irrelevancies; one must extract the pertinent material without doing too much violence to context. It is exhilarating to discover the way these pieces on any particular topic build and comment on one another, although one hardly finds total consistency among them. I have tried to

12. *CL*, III, 313–314.

13. Unsigned review, *Edinburgh Review*, 28 (1817), in *The Critical Heritage*, p. 304.

14. This problem will be remedied by the new edition, *The Collected Works of Samuel Taylor Coleridge*, under the general editorship of Kathleen Coburn. As Bollingen Series 75, it is published in the United States by Princeton University Press, and in Great Britain by Routledge & Kegan Paul. It will include such previously unpublished works as the Logic, the Opus Maximum, and the Marginalia. As of the present writing, the *Lectures 1795*, *The Watchman*, *The Friend*, and the *Lay Sermons* have appeared.

preserve the most provocative thought, not necessarily the thought most representative of or most consistent with ideas expressed elsewhere.

The structure of this book follows informally, chapter by chapter, some of the major traditional topics of moral philosophy: freedom, duty, virtue, historical and comparative analysis, and metaethics. The structure also attempts a dramatic representation of Coleridge's mind. One should not so much write on Coleridge as with him—his was a mind always in motion, always, as he might say, thinking in some direction. His fear about his own work was that it eddied and did not strictly progress. While I have attempted to find principles of progression in his thought, I have not pursued them to hard-and-fast conclusions that would do violence to the speculative tenor of his mind. An eddying effect will, I hope, to some extent remain, for he was often circling around his own conclusions, often qualifying or undercutting them. This will be especially noticeable in Chapter 2, where his reflections on duty will be seen to be tenuous and contradictory, though a definite direction will emerge. To give a sense of the rich contexts of his thought, I have sometimes quoted more than the argument would strictly require. The quotation is desirable, too, because much of it either has not been in the public domain or has never been singled out for special comment. Not the least important service one can do Coleridge is to find an appropriate context for his scattered insights.

Hazlitt's comment really missed the point. Coleridge was hardly "confident," as the pomposity of his public stance revealed. And paradoxically his nonachievement sits there as the thing he achieved. The antibook that is the *Biographia Literaria*, the scores of notebooks and other manuscripts, the letters and marginalia, the journalism, add up to a corpus to compare with that of our most prolific men of letters. What the corpus needs is critical and scholarly rehabilitation.

I have also been conscious that I am dealing with a drug

addict and a thief. Drug addiction can explain so many of Coleridge's problems and ideas that it ends up explaining few of them. Perhaps most of his talk about will, habit, indolence, dread, and nightmares stemmed from his experience with opium. But it should be remembered that many of these problems were evident before he became addicted. Alethea Hayter in *Opium and the Romantic Imagination* (1968) concludes that "opium was a symptom, not a cause of Coleridge's tragedy."[15] In addition, we would be committing a kind of genetic fallacy to insist that our knowledge of origins explains (or explains away) the categories to which Coleridge in his agony made reference. Dread has still the properties of dread, even when it can be said to have been drug-induced.

His plagiarisms, back in the news again, present a more serious obstacle. I discuss the difficult moral and scholarly questions they raise elsewhere in the book and will make only a procedural point here. The argument that his plagiarisms are, as Thomas McFarland suggests, symptomatic of an unusual "mode of composition" or a form of "compulsive intellectual symbiosis" would permit one to assume it is still Coleridge who is doing the thinking even when he is borrowing from the works of other thinkers.[16] Although such an argument would only with difficulty cover such a gross and extended theft as that from Schelling in *Biographia Literaria*, Chapter XII, which smacks more of parasitism than symbiosis, it is useful when applied to sources that Coleridge has absorbed and redirected in some way, and it eases one's anxieties about employing material that might ultimately be traced to German sources not yet identified. I do sometimes use material that strongly suggests origins in Kant, Schiller, Fichte, Schelling,

15. *Opium and the Romantic Imagination* (Berkeley and Los Angeles: University of California Press, 1968), p. 207.
16. *Coleridge and the Pantheist Tradition* (Oxford: Clarendon Press, 1969), pp. xxiii–xl; 1–52.

or the Englishman Joseph Butler when the material supplies a bridge in exposition or when it demonstrates a significant affinity with such thinkers. What I would emphasize is that my focus is Coleridge's sense of his own moral situation; the source of his commentary is therefore less important than its application, his own or mine. A passage borrowed or stolen can occasionally illuminate his own moral universe. Some passages employed here will sooner or later be found out as plagiarisms, but their usefulness will not necessarily be undermined.

Even so, I have tried to exclude most, if not all, material that I have found to be directly translated or paraphrased from works of other thinkers, or that to my ear lacks a true Coleridgean accent. I draw most frequently on the private notebooks and letters, and here the plagiarism question is not so menacing. Coleridge was closer to his own experience in them, his writing more spontaneous and more analytic than in works he published. It is true that even in notebooks and letters he sometimes translated from other writers without acknowledgment, as if hoping that future editors would not track him and the discourse could be claimed as his own. And perhaps, in a complex psychological process embracing both intense intellectual sympathy and self-delusion or even bad faith, he could think of this material as his own if only he so appropriated it. But there is much genuine Coleridgeana that remains if one is attuned to the distinguishing qualities of his thought—its speculative probing, rhetorical color, subtlety, and its rootedness in personal experience.

Carlyle thought Coleridge lost in a Kantian "haze-world" of "vacant air-castles and dim-melting ghosts and shadows."[17] A glance at the prospectus of the "Logosophia," with its talk of the "Tetractys," the "Pleroma," and the "Jahagean Ult et Penult with great augmentations," might suggest he was lost

17. *Coleridge the Talker*, p. 117.

in something far worse.[18] A contemporary critic complained
that Coleridge's abstractions turned "all things into their
ghosts." We will find, however, that much of his moral writing, especially in the notebooks and letters, has a concreteness
and animation that remind us time and again of the man who
wrote "Frost at Midnight." The material I shall consider
originated in immediate moral problems, and although the
experiential promptly led him to the theoretical, the theory
was given ballast and color by the urgency with which he
sought contexts for his irresolution, dread, and physical suffering. Part of this tangibility came from the development of a
rhetoric of psychological description. He wrote analytically,
and ruthlessly, of the dynamics of envy, projection, and need
of confirmation. The transcendental mode of description derived from Kantian epistemology retained its hold on him, but
Coleridge came into his own when he observed the human
mind and behavior directly. Kant he thought a wretched
psychologist, while Fichte's "crude *Egoismus*" or "I itself I"
yielded only to a "super-postulate," "X,Y,Z, the God Infini-
tivus!" Coleridge's inquiring eye and rhetorical daring invested
his own ghosts and shadows with an engaging tangibility.

18. *Coleridge on Logic and Learning*, ed. Alice D. Snyder (New Haven:
Yale University Press, 1929), pp. 3–8.

1 | Freedom and Alienation

The Loveless Observer

Coleridge's notebooks and letters reveal alienation in his relationship with Wordsworth long before and after their official falling out and reconciliation in the years 1810–1812. In 1803 he writes to Thomas Poole, a tanner in Nether Stowey and his close friend, that Wordsworth has undergone "Self-involution" from "living wholly among *Devotees—*having every the minutest Thing, almost his very Eating & Drinking, done for him by his Sister, or Wife." He trembles "lest a Film should rise, and thicken on [Wordsworth's] moral Eye."[1] And in 1819 he complains of Wordsworth that the "admiration of his writings is not merely his gauge of men's *taste*—he reads it as the index of their *moral* character. And yet in his commendations of friend or contemporary, this same Atticus [Wordsworth] is as nice and deliberate a *balancer* as if his judgment were at that moment passing its ordeal before the eye of the whole world." Wordsworth's "chilly, doubting, qualifying *wiseness*" had, in the early years of their friendship, discouraged his own literary efforts

1. *CL*, II, 1013.

when he had requested his friend's judgment with "a timid
and almost girlish bashfulness." Instead of encouragement the
author of "Tintern Abbey" had, in his qualified praise, sent
him the kind of "sand-blast from the desert, that in its passage
shrivels up the very marrow in a man's bones, like the pith
in a baked quill!"[2]

The "Film" over the "moral Eye" suggests that, for
Coleridge, Wordsworth's error is as much one of perception
as of feeling. He knows the film threatens to cover his own
eye, too. Of his unhappy marriage to Sarah Fricker, he writes,
"To love is to know, at least, to imagine that you *know* (not
always indeed *understand*); what is strange to you, you cannot love (Mrs. C. is to me all *strange*, & the Terra incognita
always lies near to or under the frozen Poles)."[3]

The refusal to know and the act of passing judgment are,
for Coleridge, closely related means of alienation. Judgment
of another, whether of character, intellect, or work, implies
distance between judge and defendant; to be judged is to be
alienated. In passing judgment, one can only with great
difficulty avoid a blurring of vision by envy. A very
young Coleridge writes with a solemnity beyond his
years, "When a man is attempting to describe another's
character, he may be right or he may be wrong—but in one
thing he will always succeed, in describing himself. If he
express simple approbation, he praises from a consciousness of
possession—If he approve with admiration, from a consciousness of deficiency."[4] In the first instance he "egotizes in
tuism." The moral judge proves his own pharisaical cruelty

2. *CL*, IV, 966–968. Titus Pomponius Atticus (109–32 B.C.), friend and
correspondent of Cicero, is known for his political neutrality, prudence, and
is indeed a "balancer" in his judgments. Coleridge disguises very thinly in
this letter the fact that he is speaking of his relationship with Wordsworth.
The fairness, or lack of it, of his own sometimes harsh judgments of
Wordsworth is not my concern in this study.

3. *N*, I, 1816.
4. *N*, I, 74.

when he feels "joy at a Vice in another which by point blank Contrast reminds him of a Pet Virtue in himself."[5] The mechanism of envy works deviously to make the egotist less despised than the flatterer. An otherwise offensive egotist may in fact impart pleasure to others, because he unintentionally reminds them of their own prudent humility. "Envy is sopped by the unamiable Light, in which the Egoist shews himself—." As for flatterers—and Coleridge has himself in mind—"the violence of praise is an effort of the mind to disguise its own envy from its own consciousness—& to bully it out of their Hearts by giving it the loud *Lie*, which is retorted from within by the whispered—you lie."[6]

In these and comparable passages, Coleridge describes a relentlessly nasty world in which one's best-intentioned gestures are likely to be tainted with bad faith. The eye we cast on others is, alternately, malign and disingenuous. The Mariner's shooting of the Albatross, whatever one says about his motive, is overt, tangible, and direct—so much so that it does not altogether typify Coleridge's vision of how evil is manifested. More illustrative would be the shrunken serpent's eyes of Geraldine, full of malice and dread. Evil is discovered in subtle intonation or the head's tilt. Coleridge's analysis of gesture and intonation in his notebooks is nearly Jamesian, and, with regard to what is behind gesture, he would fear the truth of the Prince's melodramatic declaration to Maggie in *The Golden Bowl* that "everything's terrible, *cara*—in the heart of man."

In friendship he finds a protective cover from unspecified harm, but the cover itself always threatens to become the enemy. To Poole he writes, "Indeed my Soul seems so mantled & wrapped round by your Love & Esteem, that even a dream of losing but the smallest fragment of it makes me shiver—as tho' some tender part of my Nature were left un-

5. *N*, I, 1816.
6. *N*, II, 2830.

covered & in nakedness.''[7] The fragility of the bond and his own vulnerability are offered up as temptations to betrayal. One senses his extravagant professions of love for such men as Poole, Southey, and Wordsworth mask a hostility; on some level he wishes to bring about a rupture. Whatever the psychological sources of his behavior may be, the patterns are clear. The threat of alienation, of the death of friendship, is countered by either apology or hostility. He fears that his sins of omission—his failure to answer letters promptly, for example—may be misinterpreted as positive violations of a bond. His letters often open with an elaborate and awkward apology for his unreliability in all matters except constancy of love. Apology is indeed his most characteristic mode of address. On the other hand, his sensitivity to any coolness in another's regard can prompt the hostility that we have seen in his relationship with Wordsworth. Apology and hostility are two sides of the same coin: both are fearful expressions of the chronic and generalized sense of guilt that persists even when he declares himself not guilty and free of malice.

In freeing his accuser's moral eye of its film, Coleridge hopes to remove a stimulus of his own guilt. He analyzes the perceptual error that must be corrected:

Hazlitt has made the usual mistake of loveless observers—Seeing weakness on the surface of a Character, he has made no allowance for Strength: tho' seeing characteristic Strength (as in Wordsworth) he would be apt enough to make allowance for undiscovered but certainly existing Weakness—In every character, that commands notice or is worth talking of, there is Strength & Weakness, tho' in very different ratios of inversion.[8]

Liberality in moral judgment should be based not on sentimental presumption of innocence but on imaginative assessment. The occluded eye of the loveless observer is likely to

7. *CL*, I, 235.
8. *N*, I, 624.

be mistaken because it is unimaginative. In notebook entries of 1803 he explores in some detail his own misjudgments of Southey and Wordsworth. With regard to his earlier falling out with Southey over Pantisocracy (the utopian community on the Susquehanna that the two planned in 1794–1795), he reasons that instead of taking offense at "one or two *Actions*," he should have asked what Southey is "on the whole." Actions of Southey that had been prompted merely by passion and lack of prudence had been magnified "under the warping and amid the bedimming Glare of [Coleridge's own] Passion," and Southey had fallen into the same error regarding Coleridge. This reflection gives rise to his often reiterated distinction between doing and being. One should ask "not what C[oleridge] has *done?* or what has S[outhey]*done?*—but— . . . what *is* C. or S. on the whole?"[9] (He later decides that what Southey is, is, if anything, inferior to what he does.)[10]

The entry on Wordsworth explores the difficulty of "calmness and dispassionateness" in moral judgment. Its proposed cure for alienation is roughly the same. Instead of becoming obsessed with another's faults, we should ask, "What *is* [he] on the whole?" We should understand his "whole complex mixed character . . . intensifying our Love of the Good in it, & making up our mind to the Faulty."[11] One should consider the whole "person," not the misleading evidence he may give of himself in gesture or act.

But Coleridge's sketch of the conflict itself in this entry is more vivid than this somewhat pious resolution, and it suggests why alienation is not so easily remedied. The scene is a distressing one of two great poets in silent, envious competition. His latent "envy" confronts Wordsworth's deep-seated "selfishness." Coleridge thinks he has sacrificed his own poetic career for Wordsworth's. Wordsworth, while taking Cole-

9. *N*, I, 1605.
10. See, e.g., *N*, I, 1815; *CL*, III, 316.
11. *N*, I, 1606; cf. *N*, III, 4188.

ridge's adulation as his due, has not reciprocated. Coleridge records, though the context is uncertain, Wordsworth's "*up, askance, pig look, in the Boat &c.*" When he hears thereafter that Wordsworth has written a good new poem, he feels "little ugly Touchlets of Pain & Shrinkings Back at the Heart." The source of this envy, or, as he thinks it may be, simple resentment, is diagnosed as "the instinct of all fine minds to *totalize*—to make a *perfectly congruous whole* of every character—& a pain at the being obliged to admit incongruities." Just as Prime Minister Pitt's occasional wisdom had caused him pain by subverting his "*Theory* of Pitt's Contemptibility," so Wordsworth's fine new poem had seemed to undercut Coleridge's for the moment negative "totalization" of Wordsworth in terms of his selfishness. Envy, or "Pain at the excellence of another," arises not from the excellence itself but from its incongruity with a preconception. And the envy grows with the inevitable sense of "Self-degradation" relative to the object, a sense that is all the more powerful because obscure.[12]

Coleridge elsewhere describes this envy or resentment as "an uneasiness at a non-harmony, the wish not to see any thing admirable where you find, especially in the moral character, any thing low or contemptible, and the consequent wish to avoid the struggle within."[13] He would like to think the novelist Richardson nothing but contemptible: "His mind is so very vile a mind—so oozy, hypocritical, praise-mad, canting, envious, concupiscent." Yet he admits with vexation that he must admire many things about Richardson. If his conception of Richardson does not grow to accommodate the con-

12. Ibid. Coleridge is, of course, more likely to totalize in the opposite direction when judging Wordsworth. In 1819 he speaks of his former error: he "had separated [Wordsworth's] excellencies from their dross or alloy, in the glow of his attachment, and then recast them into a whole, in the mould of his own imagination" (*CL*, IV, 968).

13. *N*, II, 2471.

tradiction, if he does not engage in the "struggle within," then he is unjust and unimaginative. The act of totalizing is dangerously related to one's capacity for abstraction; it is "an instinct of all fine minds." To predicate a person in his totality in terms of a few hints of his nature abstracted from the "obscure Manifold" of characteristics that makes up the personality is an act of intelligence that ironically narrows one's moral view. As Blake might suggest, generalization and restriction are products of the same debased mentality, and both are opposed to imagination. Any one action, when *"plucked out* of its Context," defines the person "only in your mind by virtue of Abstraction; but in the man himself is only a basin full of the Billow rolling on."[14]

The impulse to totalize is at the bottom not only of moral judgment but of action generally. Coleridge notes he adds wood to the fire to make it more symmetrical, even if he is going to bed and no longer needs a fire. Anything "fragmentary" prompts one to an act of completion, and one's powers of abstraction can go against all reason.[15]

What is the distinction between "totalizing" another person and judging him "on the whole"? In either case, one makes a total evaluation of another, but totalizing is a brutal, reductive procedure based on fragmentary knowledge, while judging on the whole is a way of making allowances and of imagining his "whole contexture."[16] It is difficult, however, to maintain the distinction in theory and in practice. Coleridge admits that even in love relationships the essence of another person can be only surmised; manifestations of self in gesture and intonation are most of what we have to go on. Judging someone "on the whole" or sensing out his "whole contexture" is more imaginative, tactful, and intuitive than "totalizing,"

14. *N*, III, 3419.
15. *N*, II, 2414.
16. *N*, III, 3419.

but it is also more demanding and precarious, and it too is necessarily based on imperfect, fragmentary knowledge. His prescription for liberalizing judgment is perilously close to the problem it would solve. Wordsworth's treatment of him suggests that liberality is tenuous and short-lived; even the philosophic poet ceases to make allowances and to regard him with a kind and open eye. Because imagination is such a fragile component of judgment and such a labor too, the moral view easily narrows. Judgment inherently tends to reduce personality to the confines of mere interpretation.

Indeed Coleridge senses the ubiquity of the loveless observer—it is what we all tend to be. We allow the moral eye to harden and occlude, to lose its imaginative power, because reductionism in judgment of others is the simplest way of warding off encroachments on our intellectual and moral complacency, on what he calls "the sphere of easy comprehension." The loveless observer is there implicity on almost every page Coleridge writes. The history of his closest friendships insists on the primacy of alienation, as if friendship were defined largely in terms of its contrary. The broken friendship of Sir Leoline and Lord Roland de Vaux of Tryermaine in *Christabel* becomes an essential metaphor of Coleridge's life. After his breakup in 1810 with the Wordsworths, he reviews the history of their friendship with great bitterness. Wordsworth's love for him has dulled because he "has procured other enthusiastic admirers" and has subsequently subjected Coleridge to unfair moral scrutiny, an "accursed analysis or rather anatomy of a friend's Character, as if a human Soul were made like a watch, or loved for this & that tangible & verbally expressible quality!"[17] It may be that he checked love himself by his "want of reliability in little things, the infliction of little pains," but, more important, his very devotion to his friend blinded Wordsworth and destroyed

17. *N*, III, 3991.

the friendship. The dismal import of this failure is that "even in Love & Friendship we gain only what we arrogate."[18] He recalls that as many as twelve years earlier his friends had closed ranks against him. The "rascal" and "madman" Charles Lloyd—a minor novelist whom he had tutored and who parodied him in his novel, *Edmund Oliver* (1798)—may have tried to convince the Wordsworths that he, Coleridge, was a "villain." By such tactics, Lloyd had driven him to opium for the first time, he says, and had prevented him from finishing his *Christabel.* (They were to become somewhat reconciled later.) But outrageously the Wordsworths seemed at this time to defend Lloyd against him. If they did not perceive his inner worth and literary genius, who would?

Alienation seems all the more likely when individuality is highly developed, when one is distinguishable from others. "It is a sense of *Un*kind, and not the mere negation but the positive opposite of the sense of *kind.* Alienation, aggravated now by fear, now by contempt, and not seldom by a mixture of both, aversion, hatred, enmity, are so many successive shapes of its growth and metamorphosis." What one does not understand, one cannot love, and how is understanding possible? One who sees genius in another "either recognizes it as a projected Form of his own Being, that moves before him with a Glory round its head, or recoils from it as from a Spectre."[19] Coleridge feels himself to be such a gifted spectre surrounded by those who recoil. He often speaks as if he has been unjustly singled out and as if he alone is still able and willing to love, but he knows that everyone is subject to the other's "look," as Sartre would say, that does not penetrate beyond one's uncertain efforts at self-representation. The society of

18. *N,* III, 4006.
19. *AR,* p. 220n. I use a first edition presentation copy of *Aids to Reflection,* now in the Berg Collection, which Coleridge gave to John Hookham Frere. This copy contains marginalia and many textual emendations in Coleridge's hand. The latter are incorporated when pertinent.

loveless observers sits in judgment on each of us, but ironically it is made up of all of us: we cooperate in framing the cruel arena in which human action is to be played out and judged.

Moral Necrosis

The cruelty of the moral judge is no more disturbing than the infirmity of the moral agent. Coleridge's plea to the loveless observer is that he judge according to what one is, not what one does. He tells his disapproving and literal-minded older brother George that all would be forgiven if only his inner life, or what he *is*, could be made manifest.[20] But his distinction between being and doing tends, he discovers, only to compound the incrimination, because, as he might have guessed, he is even less successful at being than at doing.

Coleridge develops and refines that aspect of the Romantic ego which applauds its own hidden fertility and sustains the mystique by a certain retentiveness. He takes pride in thinking that he is *"wiser behind* the Curtain than his own actions before it."[21] The person he calls the *"commanding* genius" reveals a weakness in his very need to step before the curtain; he lacks the "creative, and self-sufficing power of absolute *Genius*."[22] Because the commanding genius requires confirmation of his powers, he builds temples and aqueducts, or goes on the rampage like Napoleon and Nimrod.[23] But the absolute genius rests "content between thought and reality, as it were in an intermundium of which [his] own living spirit supplies the *substance*, and [his] imagination the ever-varying *form*."[24] At times Coleridge would like to think himself one of these and would carry the self-sufficiency of noble conception to

20. *CL*, III, 102–105.
21. *N*, I, 1602.
22. *BL*, I, 20.
23. *Lay Sermons*, ed. R. J. White (Princeton: Princeton University Press, 1972), pp. 65–66.
24. *BL*, I, 20.

its logical extreme: he would luxuriate in nonachievement and lack of public applause. The discrepancy between promise and fulfillment would be annulled if the promise were all. Is it not comforting that there is "something inherently mean in action"?[25]

But his reluctant admiration of those who do act, or of those who, like Wordsworth, do write poems, is everywhere apparent. He solves no problems with this suspect distinction between "commanding" and "absolute" genius. Even absolute geniuses require confirmation of their powers in, for example, art or literature. Coleridge quotes from his own works frequently as if to convince himself that they do exist. Self-sufficiency is probably a specious ideal. For better or worse, we all need "outward confirmation of that *something* within us, which is our *very self*."[26]

The manner in which the need is manifested does, to be sure, relate directly to the sense of one's own powers, and the weaker one feels oneself to be, the more one is likely to seek confirmation both compulsively and fraudulently. Coleridge's seeming vanity is, he thinks, related to his fear that he has no real power within; to exact confirmation from others, he maneuvers them into praising him. His "faulty delight in being beloved" is perceived incorrectly by others as vanity. The fraud in his demand for love is that he offers no particularized love in return but only a generally extended sympathy.[27] This same need of confirmation deriving from internal weakness can take an opposite turn and produce a villainous *"ossificatio cordis"*:

The ultimate or predisposing Cause a restless craving videri quam esse, even to themselves—2. thence a seeking from others for a confirmation of that, which, if it had had any other existence but in the Wish, would like Light have been it's own & only possible

25. *N*, I, 1072.
26. *BL*, II, 188.
27. *CL*, II, 959; cf. *CL*, III, 277.

Evidence—3. thence unquiet & insolent Positiveness, the infallible
symptom, because the necessary Effect, of inward Uncertainty—
4. and thence as the proximate Causes, pompous and irritable
Vanity, with vindictive *Envy*, which before the occasional
Looking-Glass of Conscience tries to hide it's own face from it's
own Eyes by assuming the Mask of *Contempt*.[28]

Though Coleridge is not expressly referring to himself here,
he could probably so describe the growth of his resentment
toward Wordsworth, who he thinks has refused to confirm
him in his powers. The need for confirmation afflicts just
about everybody, even the seemingly self-sufficient, and
whatever form it takes qualitatively—whether political rampage, the compulsive demands one makes on others in social
contexts, artistic creativity, or love—it insists on active commitment to the external world.

That "being" is primary and "doing" only epiphenomenal
is at times a useful fiction for Coleridge and one that inspires
his early poem, "Reflections on Having Left a Place of Retirement" (1795). But even here he perceives the retreat from
active life as a temptation to be resisted. From the top of a
"bare bleak mountain speckled thin with sheep," the poet has
an intense vision of God's omnipresence and exclaims, "No
wish profan'd my overwhelmed heart. / Blest hour! It was a
luxury,—to Be!" William Empson and David Pirie, in their
selection of Coleridge's poetry, delete the remainder of the
poem, which indeed degenerates into moralizing on how such
"feelings all too delicate for use" must give way to positive
action.[29] The fact that the poem degenerates when it turns to
the rigors of doing may indicate the poet's inability to conceive of himself as doer. But he does argue, nonetheless, that

28. *CL*, III, 529–530.
29. *Coleridge's Verse: A Selection*, ed. William Empson and David Pirie
(London: Faber & Faber, 1972), pp. 104–105, 218–219. Quotation of poetry
and plays, unless otherwise indicated, is from *The Complete Poetical Works
of Samuel Taylor Coleridge*, ed. Ernest Hartley Coleridge, 2 vols. (Oxford:
Clarendon Press, 1912; rpt. 1962).

the romance of "being" contains a real and complex threat. Here the threat is the extinction of moral energy and the injustice of dreaming away the "entrusted hours / On rose-leaf beds," while others toil and bleed in social and political struggle.

In 1799 he writes from Germany to his wife (perhaps reassuring her that a vacation away from her is not all delectation) that his "Imagination is tired, down, flat and powerless. . . . I have, at times, experienced such an extinction of *Light* in my mind, I have been so forsaken by all the *forms* and *colourings* of Existence, as if the *organs* of Life had been dried up; as if only simple BEING remained, blind and stagnant!" He feels himself companionless in a desert of sand "where his weary Halloos drop down in the air without an Echo."[30] Deprived of the kinds of confirmation that imaginative investment in his surroundings would provide, he experiences the stagnation of being. The "absolute Genius," who could subsist on imagination alone, is a fiction—the imagination would soon go flat if not actively engaged in and nourished by nature and the society of other human beings.

It might surprise one to hear from the thinker who has given us so many of our notions of Romantic consciousness that "Thought or the Act of Thinking has no *transitive* power," and that the mind in itself does not create a "drawbridge from Thought to Thing."[31] He complains of his habit of never finishing but always advertising his literary projects, wasting his life away, "always *going to* do that & that, *never set down at it.*"[32] The "Act of Thinking," which is what in part he means by an elevated state of "being," mocks its own insufficiency if it sets nothing in motion. Such a *"thinking disease"* produces mere self-involuting feelings "instead of Actions, Realizations, *things* done & as such externalized &

30. *CL*, I, 470–471.
31. *N*, I, 1500n.
32. *N*, II, 2361.

remembered. On such meagre Diet as ⟨feelings evaporated⟩ embryos interrupted in their progress to Birth, no moral Being ever became Healthy."[33] That the "Act of Thinking has no *transitive* power" extends sadly to self-analysis, which alone cannot provide a link between being and doing. He notes "the Evil (occasionally) of Acknowlegment by its affinity with Acquiescence."[34] A hypochondriacal or intemperate person makes "endless fruitless Memoranda" advising himself against bad habits, but this only results in the "lazy Contemplation of his own Weakness."[35] Self-knowledge of this kind substitutes for making amends, and consciousness remains divorced from will: "Video meliora proboque, / Deteriora sequor—was the motto of my Life."[36]

An inability to unite being and doing is therefore the broad diagnosis Coleridge offers for his indolence and unhappiness. Socrates, he writes, postulates the highest state as one in which "perfect Well-*being* is one and the same with well-*doing.* . . . A spirit made perfect is a self-ponent act, in which (or whom) the Difference of Being and Doing ceases."[37] And he writes that "to be and to act, two in Intellect . . . but one in essence = to rest and to move."[38] His ideal self-image is the pyramid, which, though absolutely steadfast, contains the suggestion of movement, of "positive rapid energy."[39] The pyramid is the emblem he uses in conjunction with those emphatic initials, STC, the "estecean," which suggests the Greek for "he hath stood."[40] He admires those who command reality, who can stand with self-sufficiency and shape them-

33. *N*, III, 4012. The brackets indicate a passage added later by Coleridge.
34. *N*, II, 2458.
35. *N*, II, 2474.
36. *CL*, IV, 626. "I see and approve of the better, and I follow the worse."
37. *PL*, p. 409n34.
38. *N*, II, 2342.
39. *N*, II, 2343.
40. Έστησε. See *Poetical Works*, I, 453; *CL*, II, 867. E. L. Griggs notes that the Greek is more properly translated, "He hath placed."

selves in the "self-ponent act" to their conception of themselves. Perhaps others should judge us for what we are, not what we do, but in the healthy moral agent there is a continuity between being and doing. In a notebook entry of 1830 he writes that morality is a "*doing* of truth, a conversion or rather a completion of Light into Life."[41] Such, at least, is his account of the *healthy* moral agent in general terms. This ideal stands in monumental mockery, however, of his own fractured reality. And we shall see that he clings, in spite of everything, to the notion that there is something almost meritorious in the state of dissociation that brings on all his suffering. To unite being and doing is, of course, an incontrovertible ideal, but he continues to find something perversely moral in paralysis.

As evidence of this ambivalence, one notes that he tends to regard his madness as of a high order—it is almost honorable. In the *Lectures 1795* and in *The Friend* (1809–1810) he tells the Allegory of the Maddening Rain. This rain falls on all inhabitants of an imaginary Eden except the prophet who, on the word of a mysterious voice, predicted the rain and who alone has sought refuge in a cave. Upon leaving the cave he witnesses wretched people worshipping minerals, murdering and enslaving one another. Since the sane prophet stands motionless through all this, the others inquire of each other, "Who is this man? how strangely he looks! how wild!—a worthless idler! exclaims one: assuredly, a very dangerous

41. MS Notebook 47 (1830), f. 34ᵛ. Coleridge kept notebooks for most of his adult life. Kathleen Coburn has been preparing an extraordinary edition of them, already cited. The third volume, published in 1973, brings the edition up through March, 1819. The earliest entries date from 1794. The British Library has the notebooks of the series 1–55, with the important exception of Notebook 29, which is in the possession of the Berg Collection, New York Public Library. The Berg Collection also has Notebook Q (1833–1834). Victoria University Library, Toronto, has the notebooks of the series 56–65 and a few others, F, L, M, N, P. I have examined all notebooks not yet published (1819–1834) in preparing this study. My largest scholarly debt is to Kathleen Coburn's Notes on the Notebooks.

madman!" cries another. The prophet, apparently unable to bear his sanity amid the madness, jumps into the water and himself becomes mad.[42] Coleridge links the greater sanity in this allegory with what is conventionally called madness. It appears in the eccentric prophet as idleness, imagination, and the refusal to participate. The paralysis of the prophet is morally superior to the activity of the mob, though paralysis in the end proves itself to be what it is: a self-defeating challenge to active evil.

These revaluations are suggestive. Coleridge's sins, which he says are venial and omissive, may be symptomatic of a reluctance to be conventionally sane, as the convention itself is madness. I do not mean to argue that he deliberately separates himself from normative behavior with his own kind of antic disposition; we see him frequently trying to be as normal as everybody else. And his paralysis is on the simplest level "caused" by opium. Yet there is an element of self-vindication in the way he begins to interpret his suffering. He senses that something in him has balked, has refused to go along. Inactivity, the state of motionless "being," is superior to activity, or "doing," in the sense that one is likely in this world to act badly.

He insists he has at least avoided active evil; instead his character is "in a moral *marasmus* from negatives—from misdemeanours of Omission, and from Weakness & moral cowardice of moral Pain—."[43] Like Hamlet, to whom he compares himself, he is too meditative. But in line with the paradoxes above he plainly admires Hamlet's imbalance. It is a meditativeness that implies great moral awareness, even though it comes between the agent and his act. He defends Hamlet from Samuel Johnson's charge that the Prince hesitates to kill

42. *F*, I, 7–9. Cf. *Lectures 1795: On Politics and Religion*, ed. Lewis Patton and Peter Mann (Princeton: Princeton University Press, 1971), pp. 215–217.
43. *CL*, III, 48.

the praying King out of calculating fiendishness. Rather, Hamlet is displaying real reluctance and procrastination, which he covers up with the pretext that to kill the praying King would be to purge the King's soul. Hamlet's inaction comes from "great, enormous, intellectual activity." In this context Coleridge quotes Oswald's speech in Wordsworth's *Borderers* (1795–1796): "Action is transitory, a step, a blow," whereas "Suffering is permanent, obscure and dark, / And shares the nature of infinity." Hamlet's excessive meditativeness illustrates an imbalance between "passive impressions and the mind's own re-action on the same," a lack of correspondence between mind and nature. When Hamlet tells Gertrude he knows not "seems," and he has "that within which passeth show," Coleridge comments that the speech reveals Hamlet's "aversion to externals, the betrayed habit of brooding over the world within him, and the prodigality of beautiful words, which are, as it were, the half embodyings of thoughts, that make them more than thoughts, give them an outness, a reality *sui generis*, and yet retain their correspondence and shadowy approach to the images and movements within." The point is that the "outness" language provides is, in Hamlet's case, an illusion that corresponds only to a rich and agonized internal reality. The outward objects have acquired as they have passed through Hamlet's brain "a form and color not naturally their own." Hamlet's excessive meditativeness "wastes[,] in the efforts of resolving[,] the energies of action." Coleridge might say the same of himself. He suffers from an over-abundance of consciousness, which indicates that a "prerogative of the mind is stretched into despotism." Madness of a high order indeed, Hamlet's and Coleridge's is a madness whose merit is a richness of consciousness for which the world has no correlative. In this state of mind, "realities must needs become cold."[44] Both men suffer the stagnation of being—

44. *Shakespearean Criticism*, ed. Thomas Middleton Raysor, 2d ed., 2 vols. (1930; rpt. London: Everyman, 1960), I, 28–36.

they cannot set about doing—but their madness is neither evil nor inane.

Even when he does not link madness with this kind of heightened awareness, Coleridge thinks no stigma should be placed on it. "The Reason of Law declares the Maniac not a Free-Agent; and the Verdict follows of course—Not guilty."[45] He objects to "the exquisite Superficiality, and *commonplace moral-essay* character of our numerous French, Scotch and English, great and small, Treatises on the *Passions*."[46] And in connection with the futility of offering sober moral advice to a drunkard, he calls for a "Maison de Santé . . . for Lunacy & Ideocy of the *Will*—in which with the full consent of, or at the direct instance of the Patient himself, and with the concurrence of his Friends, such a person under the certificate of a Physician might be placed under medical & moral coercion."[47] To be sure, Coleridge reproaches himself on moral grounds for his opium habit, but almost always with qualifications: he was seduced into the habit ignorantly, he does not take opium for pleasure but only to escape pain, he has at least made efforts to rid himself of the habit. What he needs is not moral commonplaces but a "Gymnastic Medicine," a "system of forcing the Will & *motive faculties* into action."[48] This early call in 1808–1809 for psychotherapy demonstrates his close alignment of psychological with moral categories. There may be, as Wordsworth says, a derangement in his "moral constitution," but, at worst, this may be only an opium-related psychophysical disturbance for which he is not morally responsible. At best, it may be some kind of profound refusal, such as is seen in Hamlet, to be conventionally sane, active, trustworthy. In neither case does he accept total culpability, and he thinks his case begs for a more comprehensive assessment of what constitutes moral worth and failure.

45. *AR*, p. 262.
46. *IS*, p. 65.
47. *CL*, VI, 934.
48. *N*, III, 3431.

But though he sees something almost meritorious in his plight, he finds himself implicitly censured in the greatness of his suffering. He senses that he is found guilty and severely punished, in spite of the fact that he is not really culpable. Absurdly, he responds to unwarranted punishment with unwarranted feelings of guilt. The punishment is not *for* the opium habit, it *is* the habit. "The Pains of Sleep" (1803) explores the contradiction between guilt and culpability. The poet goes to sleep in the spirit of love and "reverential Resignation," with the feeling that though he is weak he is surrounded by "Eternal Strength and Goodness." He promptly has a nightmare of profound, objectless guilt:

> Deeds to be hid that were not hid,
> Which, all confus'd I might not know,
> Whether I suffer'd or I did:
> For all was Horror, Guilt and Woe,
> My own or others, still the same,
> Life-stifling Fear, Soul-stifling Shame!

Upon awakening the poet decides that such punishments are due "to Natures, deepliest stain'd with Sin," those who nourish a "self-created Hell," and who "know and loathe, yet wish and do!" But he does not accept the punishment as due *him*. The "Fiends" can mock those who are truly sinful,

> But I—Oh wherefore this on *me?*
> Frail is my Soul, yea, strengthless wholly,
> Unequal, restless, melancholy;
> But free from Hate, and sensual Folly!
> To live beloved is all I need,
> And whom I love, I love indeed.[49]

Because the poet suffers punishment he has not earned and feels guilty for no good reason, the poem contradicts the premise of "Eternal Strength and Goodness" with which it began.

49. *Coleridge's Verse*, pp. 200–201. This edition incorporates lines of a more personal nature that Coleridge adds in a letter to Southey (*CL*, II, 982–984).

The distinction between guilt and culpability is explored more analytically in a critique of Edward Williams' *A Defence of Modern Calvinism* (1812), a work that deduces, says Coleridge disapprovingly, "that the inability to will good is no excuse for not doing so." His refutation is revealing for what it does not refute. Before we cast blame, we should consider the origins of the vice, for "our conscience never condemns us for what we cannot help unless this *'cannot in praesenti'* is the result of a *'would not a preterito.'*" If a man is created with an inability to love God, he can no more be blamed than "a rattle snake for his Poison."[50] Likewise murder committed in madness is not blameworthy. Coleridge is in effect reiterating Aristotle's distinction between voluntary and involuntary actions. With the latter, "praise indeed is not bestowed, but pardon is, when one does a wrongful act under pressure which overstrains human nature and which no one could withstand."[51] We can fall into habitual immorality unsuspectingly, just as he falls into drug addiction. But it is significant that Coleridge begins his argument by stating that vice, or habitual immorality, while in any single act less reprehensible than a crime, is "more hopeless and therefore of deeper Evil than any single Crime, however great."[52] The obvious deduction, although he does not explicitly make it, is that one may not be responsible for one's "deeper Evil," one may be found profoundly guilty without being culpable.

This is exactly how he feels about his opium habit. His meritorious indolence and moral sensitivity have only worsened the self-perpetuating punishment that is his habit. Indeed, he feels crippled by this "deeper Evil" *because* of his goodness, his lack of active aggression and of hatred. "Oh wherefore this on *me*?" A verdict of guilty plus severe punish-

50. *CL*, IV, 553.

51. *The Nicomachean Ethics*, trans. and ed. Sir David Ross (London: Oxford University Press, 1925; rpt. 1959), p. 49 (III.1).

52. *CL*, IV, 553,

ment without culpability is unjust, but from Coleridge's perspective this injustice seems to be in the nature of things. Feelings of guilt persist for all the self-vindication; his conscience absurdly compounds the injustice by becoming an avenging demon. The loveless observer who confronts him in Hazlitt, Southey, or Wordsworth begins to permeate the nature of things, while he cooperates in his own persecution through unreasonable paralytic guilt. The moral agent is punished and paralyzed by the enlargement of moral consciousness itself, which registers the deeper evil so sensitively that his power to control it is inhibited.

The implicit argument of his paradoxical reflections on his dilemma as moral agent is clear now. The union of being and doing is of course the ideal of the healthy moral agent. Coleridge feels, however, that as a "creature of mere *Impact*" he has at least avoided active evil. Correlative to this reluctance to act is a heightened moral consciousness that is his own version of thinking too precisely on the event. Neither this reactivity nor this extreme meditativeness is in itself so damnable that it should bring down on him the avenging angels—and in fact each is in some ways commendable, almost moral. But each has invited the kind of suffering that seems indistinguishable from great punishment. His passivity has augmented itself in the opium habit, a habit that he only fell into; his moral consciousness has augmented itself in guilt, but guilt for what crime? Coleridge, who wishes, as he says, only to love and be loved, cannot help but think that he is being punished for being moral. I suggest that this thinking is behind much of his baffled sense of justice. It accounts for the "mild astonishment" that Carlyle sees in his sorrowful deep eyes. What kind of world is it in which the more highly developed moral consciousness should be equated with pain and paralysis?

To make matters worse, the same suffering that shares "the nature of infinity" is in no way eventually rewarded in this world; the prisoner is not released. One of the more painful moments in Coleridge's life, for example, comes at the end of his voyage to Malta in 1804 to seek a cure for his opium addiction. His account of his journey by ship echoes at many points the experience of the Ancient Mariner, and indeed he revises a passage of the poem en route. Having left, or perhaps run away from, Sara Hutchinson (his would-be mistress for many years), the Wordsworths, and his own family for uncertain employment abroad, he is lonely amid his shipboard acquaintances and physically wasted. He becomes so badly constipated that a surgeon from a companion ship is sought to administer an enema. Coleridge contends with the "endless Flatulence, the frightful constipation when the dead Filth *impales* the lower Gut—."[53] After several weeks of such extremity in bad weather and with many delays, he arrives with new hope in Malta where he is to report to Sir John Stoddart, a lawyer who has invited Coleridge to visit him en route to Sicily. Reading the horrifying notebook entries of the passage to Malta, we rather feel that Coleridge is owed something for his perseverance, that Malta will promptly and warmly welcome him. But after docking, "I came to Stoddart's—neither he nor Mrs. S. at home/the sister was, but not knowing it to be me, did not come down/—In above an hour she came down/O ipsissima!—would not let the Servant, after 2 hours & a half go to the next street to inform St. of my arrival/. *No! There was no occasion!!—.—.*"[54] The coup de grâce, though, is the abundance of white poppies he soon notices on the island. The addict studies the plant closely and calculates the value of the opium yield per square foot.[55] It is in keeping with a baldly ironic fiction that Cole-

53. *N*, II, 2085, 2091.

54. *N*, II, 2099. For recent accounts of Coleridge's journey to Malta, see Donald Sultana, *Samuel Taylor Coleridge in Malta and Italy* (New York: Barnes and Noble, 1969), pp. 113–141; and Alethea Hayter, *A Voyage in Vain: Coleridge's Journey to Malta in 1804* (London: Faber & Faber, 1973).

55. *N*, II, 2189.

ridge, after sailing thousands of miles to escape the drug, should encounter it head-on at its source.

The Abyss of Will

Is Coleridge depraved or isn't he? His answer is that he is, to the extent we all are. To be sure, he sometimes speaks like a moderate on the question of human depravity. That the author of *The Ancient Mariner* is also the forerunner of the Broad Church Movement seems incongruous. Is not the latitudinarian good sense he occasionally professes out of place in a man who speaks of "motiveless malignity" and the "strange lust of murder in Man," and whose Christabel begins to turn into a serpent? How does this moderation fit his theory of will, which argues the evil of the active human will?

Although he is at times inconsistent, much of the inconsistency disappears if one keeps in mind that Coleridge believes a human being can participate simultaneously in more than one moral condition. In a late notebook entry he lists the "four states" of man:

1. The Man i.e. the Spiritual Man, the Finite Rational, the Image of the Absolute.
2. The Beast, the Finite Irrational.
3. The Fallen Man, the Spirit sunk into & partaking of the Bestial = the Will by Self-determination become a *Nature*, and thus at once corrupting the innocent Nature as an alien ingredient and corrupted *thro'* it. Briefly, state the 3rd is The Natural Man.
4. The Fiend, the Spirit creating itself to evil = the Mystery of Evil, a Spirit inverted, and not as in No. 3. simply corrupted and adulterated by combination with the inferior.[56]

The distinction between fallen and fiendish is crucial. He comes to identify the origin and nature of evil with some-

56. MS Notebook 48 (1830), ff. 19^{v}–20.

thing more basic and frightening than fallibility, and yet, like fallibility, near at hand. While most people are fallen rather than fiendish, even some of Coleridge's friends occasionally take on the demeanor of fiends. Indeed, "I dare not deny the possibility of a finite Person *willing* evil irrevocably and beyond the powers of Repentance, & Reformation—Nay, the *Idea* is indispensable in Morality—."[57]

Radical evil is not merely the overwhelming of reason by the passions; in its pure form, it is a positive, willful malignity. Temptability, paralysis, and failure are marks of the fallen "Natural Man," and his own marks, Coleridge would hasten to add. But the more radical evil—"Evil, be thou my good"— informs the imagery of his best poetry and indeed of his dreams. It attaches in a nightmare to a child, as if to discredit Romantic faith in childhood and natural piety. He dreams that he had spoken to one "most lovely Child, about 2 years old or 2½—and had repeated to her in my Dream, 'The Dews were falling fast' &c—and I was sorely frightened by the sneering and fiendish malignity of the beautiful creature/from the beginning there had been a Terror about it, and proceeding from it/—." Evil is not fallen innocence, because the child has not fallen, and those who have fallen are not necessarily malignant. In fact, fiendish evil is marked by a lack of temptability or passion; it is the motiveless malignity of Iago and Richard III, the passionless energy of Napoleon and Robespierre, the inexplicable sneering of the beautiful child. Even worse than the child's "malignant will of the external Form" is a hate and horror detached from form, "an *abstract touch/* an *abstract* grasp—an *abstract* weight!"[58] In his worst nightmares the malignant will attacks Coleridge through no perceived physical agency and, in a most hideous union of op-

57. MS Notebook 30 (1823–1824), quoted by J. Robert Barth, *Coleridge and Christian Doctrine* (Cambridge, Mass.: Harvard University Press, 1969), p. 119n.
58. *N*, II, 2468.

posites, is sensed abstractly. In these nightmares he sees that evil has an arcane source, that it is somehow both tangible and illusory, and that it has a power and fascination before which one may be helpless.

That evil is implicit in the nature of the human will is a possibility Coleridge explores over many years. His conception of will remains primarily metaphysical, though it also adumbrates modern psychological theories. The relation of will to the psychological processes of feeling, perceiving, and thinking is the subject of an 1804 notebook entry. Willing would not be a separate activity if it merely united aspects of these processes, as wishing does. But he is attracted to the idea that will is "the Being itself, the absolute I or Self, not a modification or faculty—."[59] Despite backing off from this view in 1804, he eventually adopts it as a frequent equation in his writings.[60] To seek beneath the empirical personality for a "root" or "core" or "radical power" is a familiar Romantic maneuver. He praises Fichte for "having prepared the ground for, and laid the first stone of, the *Dynamic* Philosophy by the substitution of Act for Thing," but unlike Fichte, Coleridge does not perceive will as the pure activity of a supraindividual cognitive ego.[61] More in line with the later Schelling, he finds it to be the mysterious reservoir of power that determines each of us to be this or that person. It is our individuality, the primordial energic principle, the ground of selfhood and freedom, and, he will suggest, the source of evil.

Although Coleridge identifies the core of self with will, the core is not the entirety of the self, which is a plurality of activities and which develops in time through the interaction of will with reason. The relationship between these two powers is of great interest to him, and he is at pains in the

59. *N*, II, 2382.
60. E.g., *PL*, pp. 224–225, 364–365; *N*, I, 1717; *N*, II, 2058; *CL*, V, 406; *CL*, VI, 641; *AR*, p. 136.
61. *CL*, IV, 792.

Opus Maximum and elsewhere to explain it. Since will is the ground of reality, he argues that it is prior in a nontemporal sense to being, and by extension to reason or human consciousness. It is futile to call him either voluntarist or rationalist, because for him will and reason are basic contraries of moral struggle: reason is impregnated, made active by will, and will is directed, trained up by reason. It is only in the Absolute Will, or God, that will and reason are not in conflict. Reason, or consciousness of universal law, is "incompatible with individuality or *peculiar* possession." It is potentially the same in all persons, just as the truths of geometry do not depend on individual interpretation. The "abysmal mystery" of will, however, is "not only capable of being conceived of as different & even diverse Wills, but we are under the necessity of so conceiving it in its relation to reason." Will deprived of reason must be an erring will, whereas reason deprived of will, no matter how much knowledge it embraces, "would constitute no personality in the possessor. We should find ourselves incapable of contemplating such a subject otherwise than as a living machine, an automation."[62] The human personality develops its freedom both by the light of universal law, perceived through reason, and by its own mainspring or vital power, the personal will.

Not surprisingly, Coleridge hopes that will and reason can to a degree be coordinated; this is what the moral hope is, and the means of coordination he envisions will be examined throughout this study. But he fears that the will's tendency

62. OM, B_3, ff. 164–187. The Opus Maximum was dictated by Coleridge mostly to Joseph Henry Green at Highgate, probably in the late teens and early twenties of the nineteenth century. Three clasped vellum volumes now in the Victoria University Library are the principal texts, with others in the Huntington Library and the Berg Collection. Those volumes in Toronto tentatively labeled II and III are most pertinent to this study, though the order of these volumes has been reversed. Vol. III will be referred to as OM, B_2 and Vol. II as OM, B_3. B_2 is Coleridge's most direct treatment of moral philosophy. The Opus Maximum is now being edited by Thomas McFarland and will be published in *The Collected Works*.

to maximize its individuality, its irrational and evil potential, may be too much even for the reason whose role he does so much to exalt. It is this complex response to the will's power that defines his unstable humanism and that leads eventually to collapse for him of the humanistic ideal.

It is essential to note that will is by definition unconscious. To be sure, he sometimes speaks of "conscious will" or "intelligent will," but here the will's coalescence with reason is presumed; a will wholly conscious is close to what Coleridge means by "conscience" or "higher reason." And when he speaks of "responsible will," he means simply that the will, and not something else, is accountable for its own acts because it has originated them. He often uses the adjective "unconscious," but not specifically in connection with will. As Owen Barfield has demonstrated, by "unconscious" Coleridge describes not so much a Freudian, or I might add Jungian, power, but more often that part of living nature, found in plants, animals, and the unreflective mass of mankind, that has not yet risen to consciousness.[63] Coleridge does have his own version of an unconscious power in man, however, and that is found in will. Gian N. G. Orsini has written that the "modern enthusiasm" to find pre-Freudian insights in Coleridge "is misplaced." Whereas Freudian depth psychology is based on the irrationality of the unconscious, Coleridge's version is transcendental, Orsini argues, and the unconscious is the "gateway to the spiritual and even to the divine."[64] Orsini's objection itself might suggest that the modern enthusiasm could simply realign itself on Jungian instead of Freudian principles; but it is clear even in the fact that Coleridge at times anticipates both Freud and Jung that the parallels with either must be inexact. If we take will to be his version of the unconscious, we must question whether the unconscious is so accessible a gateway to the divine in any

63. *What Coleridge Thought*, pp. 95–96, 117–119.
64. *Coleridge and German Idealism*, p. 188.

event, because it is precisely in the development of this spiritual power, the individual will, that one separates oneself from the divine; indeed, in Coleridge's view, the very act of becoming human entails this separation. The human will is for him not a collective but in its nature a frighteningly individual unconscious.

The will is anterior to, or more suggestively *beneath*, reason, he argues, and is therefore unknowable; the self is ultimately unknowable to itself. He speaks, significantly, of the "limits of human Consciousness" which do not extend "to the first acts and movements of our own will—the farthest back our recollection can follow the traces, never leads us to the first foot-mark—the lowest depth that the light of our Consciousness can visit even with a doubtful Glimmering, is still at an unknown distance from the Ground."[65] He does not go so far as Schopenhauer in emphasizing the limits of consciousness relative to the arcane powers of the will, nor does he develop an encyclopedic metaphysics of will in which the entire universe is a painful or purposeless striving. Coleridge attempts to reconcile his thinking with Christianity, where Schopenhauer looks to Eastern religion for a therapy of quieting the striving will. Schopenhauer and Freud are closer to each other than either is to Coleridge, because for both the reason is more an adaptive instrument than it is the visionary power that Coleridge takes it to be, if it combines creatively with will and becomes the *higher* reason of the truly enlightened self. What we do find in Coleridge, however, is recognition that the very structure of the human personality lends itself to neurosis, that the self in identifying with consciousness alone deprives itself of the creative power of its own ground, and that the integration of will and reason in the whole personality—where, as he writes in the Opus Maximum, the "*Will* has to struggle upward into *Free-Will*" through the light and

65. *AR*, pp. 72–73.

tutelage of reason—is achieved against great odds, and for him not achieved at all.

In his discussion of motive and impulse, volition and will, Coleridge explores his neurosis. The questions that disturb him are to what extent consciousness can direct will, and to what extent we can free ourselves of physical causation. Hobbes had given a dismal answer to the second question when he defined "motive" as "thing," and had argued, according to Coleridge, that mind is only matter in motion. Coleridge disputes that motives are subject to physical causation, though he limits their power in his own way. A motive is "not a thing, but the thought of a thing" or, more precisely, "a determining thought." He is thinking here of "motive" not as a push from within but as a consciously perceived object of interest without. As a determining thought, a motive is one among the larger class of "thoughts," and thoughts are unlike things in that one cannot tell where one thought ends and another begins. A motive he likens to "an ocean billow," and argues that just as by this we mean "no more than a particular movement of the sea, so neither by a thought can we mean more than the mind thinking in some one direction. Consequently a motive is neither more nor less than the act of an intelligent being determining itself, and the very watchword of the necessitarian is found to be in fact at once an assertion and a definition of free agency i.e. the power of an intelligent being to determine its own agency."[66]

Motives, nevertheless, are not themselves the fundamental mainspring of human action. "It is not the motives govern the man but it is the man that makes the motives: and these indeed are so various mutable and chameleon-like that it is often as difficult, as fortunately it is a matter of comparative indifference, to determine what a man's motive is for this or that particular action. A wise man will rather enquire what the

66. OM, B_2, f. 40. The amanuensis mistakenly wrote "a notion below" for "an ocean billow."

person's general objects are—What does he habitually wish."[67] The more fundamental principle is, in other words, will, the abiding and ultimately incomprehensible predisposition of the self, which Hobbes had thought to be only the last desire in deliberating.

The various competing motives are arbitrated by the "volition," the capacity of consciously choosing which motive to yield to and of enlisting "impulses" to initiate physical movement.[68] While motives are objects of conscious deliberation, impulses, more intimately connected with will, are unconscious expressions of energy and more powerful than motives. The volition would choose a haunch of venison as a suitable object or motive answering to hunger. The venison would be of greater potential benefit, and therefore provide a stronger motive, to a sick man than to a healthy. But the healthy man, with his greater appetite or impulse, is more likely to consume it.[69] The unconscious will is thereby revealed to be essentially more powerful than conscious deliberation.

How does Coleridge apply this rather academic terminology to his own case? As a sick man, he knows his impulses have been diverted from the beneficial venison to opium. What he derives from opium is not the augmentation of life but only a minimal continuance of it, the death-in-life of the addict which is "the worst state of Degradation! It is less [than] a Suicide."[70] He explains, anxiously, that there is no positive motive, like pleasure, for taking opium. And even the wish that physical and psychic pain cease is not what really drives him. "This is indeed the dread punishment attached by nature to habitual vice, that its impulses wax as its motives wane. No object, not even the light of a solitary taper in the far distance, tempts the benighted mind from before; but its own

67. OM, B₂, ff. 55–56.
68. AR, pp. 258–259n.
69. OM, B₂, f. 56.
70. N, II, 2557.

restlessness dogs it from behind, as with the iron goad of Destiny."[71] In compulsive or habitual behavior, the will discharges itself blindly and relentlessly. Coleridge may be wide awake to what is happening to him, and he insists that his purely intellectual faculties are unimpaired. But his mind is nonetheless "benighted," in that it is not performing its function of directing the impulses of will to proper ends.

This diagnosis suggests why he does not precisely think of himself as "weak-willed." Indeed, his has been a life of "unremitting effort." This is the person who selects as an appropriate object of his will the writing of encyclopedias, after all. The "desynonymization" (his coinage for the act of distinguishing between words originally thought to be equivalent) of "power" and "strength" is pertinent here: he does sense power at the core of his being, "*the vital* works vehemently." But his ability to effect what he wills, to strong-arm his way, is radically cut off: "My *Strength* is so very small in proportion to my Power."[72] With the Mariner's inspirited dead crew, he raises his limbs "like lifeless *Tools*."[73] Deeply resented is the glib advice from Joseph Cottle, the Bristol publisher, who tells him that he should simply resolve to give up the opium habit. "You bid me rouse myself—go, bid a man paralytic in both arms rub them briskly together, & that will cure him. Alas! (he would reply) that I cannot move my arms is my Complaint & my misery."[74] Possessed both of strong will and highly developed consciousness, he sees his problem as one of dissociation.

The faculty that would normally coordinate consciousness and will in action, volition, has been sabotaged.

By the long long Habit of the accursed Poison [opium] my Volition (by which I mean the faculty *instrumental* to the Will,

71. *F*, I, 105–106.
72. *N*, III, 3324.
73. *N*, II, 2557.
74. *CL*, III, 477.

and by which alone the Will can realize itself—it's Hands, Legs, & Feet, as it were) was compleatly deranged, at times frenzied, dissevered itself from the Will, & became an independent faculty: so that I was perpetually in the state, in which you may have seen paralytic Persons, who attempting to push a step forward in one direction are violently forced round to the opposite.[75]

Crazed by opium which has, with its own imperatives, preempted the deliberative role, volition no longer coordinates impulse and motive, will and consciousness. The paradoxical result is that though Coleridge is driven by the ever-increasing impulses of a powerful will, he exists in a paralyzed and energyless state. The will sends out a "galvanic fluid" that results in a simulacrum of real motion: the compulsiveness that is identical with loss of freedom. The "Spirit of Life that makes Soul and Body one" is wanting. Though as a drug addict he is one who has strong impulses and weak motives, as a poet and philosopher he finds this imbalance tragically reversed. The motives, or things he would accomplish, remain strong, but the coordinate impulses are here totally lacking; they have wasted themselves in the destructive habit. A "good" habit—let us say the habit of writing competent verse or of playing the piano well—is one in which will and consciousness have developed together harmoniously, as we shall see in Chapter 3. But Coleridge, the apostle of wholeness, is slave to a "*free-agency-annihilating* Poison," and experiences the agony of "a continually divided Being."[76]

He is fascinated and repelled by extravagant acts of will, whether statesmen's or poets', in part because he is so incapable of them. In Donne he sees "the will-worship, in squandering golden hecatombs on a Fetishch, on the first stick or straw met with at rising—this pride of doing what he likes with his own, fearless of an immense surplus to pay all lawful debts to self-subsisting themes." In both his personality

75. *CL*, III, 489.
76. *N*, II, 2557.

and art, Donne exhibits "the impulses of a purse-proud opulence of innate power!"[77] The exercise of will verifies Donne's sense of his own power, while it creates as fine a poem as "To the Sun Rising."

But the exercise of will is not always so beneficent, and we have yet to explore precisely why the will is evil. Coleridge thinks Shaftesbury errs in treating honor as a virtue, because it is in fact a "moral heresy." It is not true morality but "the ghost of virtue deceased." Duelists make their pledge as an act of will "for *the will's sake*." The will proves to itself "its own power of self-determination, independent of all other motives." He writes, portentously, that the exercise of will is "the condition of all moral good while it is latent, and hidden, as it were, in the center; but the essential cause of fiendish guilt, when it makes itself existential and peripheric—si quando in circumferentiam erumpat."[78] Prisoners sometimes deny, prior to execution, having committed some act already proved which has no bearing on the main offense; no benefit can come from the denial, which is prompted simply by will for will's sake. They make the gesture as a final free act, even though it is one that entails an obvious lie.

Coleridge's is the first English use of "existential" in something approximating its modern sense.[79] Barbara Rooke, editor of *The Friend*, suggests that the talk of center and circumference is reminiscent of a distinction Bacon makes between two kinds of knowledge.[80] I think that a more direct influence here is Schelling, whose *Das Wesen der menschlichen Freiheit*

77. *Coleridge on the Seventeenth Century*, ed. Roberta Florence Brinkley (Durham, N.C.: Duke University Press, 1955), p. 523.

78. *F*, I, 425–426n. ". . . whenever it erupts into the circumference."

79. This footnote was included in the 1818 revision of *The Friend* and did not appear in the 1809–1810 periodical. The *OED* would appear to be mistaken in dating Coleridge's use of "existential" as 1809–1810.

80. She alludes to Bacon's distinction in *De augmentis scientiarum* (VIII, 2) between the kind of knowledge that moves "a centro ad circumferentiam" and the kind that moves "a circumferentia ad centrum."

(1809), among other works, leaves its mark on Coleridge's most provocative comment on the origin and nature of evil. In his marginalia to this work, Coleridge objects to the "uncouth mysticism," the metaphoric use of "center," "periphery"—but not so much that he does not on occasion, as we have just seen, adopt the vocabulary himself.[81] Schelling's great work, much too complex even to summarize here except in its relevance to Coleridge, argues that evil is implicit in the idea of human freedom. The human will is anchored in the irrational creative ground, the power of darkness, which is said to be a part of God's reality that is not identical with God himself. So long as the human will remains indifferent and inert, in the "center" of reality as given, evil does not arise. But the human will may seek to realize itself more fully by appropriating the dark creative ground of its existence to its own ends on the "periphery" of God's reality. "Self-will may seek to be, as a particular will, that which it is only in its identity with the universal will. It may seek to be at the periphery that which it is only insofar as it remains at the center (just as the quiet will in the calm depths of nature is also universal will precisely because it stays in the depths). It may seek to be free as a creature." To exult in our selfhood is an act both of freedom and of evil, because we have sought to raise our finitude to a state independent of God, and a self independent or "free" of God is definitionally evil. But the frightening truth is that "activated selfhood is necessary for life's intensity," whereas the goodness of remaining in the "center," of choosing not to be independent of God's will, is lifeless. Schelling describes the process of willing independence—from inert goodness to activated "creature-will," and

81. The marginalia to Schelling's work are published as an appendix to *Biographia Literaria*, ed. Henry Nelson Coleridge, in *The Complete Works of Samuel Taylor Coleridge*, ed. W. G. T. Shedd, 7 vols. (New York: Harper, 1853), III, 691–699.

eventually to the union of finite will with God in a dynamic sense, God as creative will, not restrictive fate. Prior to this ultimate union, the suffering that results from the self-contradictory nature of the effort to create the independent self is both the source of evil and the tragic circumstance of life's intensity.[82]

Coleridge's analysis of the nature and origin of evil is similar in many ways to Schelling's, as Schelling's is to that of Jakob Boehme, who describes evil as the centrifugal falling away from God, the center, when the one becomes the many.[83] The absolute will, or God, writes Coleridge, is that which is "essentially causative of reality," the irreducible ground of all that is. Because he does not wish to suggest that God originates evil (and he is more orthodox than Schelling on this point), he argues that evil originates in the human will and that it is by definition not part of God's reality. Evil is illusion and self-contradiction, not reality. It originates when the human will recoils in upon itself in an effort to find "a center by centrifuge" apart from the absolute will. Indeed, the goodness of the human will is "to deny itself, to sacrifice itself, as a finite Will" to the will of God. The human will must be potentially evil in order that it be a will, but the moment it attempts to actualize itself as something real in and by itself, it progresses from merely potential to actual evil. The fiend attempts to will himself absolutely real apart from God's reality, an attempt that is self-contradictory since all reality *is* God. Satan falls away from God therefore "as a Precipitate" in an act of "inherent self-frustration." The fiend is a "hidden Fire, for ever seeking a base on which it

82. *Of Human Freedom,* trans. James Gutmann (Chicago: Open Court, 1936), pp. 40, 78–80.

83. Boehme's argument is best developed in *Sex puncta theosophica* (1620), *De signatura rerum* (1622), and *Mysterium magnum* (1623). We know that Boehme, unmediated by Schelling, exerts his own influence on Coleridge's conception of will.

may actualize and finding it only to convert it into its' own essence, which is necessarily baseless."[84] The proper symbol of Hell is fire, which is a craving for reality that results only in insubstantiality.[85] Evil arises whenever one attempts to make a "self that is not God." Most human beings have not so utterly divorced themselves from good; though temptable and fallen, they can still potentially rejoin God's center. The fallen human being is thus somewhere between the center that is God's will and the periphery that is self-will.

This argument with its appalling implications is a key to Coleridge's moral thought. It is a theoretical treatment of the fear that dogs him. We can extend the argument informally to suggest that the very act of developing humanity in one's moral capacity as a free agent is prideful; rather one should resign the human will to God's will in "a continual sacrifice." Since human freedom means in its essence the freedom to separate oneself from the will of God, the free and active personality is by definition presumptuous. If all manifestation of human will and energy in action reenacts to some degree the presumption and self-contradiction of Satan, then the alternative, as James Boulger points out, is not to act.[86] The lifeless sacrifice of self to absolute will seems to be the gloomy prescription. Coleridge writes that "our souls are infinite in depth, and therefore our sins are infinite. . . . I have called my soul infinite, but O infinite in the depth of darkness, an infinite craving, an infinite capacity of pain and weakness, and excellent only as being passively capacious of the light

---

84. MS Notebook 26 (1826), quoted by James Boulger, *Coleridge as Religious Thinker* (New Haven: Yale University Press, 1961), pp. 154–157. I am summarizing Coleridge's extensive argument, which is found, in various versions, in Notebook 26, OM, B_3, the dissertation "On the Divine Ideas" in the Huntington Library, and elsewhere. For other treatments of it, see Barth, *Coleridge and Christian Doctrine*, pp. 108–112; and Muirhead, *Coleridge as Philosopher*, pp. 236–244.

85. MS Notebook Q (1833–1834), f. 20.

86. *Coleridge as Religious Thinker*, pp. 158–159.

from above."[87] Freedom in its most dynamic form is freedom *from* God, as the self leaves the lifeless "center" for the "periphery" unsubstantiated by God's reality. But for the will to seek this freedom is irrational and evil, the goal futile.

We have seen that Coleridge is hardly enamored of resignation. With Schelling, he knows the spiritual death of an inactive will. With other Romantics, he sees life's intensity as a goal in itself. But this insight seems to leave him with a frightening choice: to resign the will risks dissolution of personality, to activate it risks "Satanic pride." We have returned on more fundamental ground to the stagnation of being, the delusion of doing.

Well before such figures as Byron, Carlyle, Nietzsche, and Wagner formulate it, Coleridge warns against the romance of the will. In the Appendix to *The Statesman's Manual* he writes, "In its utmost abstraction and consequent state of reprobation," the will becomes despotic by a "fearful resolve to find in itself alone the one absolute motive of action."[88] The heroics of inflated will may be glamorous, but they are at core often self-contradictory and banal. For all his heroics Napoleon exhibits "barbarian impotence and insolence of a mind lagging in moral sentiment and knowledge three hundred years behind the age in which it acts."[89] The exercise of will is here a masquerade. Napoleon is a blustering actor who relies on the readiness of others to prostrate themselves to the mighty illusion.

The moral perils of acting lead Coleridge to a suspicion even of stage acting. He suspects there may be a disparity between genuine deep feeling and the power to represent it. David Garrick and other actors are said disconcertingly to have their "emotions at command and almost as much on the surface, as the muscles of their Countenances." He recalls that

87. *CL*, III, 463.
88. *Lay Sermons*, p. 65.
89. *EOT*, II, 649.

the French, who are all actors, are proverbially heartless. Is it that it is a false and feverous state for the Center to live in the Circumference? The vital warmth seldom rises to the surface in the form of sensible Heat without becoming hectic and inimical to the Life within, the only source of real sensibility. Eloquence itself, I speak of it as habitual and *at call*, too often is, and is always like to engender, a species of Histrionism.[90]

This hostility toward the will to become more and other than what the interior self can consistently authorize suggests Coleridge would not easily accept the uses of gesture and role. But his own experience on so many levels tells him that some compromise with fraud and contradiction in the presentation of self is necessary. He is himself one whose famous eloquence is "habitual and *at call*," even to the point that his audience often ceases to hear. He fears that without some effort at presentation the interior self may go dead, because the person who fails to perform is as likely to become "heartless" as the "actor."

One might summarize the remarks on freedom and alienation thus far by saying that Coleridge is a more than usually reluctant existentialist. As one who uses the term, he is the first thinker in England to formulate what could loosely be called an existential viewpoint: one must act beyond one's essence, become more than what one is. But he hopes he can back away from the threatening truth he has himself propounded, because to act beyond one's essence risks fraud, pride, apostasy. The partial answer to the dilemma, he will suggest, is a development of consciousness that is commensurate with the will's exertion. Whether we have the fraudulent, egotistical, empty actor epitomized in Napoleon, or the great personality of a Donne or a Milton, depends largely on the quality of moral consciousness that directs and expresses the evil will.

90. *CL*, V, 239.

This preoccupation with will, evil, role, and act is everywhere evident in those of his works that have become most familiar to us. A connection between creative gesture and evil in the artist's task is implicit in the famous definitions of imagination, for example. The "primary Imagination," the creative element in all human perception, is separate from God by virtue of being finite. In that it half-creates the world it perceives, it is analogous to God's act of creation. The hint of apostasy is intensified in the artist's *willful* reconstruction of the data of consciousness into an independent self-sustaining whole. The act of "secondary" or artistic imagination is analogous to the act of the fiend, who attempts to create a reality independent of God. The fiend's enterprise is a destructive and illusory "causativeness," because it is self-contradictory—there is by definition no reality apart from God's will. But does not the artist participate in this self-contradiction? Does not the working of the creative imagination itself lead to apostasy, since it implies the insufficiency of God's creation, and the will to supplement or supplant it with one's own? Not satisfied with the world as given, the artist meddles with reality and creates another reality, the presumptuous work of art that contrives an illusion somehow more real than real. Coleridge's fear of the will and his abdication of the poet's role are thus connected at least on this theoretical level: to give up verse is to give up a kind of heresy. The poet obligingly rejoins the inert center. Coleridge's sense of failure because of his thwarted poetic powers is obvious; perhaps he senses too, as a reflex from the artistic act itself, the guilt that preys on imagination and destroys it.

"Kubla Khan," as is well known, employs a symbolism that links the creative act with the demonic. The poet in "Kubla Khan" imagines himself inspirited, not just inspired. He is one who would provoke others to cry, "Beware! Beware! / His flashing eyes, his floating hair!" The poet wills to create but can only say he *would* create "that dome in air."

The self-contradiction at the heart of creation is suggested—creation, if it came at all, would be in *air*. Vexation and nega-, tion are properties of the creative act. The chaotic and creative energies of the river that springs from the chasm die in measureless caverns and do not easily lend themselves to any shaping power. The poet wills an illusion, fears his own temerity, fears indeed his own self as he objectifies himself in the final lines as sorcerer. He becomes the alien of his own consciousness. Kubla Khan is free because he has the power of decree, but the poet has only the power of wish. In imitating Kubla Khan's act, he would prove his self-sufficiency, his freedom from Kubla Khan's creation. He would be at the center of his own circle that others would "weave . . . round him thrice." His creation would make him dreaded, his dome a product of necromancy. But limits on the poet's freedom are implied by his failure to turn wish to act, by his failure to become the object of fascination he envisions, and by his failure, one could say, to write the poem that he writes.

Coleridge's discussion of will also suggests a context for certain aspects of *The Ancient Mariner* and *Christabel*. The Mariner's shooting of the Albatross is portrayed without hint of conscious motive perhaps because acts of will, as we have seen, originate from the abyss below consciousness. The Mariner kills the bird in an act of will for will's sake. He attempts to establish a base in what is baseless, his own will.

William Empson has argued recently that we may be wrong to jump to the conclusion—which everyone including the Mariner jumps to—that killing the Albatross is an evil act. Nothing in Christian orthodoxy, Empson reminds us, rules against the slaying of animals, and to think otherwise would be to extend personality to things. The Mariner's deed would thus be, Empson might say, simply an act of will for food's sake. Perhaps, as Coleridge's comments years later to Mrs. Barbauld would suggest, the Mariner is simply the victim of bad luck in offending the Polar Spirit by taking away his pet. His suffering would then be from neurotic guilt; he feels guilty for no good reason. We and the Mariner mistakenly search catastrophe for patterns of God's justice, patterns that Coleridge himself wishes to find when he adds the glosses years later that tend to turn a heretical poem into a Christian allegory.[91]

I agree with Empson that the poet sees a destructiveness in Christianity's bad conscience, but I do not think it necessary to argue for the Mariner's innocence to make the point about neurotic guilt. One could infer that sin is real but that to feel guilty may nonetheless be neurotic and, one might add, that punishment from whatever source may be fatuous and vindictive. Even on Empson's own terms the Mariner could be both guilty as charged and neurotic in his feelings of guilt. He writes that "what redeems the Mariner is the opposite of pious self-torture; it is the return of spontaneous delight in the beauty of the world—the same protest against Christianity is here as in the synopsis for [*The Wanderings of*] *Cain.*" But of that synopsis, Empson writes that "Cain himself, of course, does feel guilt, *and no one denies that he should*, but the question is what should be done about it."[92] Cain is saved when he addresses the landscape as the Mariner does the beautiful water-snakes, not when he begins to mutilate himself and sacrifice his son Enoch. The futility of neurotic guilt is clear here, then, even though Cain is guilty as charged. We might remember the distinction between guilt and culpability. Perhaps the Mariner is not strictly culpable and therefore

91. *Coleridge's Verse*, pp. 31–42. Some literal-mindedness in interpreting *The Ancient Mariner* would support the argument of this study. If one insists that there would ordinarily be nothing so sinister in shooting an albatross, the consequences of that act in *The Ancient Mariner* become all the more sinister. The Mariner is then punished not because he has killed an albatross but simply because he has *acted*. Coleridge's theory of will is precisely that all positive human acts, and in a sense even love itself, must be said to have exercised the evil will.

92. Ibid., pp. 33–35 (my emphasis).

need not *feel* guilty, inasmuch as the poem withholds any suggestion that he consciously deliberates whether or not to kill the Albatross. But he still bears the imputation of guilt for the sin that originates in the unconscious.

The Ancient Mariner suggests, therefore, a certain righteousness, from the moral or human perspective, in the Mariner's "wicked whisper," his hatred of God. Paul Ricoeur writes that Oedipus is the "symbol of monstrous crime *and* excusable fault."[93] We could apply the remark to the Mariner. Many readers feel it unjust that punishment seems whimsical, subject to stops and starts, and disproportionate to any continuing manifest evil in the Mariner. He does, after all, feel guilty for his act and for the death of the crew; he is still capable of loving the creatures and his homeland. Why should he be held responsible in the first place for an act that originates from beneath consciousness? Why must the fever to tell the tale return again and again? Our awareness of cosmic injustice is enhanced by the one heroic quality we might impute to the Mariner—his perseverance in spite of having been singled out by crew, death ship, and total environment as the one who "had killed the bird."

The Ancient Mariner has eluded all efforts to find in it a coherent *moral* world, in which there would be an intelligible correspondence of character and fate. The point must be that the poem is constructed so as to disturb our sense of justice. The poem portrays the weakness of the moral virtues—compassion, love of one's country, sense of responsibility to the community, delight in living creatures—relative to the arcane movements of the will, which is evil in its nature. At the same time we can assume it is the will that energizes and defines the Mariner as *that one* who has been alone on the wide wide sea. It is the will that makes him persist in his own tortured being and that continually starts the fever over again, forcing him

93. *The Symbolism of Evil*, trans. Emerson Buchanan (Boston: Beacon, 1972), p. 115.

to wander outside the society he occasionally interrupts to issue an admonition. In a sense, the will *is* the Mariner. Even after the spell has supposedly broken, the hermit's boy looks at him in the rowboat: " 'Ha! ha!' quoth he, 'full plain I see,/ The Devil knows how to row.' " Is there not a suggestion that the Mariner is punished because he has literally distinguished himself? Is not this punishment implicit in the act of individuation itself, which inevitably gives rise to suffering and alienation? The Wedding Party is the community the Mariner can never join. One might say it is the "center" or "One," just as the wanderings of the Mariner are along the "periphery." His independence of God is of course illusory, for God will not be mocked. His self-contradictory freedom is appropriately conveyed as repetition compulsion, as he is forced to tell his tale again and again. And there is no suggestion that he develops the level of consciousness that would enable him to comprehend his own tale. But this demon with glittering eyes has an intensity and human concern foreign to the merry company walking to the kirk.

Coleridge's account of the origin of evil as the human will's departure from God's will at the center to the periphery that is self-will permits in theory a resolution: one can return to the center, and this too would be a mysterious act of will. Just as the Mariner, without "motive," kills the Albatross, so also, by means not of motive but of impulse directly aligned with the will, does he bless the water-snakes "unaware." Both alienation and reunion are acts of will, both originate from sources below what can be known either by Mariner or by reader. Coleridge writes that love is an act of will in the same sense that Adam's choosing evil is an act of will.[94] What one must note here, however, is that an act of alienation must precede an act of reunion, and that never to be alienated, never to leave the "center," is never to grow as a human self.

94. *N*, III, 3562n.

Thus, the shooting of the Albatross precedes the blessing of the water-snakes. The basic metaphor suggests, too, that reunion is difficult to conceive of without an element of capitulation, even though Coleridge, aware of the problem, insists that to be one with God "is no mystic annihilation of individuality, . . . but on the contrary an *intension*, a perfecting of our Personality—."[95] Reunion with God is a prospect so out of sight, so inconceivable in human terms, that it smacks of a merely verbal affirmation. In agony Coleridge has said that the human being is "excellent only as being passively capacious of the light from above." As we shall see in future chapters, he will address himself to overcoming alienation this side of paradise. It requires gradual integration of will with reason and other powers in the development of personality, and, more profoundly, the will's denial of its own separateness in love. But alienation will remain even here the essential feature of his moral vision. That the loving "impulse" of the Mariner breaks the curse only momentarily indicates a limit in the act of reunion itself. It is the Mariner's and Coleridge's fate to find human alienation more enduring than human love.

Christabel is an even more sinister poem. The heroine does nothing overtly evil, such as slay an albatross, prior to her transformation into a serpent. Here, the moral virtues of love and sympathy are not only powerless before evil, but increase vulnerability to it. Christabel's transformation is neither knowing nor voluntary nor even consciously experienced as such— and yet she becomes evil, evil without being culpable.

Ricoeur in a discussion of the symbolism of the "servile will" writes that evil as defilement has three perennial schemata. Evil is symbolized as something "positive," not simply as negation; it is the "power of darkness." Evil is also "external"—it "comes to a man as the 'outside' of freedom, as the other than itself in which freedom is taken captive." Seduction, accordingly, is something undergone, a captivity. Evil's

95. MS Notebook 36 (1827), f. 65.

external character is expressed in "magical conceptions of contagion and contamination," especially through sexual contact. The third schema is "infection," which declares that though seduction comes from without, it is self-inflicted: "it is by thinking of the yielding of myself to slavery and the reign over myself of the power of evil as identical that I discover the profound significance of a tarnishing of freedom."[96] I would suggest that Coleridge, in *Christabel*, has portrayed explicitly and comprehensively the paradoxical workings of evil as a positive, external, and infectious force. Any effort to explain the poem in terms of coherent moral logic would miss the point of the self-contradictory nature of "infection."

Geraldine, positive inexplicable evil, seduces the innocent, if somewhat eager, Christabel. Geraldine's bosom and "half her side" are "lean and old and foul of hue," the physical representation of defilement conceived, as Ricoeur would suggest, "in the guise of a stain or blemish that infects from without." When later Geraldine looks on her with shrunken dull snake's eyes, "with somewhat of malice, and more of dread," Christabel's captivity becomes infection. She becomes the serpent who possesses her, and the evil, however external, must be claimed as her own will. The narrator in his simplicity says that he does not know how the transformation has come about. Christabel's "features were resigned / To this sole image in her mind: / And passively did imitate / That look of dull and treacherous hate!" The narrator calls this "forced unconscious sympathy" with Geraldine's own malice. Whatever excuses he may make for her, the ordinary moral categories of voluntary and involuntary no longer condemn or acquit. In fact on a moral level Christabel retains her "innocence" in spite of her serpent's hiss, and her moral virtues of receptiveness and sympathy have ironically facilitated her captivity. Having made that dread point, the poem needs no other conclusion.

96. *The Symbolism of Evil*, pp. 151–157.

Kant, Coleridge, and Ricoeur all say that a human being cannot entirely become the fiend, because that would be to preempt the Devil.[97] But Christabel enacts the terrifying possibility that evil is not wholly a matter of moral choice. The process of heteronomy and defilement remains mysterious, beneath the level of conscious selection or rejection. Morality for Coleridge is largely the quality of one's consciousness, but morality cannot hope to remove the will's evil potential.

A notebook entry of 1812 finds a troubled Coleridge finally admitting that he, too, has committed profoundly evil acts, not merely omissive or venial ones. The act of admitting it might have some therapeutic value: "my Motive or rather Impulse to do this, seems to myself an effort to eloign and abalienate it from the dark Adyt of my own Being by a *visual* Outness—& not the wish for others to see it—." The entry suggests indirectly how the Mariner, Christabel, and Geraldine are all participants in evil, and how Coleridge becomes all three. His crime is to have a "sudden second sight of some hidden Vice, past, present, or to come, of the person or persons with whom I am about to form an intimacy," but this vision of evil does not come from the other person—it is projected from within. It is his own evil eye looking evil into another person, much as Geraldine does to Christabel. But like Christabel herself, the vision of evil "never deters me but rather . . . urge[s] me on." Combining the two roles, he is attracted to the evil vision he himself projects, and in so doing has "offended against some Law of [his] Being"; he has experienced the self-contradiction that is at the heart of evil. "These occasional acts of the Eγο νουμενος = repetitions or semblances of the original *Fall* of Man—hence shame & power—to leave the appointed Station and become Δαιμων and perhaps

<hr/>

97. See "Of the Indwelling of the Bad Principle Along with the Good; or, on the Radical Evil in Human Nature," in *Critique of Practical Reason and Other Works on the Theory of Ethics,* trans. T. K. Abbott (London: Longmans, Green, 1904; rpt. 1948), p. 342; and *The Symbolism of Evil,* pp. 156–157.

invading the free will & rightful secrecy of a fellow-spirit—." In code he admits that he has committed such a mental and malicious rape of Dorothy Wordsworth. It is an act both of power, as the Devil's is when he leaves his "appointed Station," and of shame. One recalls the Mariner's shooting of the Albatross when Coleridge writes that to commit this kind of act promotes in him an "inexplicable feeling of causeless shame & sense of a sort of guilt, joined with the apprehension of being feared and shrunk from as a something transnatural." The guilty reflex is not altogether earned because these are acts that emanate from the "dark Adyt" over which he has little control. In moments like this he becomes the transnatural, the devil, who is shunned by others, just as the Mariner is for his spontaneous evil act.[98]

Lovejoy has demonstrated, arguing from different materials, that for Coleridge evil must originate in man's own "noumenal ego," without reference to the empirical categories of time and space, if God is not himself to be the source of evil. "All the noumenal egos, in short, are *bad* egos," Lovejoy writes, and there is little that can be done about it. One of the deepest strains of Coleridge's being "was a sense of sin" which "gave rise to his belief in the freedom of the individual will." Indeed, a "renascence of the sense of sin and of the doctrine of human depravity is one of the most evident of the 'Romanticisms.' "[99]

Feeling, Imagination, and Nature

We have been speaking of the "Fiend, the Spirit creating itself to evil," which Coleridge connects with the mysterious abyss of will below consciousness. That the Mariner, Christ-

98. *N*, III, 4166 and n. "Noumenal ego"; "Devil" or "Daimon." I am indebted to Kathleen Coburn for pointing out parallels between this entry and Coleridge's major characters.
99. "Coleridge and Kant's Two Worlds," *Journal of English Literary History*, 7 (1940), rpt. in *Essays in the History of Ideas* (Baltimore: The Johns Hopkins University Press, 1948), pp. 254–276.

abel, and even Geraldine are not perfect fiends is much of their fascination for us. The fiend exists potentially in every human being, whatever his or her virtues. Coleridge fears that all life's intensity to some degree activates the evil will; to be actively human is to live in great peril.

In his pure form abstracted from all humanity, the fiend is the "dry sinner," who yields to no personal anguish and who pursues his business coldly and consistently. The "Natural Man" is a lesser offender, Coleridge has said, who sacrifices personal freedom through default in "partaking of the Bestial." He writes to John Thelwall, the persecuted reformer, that Aristotle

divides bad men into two Classes—the first he calls "wet or intemperate Sinners"—men who are hurried into vice by their appetites but *acknowlege* their actions to be vicious—these are reclaimable. The second class he names—*dry* villains—Men who are not only vicious, but who (the steams from the polluted heart rising up & gathering round the head) have brought themselves & others to believe that *Vice* is *Virtue*.[100]

The natural man or wet sinner does not, like the fiend or dry sinner, practice evil as a positive force based on perverse selfhood, but instead loses his independence through temptation. "*Tomorrow* I will do well—only today—it is hard never to indulge one-self—In all other things I will obey the commands; but this Fruit is fair to behold, the Serpent has eat it, and has become my Equal."[101] Since the world does not accommodate virtue, the wet sinner must be on his guard: "As he who passes over a bridge of slippery uneven Stones placed at unequal distances, at the foot of an enormous waterfall, is lost, if he suffer his Soul to be whirled away by its diffused every where nowhereness of Sound/but must condense his Life to the one anxiety of not Slipping, so will Virtue in

100. *CL*, I, 213.
101. MS Notebook 26, quoted by Boulger, p. 156.

certain Whirlwinds of Temptations."[102] This "diffused every where nowhereness of Sound" is the blur of the world's contingencies hostile to the moral life. Coleridge often sees himself as a wet sinner set upon by dry sinners; he is a well-meaning but intemperate man accused by the prideful and malicious. The wet sinner, unlike the dry, remains human. In fact, to be human implies this kind of temptability.

Coleridge does not always equate nature with sin and temptation, of course. Immersion of self in nature can lead either to sensuality and imprisonment in the world of things or to creative joy. Conversely, detachment of self from nature can lead either to spirituality or to acedia and despair. Which of these contrary possibilities results depends on whether nature itself is seen as dead mechanism or as living organism. An older Coleridge often speaks of nature as the mechanism that shackles the human being, body and mind, or as the biological force that tempts him. But for Coleridge as young poet, nature is the world of "lovely shapes and sounds intelligible" that seems infused with spirit and purpose. The two human powers that can connect one with nature in a healthy way are feeling and imagination. Each is linked with the will, yet each emerges as a familiar constituent of conscious life. Coleridge's treatment of them and their relation to the moral life is revelatory *because* of his inconsistencies, his inability to keep faith. This uncertain faith in their role as mediators between self and nature is linked to his recurring wish to renounce the very free and integrated personality that is the goal of his own humanism.

The crucial connection between human feeling, nature, and freedom is obvious in Coleridge's treatment of "joy." The joy the poet has lost in "Dejection: An Ode" (1802) is nourished by the impulses of the natural man—it weds nature to us, it is "Life's effluence," a "sweet and potent voice" that transforms the "inanimate cold world" into a "new Earth and new

102. *N*, I, 1706; cf. *N*, III, 3745.

Heaven." Joy is the felt sense of life that results from participation in the natural world. Although it derives from nature, which is nonhuman and not free, joy as a humanization of nature's energies is the animated and potent state of the human organism experiencing its freedom. The poet's loss of "genial spirits" is identical with loss of potency, with a sense of self-depletion. When he steals from his own nature "all the natural man," he extinguishes the energy that sustains imagination, freedom, and life itself. The energies that nature imparts are accordingly a cure of dejection. In "France: An Ode" (1798) the poet, despairing of revolutionary progress, finds freedom instead in an intimate encounter with the forces of nature:

> And there I felt thee!—on that sea-cliff's verge,
>> Whose pines, scarce travelled by the breeze above,
> Had made one murmur with the distant surge!
> Yes, while I stood and gazed, my temples bare,
> And shot my being through earth, sea, and air,
>> Possessing all things with intensest love,
>> O Liberty! my spirit felt thee there.

The corollary is that spiritual death results from placing "nature in antithesis to the mind, as object to subject, thing to thought, death to life."[103]

He attempts to define theoretically the moral legitimacy of the natural affective life, which can transcend its physical origins. In a treatise on the passions, he complains of Descartes' mere "grammatical Antithesis of the Terms, Action and Passion, substituted for a real definition of the Things themselves." The body-soul dichotomy has produced a dangerous divorce of physiology from psychology, whereas the truth of human passions is found in the "kennel of my Psychosomatic Ology," where the mental and the physical intermingle. A passion, although its etymology suggests passivity,

103. *F*, I, 520.

has an active mental element. His tentative definition of "passion," elsewhere called "impetite," approaches Spinoza's "positive emotion": Coleridge writes that a passion is "a state of emotion, which tho' it may have its pre-disposing cause in the Body, and its occasion in external Incidents or Appearances, is yet not *immediately* produced by the incidents themselves, but by the person's Thoughts and Reflections concerning them." He wishes to exclude from his discussion any "self-impulsions that are merely corporeal, . . . and never arrive at consciousness."[104] The passions or feelings are located in the pectoral region, which synthesizes the cerebral and abdominal functions.[105]

In an early letter to Southey, he writes of the desirability of a "well-disciplined Phalanx of right onward Feelings."[106] Feeling is an appropriate mediator between physical and intellectual states. He later goes so far as to suggest that the "best characteristic of Humanity" is the "intervening sympathies gradually shading & illuminating the interval between Soul & Body, & making a tertium aliquid of Both."[107] But in the same notebook entry he cautions that sexual lust can easily interfere with this synthesis.

His treatment of sexuality, for him more an intense feeling than a drive, reveals his reluctance to put into either theory or practice the full implications of his denial of Cartesian dualism; he is not prepared to give the body its due. His inconsistent attitudes toward nature and the natural man derive in large part, I think, from his profound repulsion by sexuality. We find none of Blake's confidence that infinity will "come to pass by an improvement of sensual enjoyment." Although he does imply in his poetry and elsewhere that

104. *IS*, pp. 63–68; cf. *N*, III, 4046. "Psycho-somatic" is apparently his transliteration and its first use.
105. OM, B$_3$, ff. 15–16.
106. *CL*, I, 138.
107. *N*, III, 4169.

sexual feeling plays a crucial mediating role between nature and spirit, one can speculate that personal sex loathing prevents him from formulating that role fully.

The "joy" of "Dejection: An Ode" is clearly a Coleridgean equivalent of libido, thought of as energy deriving from one's natural or biological being, one expression of which is sexuality. In the original draft of the ode, we find a comically awkward image of Mary and Sara Hutchinson sitting with Coleridge on a couch before the fireplace: his head is on Mary's lap, her hand is on his brow, while Sara's eyelashes play on his cheek. The poet writes:

> Such Joy I had, that I may truly say,
> My spirit was awe-Stricken with the Excess
> And trance-like Depth of it's brief Happiness.[108]

The point is not that the actual incident had sexual undercurrents, but that Coleridge is so careful to cleanse his poem of any suggestion of them. Mary is "that affectionate & blameless Maid"; joy is undreamt of by the "sensual" (and the proud) and is given only to the "pure." That he insists so much on the purity of this impregnating joy makes one wary. Some sexual suggestion does emerge from the poem (for example, the "sweet and potent voice," "genial spirits," "natural outlet," "the passion and the life, whose fountains are within"), but the poet, who, in reply to critics, denies even the sexual undercurrents of *Christabel*, denies them here within the poem itself. His diagnosis of the cessation of joy seems inadequate—as if "abstruse Research" were really all that enervating in itself. The poem describes the morbid state but only hints at etiology. Sexual repression is surely a covert theme in "Dejection: An Ode," just as sublimation is in "Kubla Khan." The fact that the original verse epistle to Sara Hutchinson contains a baroque argument for not keeping her company in the future probably betrays sexual fear.

If sublimation of sexual impulses into art is a dialectic of

108. *CL*, II, 793; cf. "A Day-Dream" (1802), *Poetical Works*, I, 385–386.

"Kubla Khan," sublimation into virtue is the wishful thinking of an 1805 notebook entry, in which Coleridge imagines—for it is doubtful that the relationship is ever consummated—a sexual encounter with Sara Hutchinson. The entry is an attack on Cartesian dualism and an analysis of sexuality, but Coleridge diverts both arguments into a defense of marriage and an attack on harlotry. Sexuality is permitted so long as it is absorbed into goodness. His own experience both of sex and of drug addiction, he seems to be saying, confirms the "Vileness of Human Nature," but he thinks those who claim that human nature is wholly evil because it contains evil are guilty of a logical fallacy. One might just as easily pronounce human nature good because it contains some good. An even worse error is committed by those who destroy the unity of human nature by making "the concupiscent, vindictive, and *narcissine* part of our nature one separate, dividuous being, and the pure will and ever benevolent *Reason* . . . another Thing." Such thinking encourages "spiritual Sloth, and instead of that best prayer of putting our shoulders to the wheel with upturned eyes, & heart, so that the co-operating muscles themselves *pray*, we stand idle & gossip to Hercules with our Tongues/The Cart will never be out of the Slough or Rut." The image of the praying muscle is in itself ample testimony to Coleridge's wish to unite the contraries of soul and body in an intensity of feeling, but it is feeling purified of sexual content. The pleasurable sensations he has felt while half asleep in early morning are not the same as concupiscence, "unless perhaps that dying away or ever-subsisting vibration of it in the Heart & Chest & eyes (as it *seems* to us) which is the symbolical language of purest Love in our present Embodiment."[109]

This sexual feeling, if he were sleeping with Sara, "would become associated with a Being *out of me*, & thereby in an almost incalculable train of consequences increase my active

109. *N*, II, 2495. Kathleen Coburn comments that "narcissine" is "not in *OED* and appears to be original."

benevolence ⟨= virtuous Volificence = benevolificence = *goodwilldoingness*⟩." The proliferation of neologisms underscores his wish that sexual feeling be transformed into an ever more active benevolence (one that approaches beneficence). His anxiety is that feeling, sexual or otherwise, may be reflexive and intransitive—it may not connect one with the world. The rhetorical distention itself suggests an effort to break through the solipsistic ego. The connection with his partner will be made through the power of moral virtue, strangely remote from its sexual base. In this process a "Husband's Hand or swelling chest" on his wife's bosom would be as "*Actively* virtuous" as his shunning a whore. He then employs a striking metaphor:

O best reward of Virtue! to feel pleasure made more pleasurable, in legs, knees, chests, arms, cheek—all in deep quiet, a fountain with unwrinkled surface yet still the living motion at the bottom, that "with soft and even pulse" keeps it full—& yet to know that this pleasure so impleasured is making us more *good*, is preparing virtue and pleasure for many known and many unknown to us. O had Milton been thus happy![110]

He has quoted his own poem here, "Inscription for a Fountain on a Heath" (1802), in which the fountain, in a cool twilight setting, sends up "cold waters to the traveller / With soft and even pulse." But instead of a cool fountain, Coleridge is speaking here of the warm pulse of sexual feeling that, through sublimation, kindles virtuous feeling "into tenfold heat and blaze—." Sexual feeling produces a euphoria that is even a "Fountain of intellectual activity." This passage is perhaps the closest Coleridge comes in his theoretical writings to treating sexuality as essential nourishment of life's intensity and human freedom, but even here the vigilant moralism indicates that it is acceptable only in its transformations.

If sexual feeling is linkage with a being "out of" oneself, to deny that feeling is to withdraw into the ego. Coleridge had despaired of ever marrying Mary Evans, his first love,

110. Ibid.

"possibly from deficiency of bodily feeling, of tactual ideas connected with the image," which would have convinced him of her reality. He speaks of the "influence of bodily vigor and strong Grasp of Touch in facilitating the passion of Hope" and then, in code, adds, "Eunuchs—in all degrees even to the full ensheathment & the both at once."[111] This passage presumably has reference to his sexual relationship with his wife. The literal sex act has become a negation of sexuality, contact without intimate touching. The next notebook entry speaks of the "imperfection of the organs by which we seem to unite ourselves with external things—."[112] These organs, sexual and otherwise, require the sense of touch and of grasp without which the feeling state which works through them becomes dim. Sarah Coleridge, he writes elsewhere, is emotionally frigid because she has so little sense of the tangible, of basic physical responsiveness.[113] He knows from his own lifeless dejection and his wife's lack of a sense of reality the consequences of deprivation and repression, but his profound distaste for sexuality prompts a turning away from his own insights.

Human nature, he fears, is permeated by sex. Much has been written on his early connection of the "streamy nature of association" with the "origin of evil." He comes to think this a false lead, because he locates the origin of evil, as I have noted, below conscious psychological process. What he most fears about the associative faculty is not radical evil but its unhesitating pursuit of sexual imagery. The problem is that "Reason and Reality can stop and stand still," but "Fancy and Sleep *stream* on." The fancy is subject to "motions of the blood and nerves." What he regards as indecencies result simply from "the position & state of the Body and its different members" while asleep.[114]

111. *N*, II, 2398.
112. *N*, II, 2399.
113. *N*, I, 979.
114. *N*, II, 2543.

Though he does sometimes argue that sexuality and love can enhance each other, he easily deserts his search for an integral relationship. Love is not a "refinement" of lust but its "counteracting Antidote." "Lust can never be transubstantiated into Love—it is the lusting Man that gradually Depositing the bestial Nature into which he had fallen, under the subliming influences of Affection, Awe of Duty, and Sense of the Beautiful is indeed transubstantiated (= born into) a *loving* Man."[115] In passages such as this one, an older Coleridge advises "depositing" sexual impulses, not transubstantiating them into "benevolificence." Even the younger Coleridge had often seen love and lust in combat, a combat that could strike a note of the mock heroic. The natural modesty of a Sara Hutchinson can save a man from the sirenlike seductiveness of a Cecilia Bertozzi, the actress who appears to be the object of a mild infatuation in Syracuse in 1804. Just when he is "on the very brink of being surprized" into some compromising act "by the prejudices of the shame of sex, as much as by its ordinary Impulses," he is "saved" by an imaginary vision of Sara Hutchinson's face![116]

Whatever his great reluctance to pursue his own insight, sexuality for Coleridge, as well as for Blake, promises liberation from the body through the body: it connects one with a reality outside the prison of the physical self. As Blake writes in *Europe a Prophecy* (1794), the sense of touch, which is most intensely exercised in sexuality, is one of the "Five windows" that "light the cavern'd Man":

> Thro' one, himself pass out what time he please, but he will not;
> For stolen joys are sweet, & bread eaten in secret pleasant.[117]

Orc is the Blakean figure who represents both sexuality and the drive for freedom. In *America a Prophecy* (1793) we find

115. MS Notebook 48 (1830), f. 8^V.
116. *N*, III, 3404.
117. All Blake quotations are taken from *The Poetry and Prose of William Blake*, ed. David Erdman (New York: Doubleday, 1965).

him in an agonizing embrace with the nameless shadowy female, dumb nature, who is impregnated by Orc's energies. But Orc, as Blake's myth progresses, gives way in importance to another power, Los, or imagination, who promises freedom of a higher order. The vegetative cycle of Orc, trapped in time and space and natural process, can be broken and transcended by imaginative vision, the cosmic pulse of the artery in which the poet's work is done. For Coleridge, also, the imagination promises release both from the imprisonment of nature and from one's own burden of self-consciousness. But here too, he will eventually part company with Blake when he questions the imagination's leading role.

What is imagination's connection with the moral life? For Schiller, the idea of freedom has an aesthetic origin in that it is through the play of the imagination that we first experience freedom in the phenomenal world. Mediating between our material and formal impulses, between passion and reason, the aesthetic or play impulse (*Spieltrieb*) freely creates its own coherent semblance of reality.[118] Many of Coleridge's comments on the imagination and much of his demonstration of it, particularly in the conversation poems, also suggest a link between imagination and freedom, though the way to freedom will be not so much through "play" as through a more generally conceived humanization. The imagination gives form to that which is alien and formless and creates within the prison of nature a liberating human context.

A notebook entry of 1811 describes what happens when human perception works on without imagination. The lesser perceptual faculty, the fancy, "may not inaptly be compared to the Gorgon Head, which *looked* death into every thing—." If natural objects, including human bodies, are perceived as shapes only and not as what Coleridge calls "forma effor-mans," or true form, then they are perceived as dead. "Life

118. *On the Aesthetic Education of Man*, ed. and trans. Elizabeth Wilkinson and L. A. Willoughby (Oxford: Clarendon Press, 1967), pp. 182–203.

may be *inferred,* even as intelligence is from black marks on white paper—but the black marks themselves *are truly 'the dead* letter.' " The fancy does have a purpose in that without it "there would be no *fixation,* consequently, no distinct perception or conception," but "modern Philosophers" of the empirical tradition have made it the ultimate faculty. The physical world is dead and imprisoning only if perception is dead. "Is it any excuse to him who treats a living being as inanimate Body, that we cannot arrive at the knowlege of the living Being but thro' the Body which is its Symbol & outward & visible Sign?"[119]

The imagination frees us from this incarceration in a fixed and dead universe. It is "the fusing power, that fixing unfixes & while it melts & bedims the Image, still leaves in the Soul its living meaning—."[120] Not only the power of the artist, it is the power of all active human intelligence to appropriate the image of nature that perception provides, to mold it according to its own design, even to the point of dimming one's view of the literal image itself. Yet this imaginative process does not distort or delude, for the otherwise dead image is said to have left "its living meaning" in the mind. The image becomes a symbol that nourishes consciousness on all levels. Articulated and enlivened by imagination, nature becomes "lovely shapes and sounds intelligible," and human mind, through its own agency, is freed from a world of dead objects.

In later years, especially during the mid-1820s, Coleridge loses faith in the imagination's redemptive power and supplants imagination with the higher spiritual power he calls "reason," but which he often equates with "faith." One should triumph over nature, not seek integration with it. Old dualisms of matter versus spirit reappear, and there is something of a contest between the phenomenal and noumenal.

119. *N,* III, 4066.
120. Ibid.

Then he speaks of imagination as a dangerous, delusive faculty.

His changing attitudes toward nature and imagination with respect to freedom can be well illustrated by a brief look at three conversation poems. In "The Eolian Harp" (1795) the poet in his peaceful, somewhat bourgeois, cottage setting has only to be receptive to the "desultory breeze," the energies and language of nature, which are so benign that the poet, "indolent and passive," placidly follows his "idle flitting phantasies." No exertion of active imagination is called for when he is confronted with "the stilly murmur of the distant sea." The poet's intoxicated and sensual passivity yields a series of enchanted associations. The eolian harp, the metaphor of mind, "like some coy maid half yielding to her lover," is swept over and "caress'd" by the desultory breeze of nature. The poet hears "a soft floating witchery of sound," as nature becomes a musical fairyland. From the fabulous the poet is led to the speculative. That "animated nature" may "tremble into thought" when swept over by a plastic and vast "intellectual breeze" is of course heretical from the point of view of a Christian dualism of nature and spirit. That he so readily capitulates to Sara[h]'s "mild reproof" suggests how fragile his faith in the heresy is from the beginning. In different ways, the poet will repeat the heresy in "This Lime-tree Bower my Prison" (1797), and "Dejection: An Ode" (1802), and he will recognize that it is vulnerable to something more personally threatening than Christian orthodoxy. The very passivity that has permitted the fancy to work so delightfully in "The Eolian Harp" will be in "Dejection: An Ode" the symptom of an imagination gone dead in an alien, even nightmarish scene.

In "This Lime-tree Bower my Prison" the poet is in a real sense a prisoner who laments that, having been left behind in the bower by his companions, he will be deprived of "beauties and feelings" that would, in the future, be "sweet to my remembrance." By regarding the future moment curiously as a potential but lost memory, he initiates the double vision that, in a Coleridgean and not Wordsworthian sense, will characterize the poem. He discovers in the course of the day that beauty and feeling rely on imagination, not circumstance. When he "lift[s] the soul" to contemplate what he cannot share, he engages the scene imaginatively and magnifies the very experiences of joy, beauty, and companionship that he feared he would lose.

The "roaring dell" where he imagines his friends are wandering is more awesome than beautiful, nature at its most elemental and surprising. The "dark green file of long lank weeds" that "nod and drip" is a "fantastic sight"—the weeds are alien and sunless indeed, yet tolerant of the intruders and in their nodding and dripping engaged as it were in some comic rudimentary form of communication. The poet imagines that the party enters the dell in midday sun and that when they reemerge the sun is sinking "behind the western ridge." The setting sun, however glorious, introduces an elegaic note; the poet fastens on Charles (Lamb) and the "strange calamity" he has endured "in the great City pent."

These two elements—of penetration into an alien and primitive dell, and of human suffering and need for consolation—make the poet susceptible to the scene in a new way. Alienation prepares him for the imagination's triumph, because he, unlike the Mariner, transforms the suffering of exposed consciousness into articulate self-consciousness, lifts the soul beyond loss, and renews, not relives, his life. After the surprise and awe at the fantastic dell that engages the "fancy" wholly, the party will be "struck with deep joy" that will redress suffering. They will stand "silent with swimming sense" until the landscape, so cleanly articulated up to now, will take on a sublime aspect and seem "less gross than bodily." One thinks of Coleridge's description of the imagination as the power which "melts & bedims the Image," yet which "leaves in the Soul its living meaning—." The body or image of nature has yielded up, through the poet's imaginative probing, its symbol, the language of the "Almighty Spirit."

Coleridge calls the imagination "worthy & dignified," and here we can see that it has undertaken, beyond the aesthetic, a moral task. Nature is said never to desert "the wise and pure." Integration of mind and nature is sought because of one's craving for correspondence—and nature, whether alien or familiar, embraces the bodies of our friends as well as things. The poet enters the minds of his friends by way of his imaginative humanization of the total scene. The last rook beating its way homeward connects him with Charles because both have seen and heard it. Both have recognized that its dissonant creeking to the imaginative observer has a "charm" because it "tells of Life." The person deprived of imagination, Coleridge has said, "treats a living being as an inanimate Body," and in so doing finds himself in a nightmare world of fixities and discord. Persons become things without interiors, remote when they are not threatening. But the imaginative act is one of appropriation, proved doubly in this poem because the sense of shared life is greatest when literal sharing is impossible. The poet has been cut off from his companions, but has for that very reason felt more companionable. Coleridge writes that the "imaginative power," which "with its permeative modifying unifying might on the Thought and Images specificates the poet," is also the source of "moral intuitions" and the "*Good heart.*"[121]

The poet in "This Lime-tree Bower my Prison" has discovered that a greater burden must be placed on the interior self to perform than he had supposed in "The Eolian Harp." In "Dejection: An Ode" he finds that the interior self may lose the power to perform, to transform the dead letter into living language. The imagination is so conjoined with joy—

---

121. *PL*, p. 452n25.

this "beauty-making power"—that it ceases to function when the other does.

The earlier draft of "Dejection: An Ode"—the lengthy verse epistle, dated April 4, 1802, that Coleridge sends to Sara Hutchinson—gives us more clues to the nature of imagination's breakdown than does the shorter, more tightly structured poem he later publishes. In the epistle the poet more insistently envisions Sara's positive response to the same scene he finds so mocking and unsupportive. In this respect the epistle more than the ode appeals to the power of shared experience, as does "This Lime-tree Bower my Prison." The fact that sharing no longer sustains the poet is thereby given greater emphasis. In lines from the epistle that bring to mind by contrast, both in import and quality, the earlier poem, where the poet's imaginative pathos embraces Charles' response to the same rook, he writes:

> These lifeless Shapes, around, below, Above,
> O what can they impart?
> When even the gentle Thought, that thou, my love!
> Art gazing now, like me,
> And see'st the Heaven, I see—
> Sweet Thought it is—yet feebly stirs my Heart![122]

Almost everything about the scene is structured to support a state of mind similar to that of "This Lime-tree Bower my Prison": the scene is beautiful, Sara is imagined to view the same crescent moon, and, as in the earlier poem, she is not physically present.[123] But none of these elements stirs him.

---

122. *CL*, II, 791. "A Letter to——," *CL*, II, 790-798.

123. The poet wishes he could be with the ailing Sara to nurse her back to the health he thinks he has undermined by a "complaining Scroll / Which even to bodily Sickness bruis'd thy Soul!" But in his vision of the future, when she is happily living with her sister and Wordsworth, he would rather not be with her often anyway: "Where e'er I am, I shall be well content! / Not near thee, haply shall be more content!" It would be better to "know" than to "behold" her happiness, since he reasons that, trapped in his own unhappy marriage, he could not be with her always. Even Sara's

The state he describes is one of dissociation of inner life from scene. He has lost "what Nature gave me at my Birth, / My shaping Spirit of Imagination!" The imagination, we have said, mediates between inner life and the objects of nature, and discovers—as he writes in a passage added to a later version of "The Eolian Harp"—

> . . . the one Life within us and abroad,
> Which meets all motion and becomes its soul,
> A light in sound, a sound-like power in light,
> Rhythm in all thought, and joyance every where—

In such a world it "should have been impossible / Not to love all things," because one discovers through imagination that the life or energy that sustains individual consciousness permeates all objects. Their seemingly alien character is thereby denied. The poet, his imagination suspended, can only "see, not feel, how beautiful" the clouds, stars, and moon are. He quotes passages from the ode to illustrate the mostly Kantian observation that, "when we declare an object beautiful, the contemplation or intuition of its beauty precedes the *feeling* of complacency, in order of nature at least: nay, in great depression of spirits may even exist without sensibly producing it."[124] The poet's detached recognition of beauty does not prevent these objects from being "lifeless Shapes." In spite of their harmonious impression on the poet's senses, they are not invested with true imaginative form, which would indeed produce the correspondent feeling of "life." Coleridge does not in theoretical discussion consider that imagination itself can bring on nightmare. In terms of his theory, then, what still operates in the poet is the Gorgon Head, Fancy, that looks death into everything. Instead of a sense of correspondence with scene and others, the fancy produces the

---

absence, therefore, is not in itself depressing. As in "This Lime-tree Bower my Prison," he would have only to "lift the Soul" to gain a deeper sense of her companionship.

124. *On the Principles of Genial Criticism*, III, in *BL*, II, 241.

nightmare world, the phantasmagoria that are out of the
poet's control and that parody the imaginative process. He
recoils from his own image-making—frenzied scenes of torture,
"Groans & tremulous Shudderings" that give way to a vision
of a screaming lost child.

The poet denies here what many Freudian critics were
later to assert, that art originates in and provides its own
therapy for neurosis. (The fundamental paradox of the poem—
that it is, as "Dejection: An Ode," a finished poem about the
impossibility of writing poetry—might indirectly reinstate the
Freudian claim, of course. The act of writing the poem has
perhaps given Coleridge something of the catharsis and self-
mastery that the poem itself says are beyond the poet's reach.)
Rather, imagination and joy are inseparable, and through
each the poet affirms his freedom. When nature no longer
seems living, its shapes only add to the claustrophobic weight
of mental incarceration. In this state he cannot make the
loving gesture with the same sense of reciprocity that makes
the end of "This Lime-tree Bower my Prison" so moving. At
the end of the verse epistle, he offers a blessing on Sara, that
she, "nested with the Darlings of thy Love," would feel

> . . . in thy Soul, Heart, Lips, & Arms
> Even what the conjugal & mother Dove
> That borrows genial Warmth from those, she warms,
> Feels in her thrill'd wings, blessedly outspread—

but he is himself excluded from beneath the dove's warm
wings.

I have said that the poem deals only covertly with sexuality.
There is another powerful theme treated obliquely in the
ode. Combined with the verse epistle, it suggests that the poet's
crisis, beyond the loss of imagination and feeling, is a moral
one. Imagination is of course a shaping power, but as we have
seen in "This Lime-tree Bower my Prison" it operates as a
power of sympathy as well, a function that Shelley later

elucidates. A breakdown of imagination, in this sense, is a breakdown of felt sympathy, of sharing, and leads to bad conscience. The ode is a conversation poem that does not really believe in conversation. Could it be that the secret message behind the epistle to Sara is that he suffers from an inability to love, and that his best gesture can only be to renounce the woman he does not deserve, in the first place, to have?

"Limbo" (1817), a short philosophic lyric, develops even further the nightmare of consciousness deprived of imagination. In the world of limbo, the human mind is losing even its capacity for alienation. In allowing itself to be crushed into the perspective of lifeless nature, it is instead *becoming* the alien; mind is becoming the material universe it should interpret and humanize.

> 'Tis a strange place, this Limbo!—not a Place,
> Yet name it so;—where Time and weary Space
> Fettered from flight, with night-mare sense of fleeing,
> Strive for their last crepuscular half-being;—
> Lank Space, and scytheless Time with branny hands
> Barren and soundless as the measuring sands,
> Not mark'd by flit of Shades,—unmeaning they
> As moonlight on the dial of the day!

Nature unredeemed by imagination is this "spirit-jail," this "blank Naught-at-all." There have been no guarantees that the imaginative perspective can be sustained. The imaginative perspective of the limetree bower is in fact more precarious than the flattened perspective of limbo, which has the stability of deadness, after all. The challenge to the self to perform, to redeem nature through imagination, is one that may not be met, and not really through any severe shortcoming of the self. Nature as jailer may militate too strongly against the self's imaginative presumption.

A letter of 1825 to James Gillman, the Highgate doctor in whose house he rooms during the last eighteen years of his life, is perhaps the older, less presumptuous Coleridge's most memorable description of the growth of the relationship of mind to nature. In youth, mind and nature are "two rival Artists, . . . each having for it's object to turn the other into Canvas to paint on." The mind has the better of it for a time, transforming nature's "Summer Gales into Harps and Harpers, Lovers' Sighs and sighing Lovers, and her Winter Blasts into Pindaric Odes, Christabels & Ancient Mariners set to music by Beethoven." But nature, that "wary wily long-breathed old Witch," takes control and "mocks the mind with it's own metaphors, metamorphizing the Memory into a lignum vitae Escritoire to keep unpaid Bills & Duns Letters in." One's projects have meanwhile become outlines never filled in. She not only "turns the Mimic Mind, the ci-devant Sculptress with all her kaleidoscopic freaks and symmetries! into clay, but *leaves* it such a *clay*, to cast dumps or bullets in."[125] The world, Coleridge writes elsewhere, is a "*spidery* Witch" that closes in on us limiting our freedom and blunting our imagination.[126] But he wonders whether this very imagination has not been in any event dangerous from the start. He objects, for example, to Wordsworth's "vague misty, rather than mystic, Confusion of God with the World & the accompanying Nature-worship."[127] Imagination may lead to the heresy of pantheism, as Sarah, of all people, had seemed to warn in "The Eolian Harp." "Tintern Abbey" borders dangerously on depicting God in the "counterfeit form of Ubiquity" interfused through all creation.[128]

Coleridge argues that a "certain vantage-point" of education and sensibility is prerequisite if country life is not to make one "selfish, sensual, gross, and hard-hearted."[129] Pastoral

125. CL, V, 496–497.
126. MS Notebook 29 (1814–1825), f. 82^V; CL, V, 414.
127. CL, V, 95.
128. OM, B$_3$, ff. 48–53.
129. BL, II, 32.

nature hardly enriches moral character, as Wordsworth had seemed to say. Nature is by turns deadener and tempter. To direct the senses of an infant to objects instead of to persons results in a reflex of these energies to the senses themselves, "like echoes from an unreceiving Rock." It is not the actual things that we begin to desire, but the "images of the things."[130] The sensualist is one who has been "enslaved by imagination." Because it lends itself to illusion, sensuality, and even religious heresy, imagination should be supplanted by faith and prayer.

The young Coleridge had believed imagination to be the free and active power of consciousness to create the world in its own image. While it had more than an element of presumption, it also created awareness that one is a member of a community of living selves. Thus its moral or humanizing power was evident along with its presumption. An older Coleridge has learned painfully that imagination may lose its visionary power, and nature its lovely shapes and sounds intelligible. It is a sorry consolation that a strong imagination begins to seem dangerous anyway, in that its participatory energies may be misdirected. On the one hand it may diffuse moral consciousness into a vague and indiscriminate pantheism, or on the other hand concentrate it into delusive sensuality. In either case it diverts moral energy from human relationship into a tyranny of natural objects.

We have seen that feeling and imagination are central to Coleridge's conception of the moral life. Both act as mediators between natural and spiritual spheres; both assert, extraordinarily, the possibility of freedom within the sphere of nature itself, and therefore challenge the limitations on freedom implicit in the Newtonian conception of nature as mechanism. When Coleridge questions their value, as we have

130. OM, B_3, f. 70.

seen him do, morality and humanism tend to give way to supernaturalism.

His suspicion of his own assertions about human value will be seen constantly in this study. Contradictions in his writings do not result from failure to see incompatible modes of thought; rather they result from the doubt or fear that unstrings his own arguments. We have heard him assert, for example, that liberal judgment of others is not only more kind but more perceptive. Still he knows that human beings are forever unknown to one another; all judgment is to a degree an injustice because we are cut off from interiors. Liberality suggests a modus operandi but does not do away with the gelid look we cast on others and receive. (He might wish to add that many people, such as Hazlitt and, on occasion, Lloyd, *deserve* the evil eye.) In his more assertive vein he has argued that what one is, is of greater import than what one does. Nevertheless, he doubts that "being" dissociated from "doing" is a healthy state, whatever its perverse rationale. In these cases doubt has added the complexity we would otherwise have missed. But doubt does not always work advantageously. He has asserted passionately in "France: An Ode" and the conversation poems that integration of self and nature is necessary for a sense of personal freedom, and that feeling and imagination are the means of this integration. Doubt will triumph here more conventionally—Coleridge fears that nature, as the source of sexuality and as the occasion of pantheism, must be "deposited."

We must keep in mind that most of his assertions are problematic and subject to qualification or even rejection. This tenuousness often makes it difficult to assert what Coleridge *thought*, but it surely indicates that he has captured something of the quality of modern sensibility. The paradoxes and contradictions in his theory are coordinate with the man himself. He has great psychological acumen, yet he is compulsively unmindful of the most important facts about himself. He is the noisy propounder of principles who leads a most un-principled life; author of the "Essay on Method," yet the most irregular of expositors; author of *Christabel* and "Kubla Khan," yet an insufferable prig at times. He is indolent and unable to get on with it, yet at least as prolific as most other major writers.

With this caution in mind, we can draw a few conclusions from the material presented so far on the question of human freedom and alienation. Coleridge fears that human freedom, if considered solely in terms of the abysmal will below the reach of consciousness, is synonymous, paradoxically, with evil potential and lack of *moral* control. The moral task might then appear to be to disarm the will as much as possible. The means of disarming are self-denial, lack of individual initiative and aggression, giving one's own interest over to that of another (as Coleridge thinks he does in his relationship with Wordsworth), development of a high degree of sensitivity to one's own evil potential, and in general a dissociation of consciousness from will. Coleridge conceives of his own life as one of continual self-denial (he claims his only sensuality has been the wish not to be in pain), and he attempts to see some moral purpose and vindication in this. But his stance is, he knows, unsatisfactory—at least in part because it does not achieve its own purpose of propitiation of the moral judge, whether that be the society of loveless observers, his own corrosive and unjust conscience, or God. His stance is unsatisfactory, too, because it seems absurdly to set as the highest moral goal the lack of human purpose. Human powers become, instead of an opportunity, a temptation.

Because he is not satisfied in theory or in his own life with a state of negation, he seeks freedom through the development of powers that lie above the arcane movements of the abysmal will. The discovery and articulation of such powers are, I suggest, his central and most difficult tasks as a moralist, because his conception of will implies the comparative weakness of moral initiatives. Morality for him is the province of all exclusively *human* traits, such as imagination, feeling, humor, creative intelligence, conscious choosing, loving-kindness. Neither fiends, beasts, nor angels possess these. The Ancient Mariner and Christabel, we have seen, do possess some of them, but not to the degree necessary to withstand radical evil, an evil that must be conceived of as within. The Mariner's humane love of the creatures is only momentary redemption, Christabel's natural sympathy opens the door to heteronomy. Coleridge as moralist wishes nevertheless to describe ways in which moral virtues may be freely developed and attain to their own kind of potency. "The *Will* has to struggle upward into *Free-Will*."

Directing his attention, therefore, to the development of the conscious self or ego, he seeks ways of freeing consciousness from its imprisonment in a world of things and from its own manacles. Two human powers that promise freedom within the natural world—feeling and imagination—are his focus. I have shown that his faith in both is tenuous, even shortcircuited, but both remain central to all further articulation of moral purpose. Both suggest that the will's drive for separateness is tempered by one's conscious and free participation in nature and in human community. All moral systems will be judged by the extent to which they permit or encourage feeling and imagination. His own task as moralist is to define what prescriptions for the moral life will best promote their free development.

In pursuing this task, Coleridge treats at length, as we shall see in Chapter 2, the central issue of duty. Perhaps a clear definition of duty will set forth the proper course of human action and the way to freedom. But he discovers that such prescriptions may entail a misapplied rationality that usurps the role of feeling and imagination. Such a conception of duty seems closely aligned with the very self-destructive constraints from which he seeks to be free. Any too rigid formulation here is a false solution to his inertia and only compounds it by not allowing feeling and imagination to issue their own imperatives. He therefore turns, in arguments we shall consider in Chapter 3, from a preoccupation with what the self ought to do to a consideration of what the self *may become*. Perhaps it is possible to enlarge moral consciousness without paralytic guilt, perhaps sympathy and love can become conscious powers that do not imply the vulnerability of Christabel.

Coleridge does not sentimentally look away from the evil will that is the cornerstone of his thought. This unconscious destructive force must be confronted, harnessed, and utilized to the extent that consciousness is able to do so. It may ruthlessly reassert its primacy, but not, he hopes, before the moral powers of humane consciousness have made their own assertions. The process he will describe may at times remind us of Freud or Jung: the unconscious is the primary force in human nature and can be ignored only at one's peril. I would suggest that we find in Coleridge the germ also of post-Freudian ego psychology. The growth of the ego—the fully developed personality or conscious self—is both the highest moral task and the best therapy.

2 | The Problem of Duty

Fixed Principles

Well before he reads Kant, Coleridge calls for "fixed principles." In "A Moral and Political Lecture" (1795) he tells the "zealous Advocates for Freedom" in his audience at Bristol that he wishes "not so much to excite the torpid, as to regulate the feelings of the ardent: and above all, to evince the necessity of *bottoming* on fixed Principles."[1] One is bemused whenever he appeals to his audience this way. After all, he is himself a family deserter, pornographer (if one reads *Christabel* the way some contemporary critics did), dope addict, and plagiarist so brazen that he sometimes lifts, as one notes in the early Bristol lectures, even his exhortations to moral principle. Sermonizing is most noticeable in public formats, where he maneuvers awkwardly and pompously before the accusing eye. In less defensive postures, to be explored in this chapter, he rejects the high moral line as in itself a threat to morality.

Walter Pater, in his fine essay on Coleridge in *Appreciations* (1889), contrasts Coleridge's passion for the "Absolute" in moral issues with the "relative spirit," which "by its constant

1. *Lectures 1795*, p. 5.

dwelling on the more fugitive conditions or circumstances of things, breaking through a thousand rough and brutal classifications, and giving elasticity to inflexible principles, begets an intellectual *finesse* of which the ethical result is a delicate and tender justice in the criticism of human life."[2] Coleridge lacks this finesse, Pater says, because his passion for the absolute leads him "to stereotype forms of faith and philosophy," to fix "one mode of life as the essence of life." Yet Coleridge's own "pathetic history pleads for a more elastic moral philosophy than his, and cries out against every formula less living and flexible than life itself."[3] Pater's view of Coleridge as moralist is forcible and precise, yet it should be seriously qualified, I think. It adheres to the more general view that Coleridge, when he gives up poetry, falls into "the high seas of theosophic philosophy, the hazy infinitude of Kantean transcendentalism, with its 'sum-m-mjects' and 'om-m-mjects,'" as Carlyle puts it, imitating Coleridge's inability to pronounce his labials properly.[4] (Carlyle is hardly one to complain of "hazy infinitude.") In moral concerns Coleridge would then be a "formalist": probable consequences and personal inclination are of little or no import in determining what is right and wrong; rather one refers to a moral principle, the authority of which is unquestionable whatever the awkwardness of its implementation in particular cases. But while Coleridge, like many sinners, is attracted to what he sees to be the certainty and discipline of formalism—behind the scourge is there not forgiveness?—he distrusts his own exhortations so much, so qualifies them and seeks their accommodation with concrete moral situations, that he becomes a provocative critic of formalism.

His ambivalence is seen in his discussions of moral principles themselves. A principle, whether moral or intellectual, differs in kind from a maxim, or a generalization from experience.

2. *Appreciations* (London: Macmillan, 1901), pp. 103–104.
3. Ibid.
4. *Coleridge as Talker*, p. 116.

Polonius is a man of maxims, which are conclusions based "upon observation of matters of fact, and [are] merely retrospective." A principle or idea "carries knowledge within itself, and is prospective." Polonius may be admirable when he gives advice to Laertes about matters of "past experience, . . . but when he comes to advise or project, he is a mere dotard. You see, Hamlet, as the man of ideas, despises him."[5] Of the Biblical prophets and their habit of "moral Ex- and De-hortations," Coleridge writes that "all genuine Morality, all applied practical vivified Moral Eloquence, is essentially prophetic."[6] Principles or moral laws are applied to particular persons and circumstances in much the same way that astronomical laws explain and predict eclipses. But maxims, or generalized private motives, may or may not accord with principles.

Assent to a principle is not simply intellectual agreement or "belief." One can assent to "the idea of man's moral freedom," for example, without being able to articulate it or without ever having thought about it. The idea "possesses and modifies" our "whole practical being" even if we denounce the idea itself.[7] Conversely, we may "believe" an idea without fundamentally assenting to it. To his austere older brother, George, the suitable recipient of such talk, Coleridge writes, "In times of old the *Principles* were better than the men, but . . . now the men (faulty as they are) are better than their *Principles*."[8] There is small comfort in this; it is true that "almost all men nowadays act and feel more nobly than they think/yet still the vile cowardly selfish calculating Ethics of Paley, Priestley, Lock, & other *Erastians*, do woefully influence & determine our course of action/."[9] A person is "more and other than his

5. *Table Talk*, ed. Henry Nelson Coleridge, in *The Complete Works* (Shedd ed.), VI, 286.

6. *N*, III, 3774.

7. *On the Constitution of Church and State*, ed. Henry Nelson Coleridge, in *The Complete Works* (Shedd ed.), VI, 33–34.

8. *CL*, III, 197.

9. *N*, II, 2627.

Belief," then, but Coleridge does not underestimate the power of mere belief in itself to corrupt by gradually taking possession of personality.

The "selfish calculating Ethics" that are taking over modern sensibility are, broadly, those whose highest value is "prudence." Prior to his reading Kant, Coleridge splutters to Southey about "WORLDLY PRUDENCE" and Southey's tendency to say "I and I" instead of "It is our duty."[10] The desynonymization of prudence and morality is, to be sure, developed along Kantian lines after he reads the *Grundlegung zur Metaphysik der Sitten* (1785) late in 1803. Kant defines prudence in its narrowest sense as "skill in the choice of means to [one's] own greatest well-being."[11] As only a means to another end, the "precept of prudence" is a "hypothetical imperative"—it cannot be commanded absolutely. The categorical imperative, on the other hand, commands certain acts absolutely as ends in themselves, quite independently of personal inclination and consequences. Whereas the principles of morality do not derive their authority from experience, prudence is, as William Frankena suggests, the reality principle, the ego coping with the world.[12] Coleridge would agree

10. *CL*, I, 164.

11. *Fundamental Principles of the Metaphysic of Morals*, trans. Thomas K. Abbott (New York: Liberal Arts, 1949), p. 33. The question of Kant's influence on Coleridge is a difficult and controversial one, which has been tackled by such scholars as René Wellek, Elizabeth Winkelmann, Arthur O. Lovejoy, Kathleen Coburn, Gian N. G. Orsini, Norman Fruman, Thomas McFarland, and many others. My main interest is to find those points at which Coleridge, in his moral writings, consciously parts company from Kant, and to describe why Kant's supposed "austerity" has, for Coleridge, both attractive and repellent aspects. Whether he really understands Kant when he disagrees, whether his departures are philosophically defensible, or whether Kant would have ready answers are interesting questions in themselves but are not my focus here and will be discussed only in passing.

12. *Ethics*, Foundations of Philosophy Series (Englewood Cliffs, N.J.: Prentice-Hall, 1963), p. 6. This is a lucid introduction to the subject of ethics, one that would prove useful and congenial to a student of literature; with that in mind, I will cite it frequently.

with Joseph Butler, who writes that prudence can be neglected
only at the expense of morality itself; people do not have the
right, says Butler, "dissolutely to neglect their greater good."[13]
Coleridge knows all too well from falling into his opium habit
that imprudence can eliminate the possibility of moral effort.
He himself therefore espouses what he calls "manly prudence"
if it does not usurp what is truly moral.

But the spirit of the age is defined precisely by such a
usurpation. Prudence has become the narrow pursuit of self-
gratification as an end in itself. For Coleridge it is a short
distance from self-gratification to sensuality. This is perhaps an
inobvious revaluation: prudence, commonly suggestive of
restraint and discretion, is a subterfuge of sensuality. His
indictment of the age of prudence is so broad that strange
bedfellows seem to him to share this covert sensual intent—
Catholics and Protestants, idealists and utilitarians, poets and
politicians.

What are these principles he thinks so necessary to the
moral life? An anonymous critic writes of "A Moral and
Political Lecture" that Coleridge "has not stated, in a form
sufficiently scientific and determinate, those principles to
which, as he expresses it, he now proceeds as the most *important point*. We confess we were looking for something
further, and little thought that we were actually come to the
Finis."[14] (We do not have to wait for drug addiction to set
in before we encounter the salient features of Coleridge's
expository prose.) Most of the fragments treating of moral
principles show a strong Kantian influence. He quotes the
categorical imperative in several contexts. With no attribution
to Kant, he writes in *The Friend*, "So act that thou mayest be
able, without involving any contradiction, to will that the
maxim of thy conduct should be the law of all intelligent

13. "Dissertation of the Nature of Virtue," in *The Analogy of Religion*,
ed. Edward Steere (London: George Bell, 1886), pp. 326–328.
14. *The Critical Heritage*, p. 24.

Beings—is the one universal and sufficient principle and guide of morality."[15] He never comments directly on the imperative or even applies it in any systematic way to specific moral problems. But it is implicitly invoked whenever he insists that one act according to universal principles.

His most explicit treatment of moral principles is a clever Kantian rewrite of the Decalogue, which is also a good illustration of his persistent effort to combine German idealism with Judeo-Christian doctrine. The eighteenth-century moralist and theologian William Paley and others, he complains, have underrated the Decalogue because they have misunderstood its intent. It focuses on the outward deed because the "Jews under Moses were men with formed Habits, & bad principles proved/—ergo, they must *unlearn* . . . they must *de*habituate[;] the Law therefore must first be *negative* . . . it must involve the principle in the *action*, in order that by legal purity the *film* may be removed from the eyes, the *obstructions* from the vessels of assimilation, nutrition &c/—."[16] The Decalogue therefore treats the disease by removing the symptoms. But each of the specific prohibitions can be translated into a universal principle, and this is what Coleridge sets out to do, in order to salvage the Decalogue as a philosophical guide to the moral life.

The first four commandments comprise the duties of man "as a moral & rational Individual—[the next three] his Duties, as a *social* being—[the last three] his Duties, as a *citizen* or member of a *State*." The first commandment, "Thou shalt have no other gods before me," can be reinterpreted as commanding obedience to the moral law for its own sake. We must obey our conscience "*exclusively* & *unconditionally*," and must be prepared to resist personal inclination. The motive for obeying the moral law is the Kantian *Achtung*, rational respect for the categorical imperative; it is a motive usually

15. *F*, I, 194.
16. *N*, III, 3293.

interpreted as having no psychological properties as such. The next three commandments supplement the first. Not making graven images is, in principle, not debasing our reason with "any mixture of *sens*uality—the sensuous Imagination." We must "consecrate & worship the eternal distinction between the Noumenon & the Phaenomenon." It would be unlike Kant to urge that we "worship" this eternal distinction instead of giving it our rational respect, but Coleridge does his share of Romantic augmentation of Kant, whom he recasts as the rescuer of a sense of the miraculous from the skepticism of the Age of Reason. Not taking the name of the Lord in vain is, when referred to its principle, preserving the "faculty of Discourse" in "strict awe & allegiance to the pure Reason." This entails keeping in mind the distinction between the dictates of conscience and the "idle sophisms" of prudential understanding. And finally, to obey the Sabbath is to obey the moral law with deliberation—to contemplate it, to think of ways of implementation.[17]

That his Moses anticipated the distinction between understanding and reason suggests Coleridge reads intellectual history with a prejudicial eye. (Pythagoras sounds suspiciously like Coleridge himself in *The Philosophical Lectures*.) Ricoeur argues that the Mosaic Law, since it pertains to the chosen people and originates in a historical event, "cannot be reduced to a formal structure of the universal conscience; it clings to the historical figure, the cultural patron, interpreted by the theology of history of the Biblical writers; and so its structure is ineluctably contingent."[18] But Coleridge's structural, ahistorical approach in this notebook entry is daring (Ricoeur might say illegitimate) precisely in its translation of the ethics of the elect into that of universal conscience. The prohibitory aspects of Mosaic Law are minimized, its particularity assimilated into Kantian formalism.

17. Ibid
18. *The Symbolism of Evil*, p. 120.

Those portions of the Decalogue that treat the individual as social being and as citizen are sanctioned by Kant's third formulation of the categorical imperative: "So act as to treat humanity, whether in thine own person or in that of any other, in every case as an end withal, never as means only."[19] The imperative is closely related to the Kantian distinction, often repeated by Coleridge, between "persons" and "things." It is the "principle indeed, which is the *ground-work* of all law and justice, that a person can never become a thing, nor be treated as such without wrong."[20] Ungrateful children, murderers, adulterers, thieves, liars, and the covetous all violate this fundamental principle. A person owed money by another can be sufficiently repaid by a third party, argues Coleridge, because the sum in question would be *"the same thing."* But if a mother has not received her son's love, she cannot be bought off by a substitute who would offer her his own.[21] Likewise, it would be absurd to offer up one's own life as substitute for that of a condemned criminal—lives are not exchangeable.[22] A late notebook entry argues that "Things have no true individuality. . . . Thence the impulse to individualize them by *property*." Persons "are essentially individual. Thence the moral impulse, & command to universalize, to reduce them to a Unity."[23]

Sartre writes that Kant does not adequately entertain the terrifying truth that in our experience with the Other, we necessarily constitute him or her as an object or thing, whose hypothetical interiority will forever lie beyond our own consciousness. The Other, in turn, is a "radical negation of my experience, since he is the one for whom I am not subject but object." Kantians, in "establishing the universal laws of sub-

19. *Fundamental Principles of the Metaphysic of Morals,* p. 46.
20. *F,* I, 190.
21. *AR,* pp. 321–323.
22. *AR,* pp. 323–325n.
23. MS Notebook 46 (1830), f. 10ᵛ.

jectivity which are the same for all, never dealt with the question of *persons*," of the diversity that implies separation. In fact, "the subject is only the common essence of these persons; it would no more allow us to determine the multiplicity of persons than the essence of man, in Spinoza's system, permits one to determine that of concrete men."[24] Coleridge comes to Kant with precisely this painful sense of the multiplicity of persons and human separateness. Perhaps Kant himself does not adequately express this sense, as Sartre says, but Coleridge nevertheless finds in Kant the liberal formula that would offer a palliative to the more corrosive aspects of human separation and alienation. The imperative that one is to treat others as persons instead of things does not offer a way of overcoming alienation, but it does offer a way of coping and of living graciously in a sinister world. If intimacy or love is not commanded, respect and toleration are. Kant, who contributes so much to the development of liberalism, is elsewhere attacked by Coleridge and many others for his "austerity" and neostoic rigorism. But Coleridge is not so reductive that he misses altogether the liberal flavor of many of Kant's teachings. The distinction between persons and things has a wealth of implications that are anything but austere.

At the same time, Coleridge finds Kant's view of human relationships limited. He believes we can demand something more than rational respect and tolerance of one another. He complains of Godwin's "total want of affectionate Enquiry" toward him, and of his own lack of particularized sympathy. To treat humanity as an end in itself is in Kant's view a rational task without any necessary affective component. One's treatment of another need not be particularized, for one owes another only the respect that would be given to any human being. Kant is not opposed to feeling, of course,

24. *Being and Nothingness*, trans. Hazel E. Barnes (New York: Citadel, 1971), p. 201.

but simply argues that it is irrelevant to the moral worth of one's maxim of conduct. Coleridge wishes, however, to retain feeling as an essential component of morality, whatever its theoretical awkwardness within a Kantian superstructure. Much of his criticism of Kant is based on his view that one's idiosyncratic needs and inclinations must have a place in moral deliberation and that the Kantian effort to "reduce to a unity" and to act and judge according to a categorical imperative can be carried so far that it divides and paralyzes the moral agent.

He therefore develops a notion of respect to include feeling and imaginative recognition of the uniqueness of the person in view: "Reverence the Individuality of your friend!" One can laugh at another's oddities, but one had best be sure that what one calls "Odd and Capricious may not be a Peculiarity connected with the individuality of the Person's Being and Character—and unintelligible to you, because its source lies deeper than Intelligence." The liberality he calls for is not an imperative to become intimate. In fact, friendship does entail the tact of keeping one's distance, allowing for another's sphere of free agency. One should not construe social relationships as a series of concentric circles with one's own ego as the single center, but as a "close neighborhood of centers," each with a circumference of its own that should not be forced to contract too much "in order to give space for the others."[25] Kant himself writes that respect tends to produce "distance" and a "limitation upon intimacy," just as love tends toward intimacy. The tension between love and respect is the difficulty of friendship.[26] While Coleridge knows the truth of that insight, he will argue that the dynamics of respect should have its own warmth. One should

25. *IS*, p. 308–311.
26. *The Doctrine of Virtue: Part II of the Metaphysic of Morals*, trans. Mary J. Gregor (Philadelphia: University of Pennsylvania Press, 1964), p. 141.

extend particularized respect, and it should have emotional as well as rational components.

We may conclude here that Coleridge is attracted to un-ambiguous moral directives—his infirmities beg for strong medicine. But the specific principles that most engage him are those that militate against illiberality, those forms of the categorical imperative that urge the human being is an end in himself and must never be treated as a means or as a thing. There is from the beginning a split in his attitude toward formalism. Rehabilitation, he often implies, comes about through resolute effort in terms of severe and absolute principles, and as one whose career begins with sermonizing, he calls for them unsparingly in the abstract. But the particularities of the moral life impose on formal argument. A morality must be found that embraces more aspects of the human being than his rational capacity. To be sure, the Decalogue can and should be universalized, as he has himself shown; but universals must then be modified by concrete circumstance, psychological complexity, and individuality. In a complicated way, he will be going in both directions at once but will emerge with a moral vision that, in its emphasis on whole-ness of personality, embraces both.

Conscientious Persecutors

Coleridge is made uneasy by those whose conduct of life is all too highly principled. He turns on his own lofty precepts when he examines more closely both the personality of those who act uncompromisingly and the consequences of their actions.

One finds many of the lofty precepts in *The Friend*, where he argues, for example, that one should do what is right and let consequences take care of themselves. Luther "did his duty, come good, come evil! and made no question, on which side the preponderance would be."²⁷ At times Coleridge tries to dismiss the question of consequences altogether: "To suppose that a man should cease to be *beneficent* by becoming *benevolent*, seems to me scarcely less absurd, than to fear that a fire may prevent heat, or that a perennial fountain may prove the occasion of Drought."²⁸ Xenophon, Nelson, and Wellington have proved, he says, that principled action is also prudent. This point is so important that he claims it has been the "main characteristic of the moral system taught by *The Friend*." For man "to obey the simple unconditional commandment of eschewing every act that implies a self-contradiction, or in other words, to produce and maintain the greatest possible Harmony in the component impulses and faculties of his nature, involves the effects of Prudence. It is, as it were, Prudence in *short-hand* or cypher."²⁹ But the very examples he uses to support this argument contradict it. Luther, he admits, did scandalize half a continent. And in a discussion of freedom of the press, he says that he is unable to recall any injurious consequences from publication of the truth, "under the observance of the moral conditions above stated."³⁰ Those conditions, however, are extensive, especially in politically sensitive matters where publication of the full truth could lead to social discontent.

Coleridge is in fact painfully sensitive to the maze of contingencies that confronts the moral agent. He worries that Thelwall, the intrepid "man for *action*," is too principled for his own good. He would prefer to see Thelwall instead "*doubting* and *doubting*," his "natural impetuosity" dis-

27. *F*, I, 64.
28. *F*, I, 315.
29. *F*, I, 150. This is a Coleridgean reconstruction of the categorical imperative. Kant is not concerned with producing harmony among the various impulses and faculties; in fact, the Romantics' primary complaint is that Kant's unconditional commandment would foster self-division.
30. *F*, I, 49.

ciplined into "patience, and salutary scepticism, and the slow energies of a *calculating* spirit."[31]

When Josiah and Thomas Wedgwood offer a gift of a hundred pounds late in 1797 to free Coleridge from wasting his genius on journalism, he refuses it. He agrees he should quit journalism but thinks he should enter the Unitarian ministry, however reluctantly, without accepting the gift. In support of his position, he argues that no decision would be without its drawbacks and moral dangers, that good and evil do not exist in any pure form. If we felt that we were acting against our principles only when we produced "*unmingled* evil," we could indulge just about any crime. "If on the other hand a man should make it *his principle* to abstain from all modes of conduct, the general practice of which was not permanently useful, or at least absolutely harmless, he must live, an isolated Being: his furniture, his servants, his very cloathes are intimately connected with Vice and Misery." In moral decisions, then, "we *must* compound with a large quantity of evil," though of course endeavoring to do good. One selects comparative, not absolute, goods. Some complicated moral arithmetic—in which he balances the moral advantages against the disadvantages of each career—hardly suggests the simplistic idea that one should do what is right, come what may.[32]

Too uncompromising a conception of moral principle is not only impractical but dangerous, as Coleridge argues in his own treatment of the authoritarian personality. To act too literally from a sense of moral principle is the greatest moral error. An essay entitled "A Good Heart" seriously qualifies his earlier plea for "fixed principles." Luther, Tom Jones,

31. *CL*, I, 339, 342.
32. *CL*, I, 364–367. John Cornwell suggests in *Coleridge: Poet and Revolutionary* (London: Allen Lane, 1973), p. 204, that the real message behind the moral arithmetic may be that the Wedgwoods should offer something larger and more permanent than the 100 pounds. They take the bait and do thereafter offer an annuity of 150 pounds.

Parson Adams are contrasted with Calvin, Sir Charles Grandison, and Dr. Harrison (from Fielding's *Amelia*)—the former act with good heart, the latter with "Pharisaic righteousness." Archbishop Laud and "the whole race of conscientious Persecutors" are guilty of a "suppression" of the good heart and a ruthless substitution for it of mere "Principles." Observation of their conduct and personality "serves to reconcile one to the fewness of the men who act on fixed Principles." Ethical rigorism leads to bigotry unless there exist a "Graciousness of Nature, a Loving-kindness," which he calls "temperamental *pro*-virtues."[33] Coleridge elsewhere asserts that "whoever supermoralizes unmoralizes."[34]

He has a notable tendency to befriend those whom he accuses of supermoralism: George Coleridge and Southey, for example. The psychological need perhaps originated, as Walter Jackson Bate suggests, in his being the youngest member of a large family, making it necessary for him to ingratiate himself with those upon whom he is dependent. One lifelong means of ingratiation is to prove himself weak as if to remind the other of his own relative strength—hence, his fascination with and resentment of those with "strong" character.[35] This ambivalence is seen very early in dealings with George, who displays the kind of exemplary, steadfast, unimaginative, and finally cruel behavior that Coleridge assumes he should imitate though he secretly detests it. George's steadfastness is revealed, for example, in his refusal to receive Coleridge and his children at his home in 1807 after Coleridge's separation from his wife, because divorce is "an irreligious act."[36] Coleridge is attracted to principles in principle, but he dislikes the censoriousness and literal-mindedness of those who invoke and act upon them.

33. MS Notebook 29, ff. 112–119ᵛ.
34. *N*, II, 2358.
35. *Coleridge* (New York: Macmillan, 1968), pp. 1–11.
36. *CL*, III, 24–25, 31, 101–105.

The problem with Southey, he writes to Godwin, is his moral purity itself. Southey has "preserved himself immaculate from all the common faults and weaknesses of human nature," but "there is a bluntness of Conscience superinduced by a very unusual Infrequency, as well as by the Habit & Frequency, of wrong Actions."[37] A notebook entry of 1804 enlarges on Southey's character, his "never once stumbling Temperance," his chastity, industry, punctuality, domesticity, beneficence. For all this, Southey is empty, the "smiles, the emanations, the perpetual Sea-like Sound & Motion of Virtuousness, which is Love, is wanting—."[38] And this lack of warmth is reflected in his remorseless persecution of Coleridge (real or imagined)—his censure of *Lyrical Ballads*, malicious remarks about Sarah Coleridge, and coldness toward Coleridge. "Perhaps even *Virtue*," he had written to Southey in 1794, "is liable to a Plethora!"

The connection between supermoralism and tyranny is clear in a figure such as Robespierre, whose vision of an ideal society may have been admirable but whose "cool ferocity" imposed evil means in pursuit of it.[39] I suspect that Southey may unwittingly have inspired Coleridge's depiction of Robespierre in the early drama, *The Fall of Robespierre* (1794), the two coauthored.[40] Robespierre speaks of his own "steel-strong Rectitude of soul" (I.117), but Tallien observes that the people are weary of his "stern morality, / The fair-mask'd offspring of ferocious pride" (I.248–249). Elsewhere, Coleridge writes that Robespierre's reign proves that "the ardor of undisciplined benevolence seduces us into malignity."[41] In a real sense, Robespierre is all-too-human, because it is a person's natural presumption to "universalize his notions"—

37. *CL*, III, 316.
38. *N*, I, 1815.
39. *IS*, p. 276.
40. Coleridge wrote Act I, Southey, Acts II and III.
41. *Lectures 1795*, p. 35; *CL*, I, 284.

a presumption that implies psychological weakness and, ironically, a narrowness of moral view. "Tremendous as a Mexican God is a strong sense of Duty separate from an enlarged and discriminating mind. . . . [T]he very virtue of the person, & the consciousness that it is sacrificing its own happiness, increases the obduracy, & selects those whom it best loves for its objects."[42] To act with assuredness of universal principle is to risk the greatest immorality.[43]

Calvin and Marat proved that there has been no more pernicious error in world history than giving "to a *general* truth, the privileges of a *universal Law*, or in other words the neglect of that golden Adage, *Summnum Jus summa injuria*," the strictest application of the law produces the greatest injustice. Calvin's general truth was to "promote the Truth," but he universalized it and acted upon it as if he were omniscient and omnipotent. Marat was willing to sacrifice 200,000 countrymen to his conception of an ideal Europe. Both forgot, says Coleridge, "that a man can only *believe* himself to *know* that any given position is true in each particular form in which he announces it, or that the means which he takes to realize this position, are the right and fit means." Even if Marat had been proved ultimately right in his calculations, he would still have been a fanatic, because the "proposal was frightfully disproportionate to the sphere of a poor fallible Mortal."[44]

Does this mean that one cannot undertake momentous action at all? Not exactly, for Coleridge argues that there is an essential difference between the actions of Brutus and Ravaillac, though they were both technically assassins. Not bothered by the circularity, he says that all "good" people in all ages have pronounced Brutus' act a noble one; everyone (who is good)

42. *N*, III, 3672.
43. Kant would similarly object to the presumption that one's own point of view is universally true. In fact, the categorical imperative is in theory a safeguard against this very presumption.
44. *IS*, pp. 128–130.

knows Ravaillac was a scoundrel to assassinate Henry IV of France. An essay written in 1811 for *The Courier* explains the distinction with reference to Samuel Whitbread's speech to Parliament against any attempt to assassinate Napoleon. Whitbread's speech declares in effect that assassination is wrong in principle and would set a dangerous precedent for fanatics. Coleridge is not arguing *for* tyrannicide (usually it is not advisable), but he says that to lay down an a priori principle here is pointless. Brutus has, after all, demonstrated that tyrannicide has on at least one occasion been moral and necessary. Could not the parallel between Caesar and Napoleon suggest another exception to the rule prohibiting assassination? Indeed, it is absurd

to seek after a general rule for actions, that do not permit a single query concerning their moral character under any other name, than that of very rare and extraordinary *exceptions* to a general rule. It is absurd too, because such an exception supposes and implies a complexity and concurrence of peculiar circumstances, each single instance being itself a species, to be tried on its own grounds, and resting its whole pretences for acquittal or mitigation of censure on its *peculiarity*.[45]

The thrust of his argument is really against the dominant role of principles in determining the moral worth of action or character. He posits a much less exacting method of moral judgment than we would expect from a rigorist. It is not Brutus' action or pursuit of principle that we admire, ac-

---

45. *EOT*, III, 830–831. "General" has the force of "universal" in this passage. He qualifies the argument in the next issue of *The Courier:* in "strict language, there can be no *exception* to a moral rule," because an "*exception* in ethics means no more than an individual act that is itself a species" (*EOT*, III, 834n). Such an act will have its "own distinguishing characters" and only appears to contradict a moral law to which it is subjoined. Coleridge seems to be close here to the notion that "exceptions" to universal principles can in theory be themselves universalized, though of course the larger the number of exceptions added to the principle, the less its clarity and usefulness. See Frankena, *Ethics*, p. 31.

cording to Coleridge, "but it is the *man*, the sum-total of his known moral being, collated with the customs and creeds of his age and country." We do not and should not decide by any universal principle, but "by the effect produced on our *feelings*, by the sum total of all the data and circumstances of the particular case." These feelings are prompted "by *realities* only, by the contemplation of actual individual cases, with all the many and nice circumstances that individualized them, and not by those meagre and shadowy generalities which may serve to elucidate a general law."[46] He now claims that in *The Friend* he has "shewn that no Principle can be applied practically without exceptions, limitations, modifications—in short, without a compromise between Science & Prudence."[47] He is not throwing away a priori principles altogether but is saying that they must make their compromise with the world.

Two letters to Thomas Allsop, his young businessman friend during his Highgate years, develop the idea succinctly. In making a moral decision or judgment one must try to separate the "principle of Right" and the "*science* of Morals" from all expediency. *But* (the word one must use time and again in discussing what Coleridge believes) he fears that his friend Allsop might, through some all too principled act, such as running into marriage, blight his "*utility* by cankering [his] happiness." "A morality of consequences I, you well know, reprobate—but to exclude the necessary *effect* of an action is to take away all meaning from the word, action—to strike Duty with Blindness." A case must be decided in its "*particulars*, personal and circumstantial, with it's Antecedents and *involved* (N.b. not it's contingent or apprehended) Consequents." Otherwise our very virtues conspire against us and "Self may be moodily gratified by *Self*-sacrifice."[48] Coleridge, to use the language of the ethicist, is moving away from rule-

46. *EOT*, III, 835.
47. *CL*, III, 540.
48. *CL*, V, 177–178, 182.

deontology to act-deontology here, that is, the rightness or wrongness of an action depends on our perception, as Aristotle says, of the particulars of a case, not on some application of universal principle. He never gives up altogether a call for principles, but they often appear to be more summary rules or guidelines than a priori truths. Indeed his initial response to the categorical imperative had been to brand it a "mere empty generalization."[49]

He admits that a morality based wholly on limitation and skepticism could make the entire world stagnate. "What then is the *reconciling* principle? This:—Take care, that your *act* is proportionate to your faculties, neither forgetting their strength nor their fallibility."[50] This final principle is quite unlike Coleridge's pleading in *The Friend* that one should simply do what he or she knows is right, come what may. He now calls for self-knowledge and coordination of capacities with actions, very unassuming advice to be sure. The ultimate imperative is, "Be ye perfect," but insofar as "ought" implies "can," he realizes that such an imperative should not weigh on one too heavily. For the sake of one's own excellence, one must realize that it can exist only in approximations.

Conscience and Consciousness

Kant writes that conscience is not a "duty" but rather an "inevitable fact." When we say that "this man has no conscience, what we mean is: he pays no attention to its verdict."[51] Coleridge writes that it is still "the great definition of humanity, that we have a conscience, which no mechanic compost, no chemical combination, of mere appetence, memory, and understanding, can solve; which is indeed an *Element* of our

49. *N*, I, 1711.
50. *IS*, p. 129.
51. *The Doctrine of Virtue*, p. 61.

Being!" We can "stupify but cannot delude" it.[52] The German word for conscience, *Gewissen*, suggests certainty of judgment, and the promise of certainty is much of its appeal for Coleridge, whose moral perplexity is chronic: "Above all things it is incumbent on me who lay such a stress on Conscience, & attach such a sacredness to it, to shew that it is no Socratic Daimon which I mean, but the dictate of universal Reason, accompanied with a feeling of free Agency—that it is *Light*—that an erring Conscience is no Conscience, and as absurd as an erring Reason—i.e. not Reason/—."[53] Similarly, Kant writes that "an *erring* conscience" is by definition "a logical impossibility."[54]

But in line with his fear of moral presumption, Coleridge disputes his own self-evident truth. It is somewhat academic to *define* conscience as unerring, and it is sentimental to assume that everyone possesses it. Have there not been many, like Iago and Richard III, who have lost all vestige of conscience, and have not others with all too highly developed consciences, like Robespierre and Marat, done great harm? Coleridge admits that an "Inquisitor's conscience prompts first to torture and then burn alive hundreds of women and children for mere words without meaning—."[55]

Coleridge's lifelong treatment of the subject of conscience reveals two divergent tendencies. When he thinks of it as the faculty by which we come intuitively to know "principles," he moralizes in a quasi-Kantian manner about its infallibility, its character as an internal tribunal that passes judgment on the self, and its power to produce "remorse," not merely "regret," when contradicted. But he is not content with these

52. *F*, II, 8.
53. *N*, III, 3591.
54. *The Doctrine of Virtue*, p. 61.
55. Bound Transcript, Notes on Lord Lyttleton's *The History of the Life of Henry the Second* (1767–71), Victoria University Library.

formulations. The other tendency is to align conscience with consciousness more generally, so that it ceases to be thought of as a separate faculty. Conscience is rather the total act of moral self-awareness, which registers universal principles less than it registers one's participation in a concrete and protean moral world. Violation of conscience is, in this case, not so much the dramatic remorse, which results from direct violation of principle through wrong acts, as it is the "guilt" and "dread" that are slow and persistent components of highly developed human consciousness.

In its first aspect, conscience is indeed no Socratic Daimon—rather it is an avenging demon, which reminds "the humiliated self-examinant . . . that there is Evil in our nature as well as Good."[56] The greatest certainty it offers is, unhappily, that one is a sinner. To contradict one's conscience is a literal *self*-contradiction, the violation of the highest part of one's nature. Self-contradiction is felt as remorse. Coleridge's neo-Jacobean melodrama, *Remorse* (1812), a revision of the early *Osorio* (1797), attempts to put all of this on stage, though the result is less than felicitous. Alvar, victim of the villainy of his brother, Ordonio, returns from exile disguised as a Moor. Not seeking revenge, he wishes to provoke remorse in Ordonio, who despite habitual treachery and misanthropy retains a conscience. (Ordonio has, suspiciously, much in common with Southey; both mistake "constitutional abstinence from vice for strength of character.") The bizarre action leads up to Ordonio's discovery of his brother's identity, whereupon Ordonio kneels, asks forgiveness, and at death cries, "Atonement!" Alvar sums it up: conscience, our "inward Monitress to guide or warn," will rule us even "against our choice" (V.i.288–289).

Ordonio's error is to think that he can simply leave his crime behind him. Coleridge writes, in Southey's copy of *Aids to Reflection* (1825), that the conscience is wounded

56. *F*, II, 8.

not by the "criminal *Deed*" but by the "sinful *Act*," which embraces the entire intentionality of the agent. Only the act, not the external deed, attaches to the will. One of the "tricks and devices of self-delusion" is to lose the act in the deed, and thereby to treat both as "past." A deed, according to Coleridge, is known by its "singleness, its detachability for the imagination, its particularity, and, above all, its pastness." The function of remorse is to unmask this strategem, to make us confess to the "continuing and abiding *presentness*" of the sinful act.[57] The implicit metaphor for conscience is frequently Kant's: conscience is the internal tribunal, "with a view to either [one's] acquittal or his condemnation."[58] So considered, conscience is necessarily divisive, because a human being is necessarily imperfect. Ordonio's conscience is compartmentalized as an organ or faculty that can be repressed for long periods in isolation from other facets of consciousness, but that eventually reemerges to pass judgment on the act, not merely the deed. The dramatic and psychological improbability of Ordonio's contrition is perhaps a result of Coleridge's own lack of conviction that conscience is so specialized and formulaic in its operation, so divisible from other kinds of consciousness, and so able to survive repression. He knows there is actually a danger in setting up conscience as a separate faculty, an isolated tribunal—can it not be wooed, bribed, and deluded as any other judge can be? Scrupulosity is closely aligned with debased egotism, the overdeveloped conscience is a form of self-preoccupation. Of Bunyan's *Grace Abounding* (1666) he notes "that mood of mind which exaggerates, and still more, mistakes, the inward depravation."[59] Many indulge in the "proud Humiliations of religious Egotism," and many, whining of their wickedness, are enjoying their "mock Consciences" and are "cuddled up & comfortable in the wrap-

57. Bound Transcript, Victoria University Library.
58. *The Doctrine of Virtue*, pp. 61, 103–106.
59. *Table Talk*, p. 332.

rascal of self-hypocrisy."[60] The conscience as tribunal is a powerful metaphor that lends itself to melodrama, self-division, and hypocrisy.

Coleridge's more provocative and difficult notion of conscience is that it is the root, not simply an offshoot or faculty, of all true consciousness. It is "the ground and antecedent of human (or *self-*) consciousness, and not any modification of the latter."[61] Admitting in the Opus Maximum that the idea is obscure, he explains that the antecedence is "in the order of thought ie. without reference to time."[62] The infant has sentience prior to the conscience he later develops. Even a cow has "consentiency" or "conpercipiency" in that it has some somnambulistic awareness of its environment. But this is neither consciousness nor self-consciousness, both of which require knowledge of "something in its relation to myself—in and with the act of knowing myself as acted on by that something."[63]

Coleridge attempts in the Opus Maximum a complicated elliptical explanation of the necessary priority of conscience to consciousness. The exposition is obscure and requires some inferences. The three persons—I, you, and he, she, it—all definitionally presuppose one another. Each exists in its relation to the others; an "I" without the "not-I" would contradict the use of language. But how do we go from language use to reality? The reality of the "thou," or another consciousness correlative to but not the same as our own, would seem to distinguish us from animals, who must have a sense only of the "it."[64]

Coleridge argues—and this idea is of profound importance to him—that to be conscious of oneself as a *self* requires a

60. *N*, III, 3591.
61. *AR*, p. 118.
62. OM, B$_2$, f. 111.
63. OM, B$_2$, f. 142; cf. *N*, III, 4195.
64. OM, B$_2$, ff. 143–144.

synchronous commitment to the reality of another. "Without a *Thou* there could be no opposite, and of course no distinct or conscious sense of the term I." To posit another being correlative to one's self requires an act of moral imagination, because the natural tendency toward self-involution, or indeed solipsism, makes the reality of the other contingent. The act of moral imagination required, then, to assert the reality of the "thou" is called "conscience." It is the "equation of *Thou* with *I* by means of a free act by which we negative the sameness [assert that the I and the thou are not identical] in order to establish the equality" [the two consciousnesses are equally real and worthy].[65]

The argument is expressed more simply in a notebook entry: "*From* what reasons do I believe a *continuous* ⟨& ever continuable⟩ *Consciousness?* From *Conscience!* Not for myself but for my conscience—i.e. my affections & duties toward others, I should have no Self—for Self is Definition; but all Boundary implies Neighbourhood—& is knowable only by Neighbourhood, or Relations."[66] One's sense of relatedness to a world of other consciousnesses is then prior "in order of thought" to a sense of self, which is what Coleridge means by "consciousness" in this context. Similarly, Fichte in *Die Bestimmung des Menschen* (1800), a likely source for some of Coleridge's thinking here, writes that it is conscience that forces us to put aside empty solipsistic speculation and to assume that there are other beings "in possession of an existence for themselves wholly independent of mine," who set a limit to our freedom by their own.[67] Coleridge calls the conscience an "act of being," the imaginative positing of

65. OM, B₂, ff. 143–146; cf. *N*, III, 4426.
66. *N*, II, 3231.
67. *The Vocation of Man*, trans. William Smith (La Salle, Ill.: Open Court Publishing, 1946; rpt. 1965), pp. 105–111. This work, among others, makes Coleridge's reduction of Fichte's ethics to "I itself I" dubious indeed.

human reality beyond the sphere of the private self and the resultant moral responsibility that falls on that self.

What is the relationship between such a conception of conscience and guilt or dread? He notes that the more highly developed the conscience, "the less loose and detachable is the consciousness of the events and objects that make up the man's experience . . . from the Self-consciousness, which is the essential and inalienable Form of his Personal Identity."[68] The provocative idea that the moral view makes experience "less loose and detachable" has a sinister underside. All objects of consciousness, all experience, become morally significant and, therefore, potentially menacing. It may be not simply one's notably evil acts that produce guilt or dread but one's entire act of being, as he discovers when in 1805 he takes an inventory of his own life.

The venerable faculty called "conscience" that puts us in touch with "principles" begins to be outstripped by a modern conception of moral consciousness. "It is a most instructive part of my Life the fact, that I have been always preyed on by some Dread, and perhaps all my faulty actions have been the consequence of some Dread or other on my mind/from fear of Pain, or Shame, not from prospect of Pleasure/—." He recalls, among other things, his horror at not being able to pay his bills at Cambridge, "a short-lived Fit of Fears from sex," the alienation from Southey, the "constant dread in my mind respecting Mrs Coleridge's Temper," and the use of "stimulants." His resort to opium was "in the fear & prevention of violent Bowel-attacks from mental agitation." This suggests that its use was indeed at some point escapist: dread, because it brings the horrors closer to one in a mental way, prompts a yearning for withdrawal. The escape from conscience has the ironic consequence of "night-horrors in my sleep," and the compounded dread of these dreams them-

68. MS Notebook 26, quoted by Boulger, p. 233.

selves. With a grotesque metaphor, he illustrates the dread that permeates all his consciousness, not simply fixing on the particular moments he has listed: "all this interwoven with its minor consequences, that fill up the interspaces—the cherry juice running in between the cherries in a cherry pie—."[69] The more dismal import of the linkage of consciousness with conscience is that any increase of consciousness, as a generalized sensitivity to one's place in the world, may bring with it an increase of dread and guilt.

One response to the burden of conscience, or moral self-consciousness, is to escape it. The Romantics' quest for self-consciousness is countered by an equal and opposite quest to free themselves from it. One means of escape is opium-eating, which, as Edward Engelberg has surmised, has a fatal appeal because it appears to offer an increase of consciousness free of conscience, imagination without guilt. Ironically, its indulgence only increases guilt.[70] Coleridge insists, of course, that he has taken the drug only to escape physical pain and not to activate his imagination. But imagination, however activated, does promise escape from corrosive self-scrutiny. Thus imagination and conscience are usually conceived of as contraries in the Romantic period. For Blake the threat of false self-consciousness, of restrictive conscience, is clear in the destructive codes of Urizen and the solipsism of Ulro. The perennial struggle between Los and Urizen is that of imagination warring against restrictive conscience. Newton P. Stallknecht argues that Wordsworth is unable to make imagination and conscience "live together," and that English poetry is the poorer for it. In the transition from "Tintern Abbey" and *The Prelude* to "Ode to Duty" and *The Excursion*, he gives up the morality of imaginative self-realization for that of

---

69. *N*, II, 2398.
70. *The Unknown Distance* (Cambridge, Mass.: Harvard University Press, 1972), pp. 33–39.

conscience and duty. His poetry goes into a decline when he sees no way of combining the two.[71] More recently, Geoffrey Hartman alludes to a wealth of Romantic literature, including *The Prelude* and *The Ancient Mariner*, to demonstrate that the Romantics' crucial purpose is "to explore the transition from self-consciousness to imagination, and to achieve that transition while exploring it (and so to prove it still possible)."[72] Seen in this light, self-consciousness (conscience) and imagination are two forms of consciousness, the neutral middle term. They are contraries that propel the dialectic of Romantic poetry. The poet struggles against paralytic self-consciousness to maintain imaginative vision, and makes that process the very subject of his verse.

It is by now a truism that the spontaneities one associates with artistic creation and myth-making may be arrested by the burden of self-consciousness, guilt, knowledge. Wordsworth and Coleridge often construe their problems this way. One of the central themes of *The Prelude* is that imagination is impaired by the kind of morbid analysis the poet practiced when he dragged "all passions, notions, shapes of faith, '/ Like culprits to the bar, suspiciously / Calling the mind to establish in plain day '/ Her titles and her honours," until finally he "yielded up moral questions in despair."[73] And in the *Biographia Literaria* Coleridge writes, though I think him only half-convinced, that it would have been preferable "had I never relapsed into the same mental disease [his early pursuit of metaphysical knowledge]; if I had continued to pluck the flower and reap the harvest from the cultivated surface, instead of delving in the unwholesome quicksilver mines of

71. *Strange Seas of Thought* (Durham, N.C.: Duke University Press, 1945), pp. 204–222, 232–237.

72. "Romanticism and 'Anti-Self-Consciousness,'" *Centennial Review*, 6 (1962), rpt. in *Romanticism and Consciousness*, ed. Harold Bloom (New York: W. W. Norton, 1970), pp. 46–56.

73. *The Prelude* (Text of 1805), ed. Ernest de Selincourt (London: Oxford University Press, 1933; rev. 1960), X.890–893, 901.

metaphysic depths."[74] He promotes the notion that he cannot be both imaginative poet and self-conscious philosopher, even though he foists both roles on Wordsworth, who is even less suited to them.

My reading of Coleridge's discussion of conscience as itself a finer form of consciousness suggests, however, that he has already in theory provided a way of reconciling the contraries of conscience and imagination. Conscience in this sense is itself an imaginative act, we have seen, because through it we assert the reality and worth of other selves; by means of logic alone, we would have to admit that others are cut off from us, that they are mere contingencies, that their reality and worth are hypothetical. The sympathetic imagination the poet directs toward his friends in "This Lime-tree Bower my Prison" is close in its function to Coleridge's description of the healthy conscience. The reality and worth of his friends are felt so deeply that he experiences the scene more intensely through their eyes in an "equation of *Thou* with *I*." The escape from morbid self-consciousness need not involve an escape from moral categories or from intense self-consciousness; in Coleridge's view, it is best achieved by the development of imaginative, sympathetic conscience.

Conscience as a tribunal is necessarily "bad," because the defendant will always be found remiss to some degree. Conscience as a finer form of consciousness may also be "bad," because any enlargement of one's moral view and of one's sense of participation in a human world makes one more sensitive and vulnerable to that world; but this is the only kind of conscience that has the power of becoming "good." We are working with a characteristically balanced Coleridgean formulation. In "This Lime-tree Bower my Prison" the "good" conscience is dominant. The author of *The Ancient Mariner*—a poem in which conscience operates by turns as tribunal and as a power of sympathy with the world

74. *BL*, I, 10.

beyond the self—is better known for "bad" conscience, of course. The most notable practitioner of bad conscience in British letters, he gives guilt and dread a prominence in the human psyche exceeding even that suggested by Milton, Bunyan, or Johnson. But good conscience as a power of active sympathy and imaginative self-realization is another facet of his moral thought, one which I will examine more closely in Chapter 3. Coleridge emphasizes that the development of the sympathetic conscience entails suffering and alienation. He sees the wisdom of Wordsworth's "Elegiac Stanzas" (1804), where the poet says, "A deep distress hath humanised my Soul." But he hopes that imaginative power need not be forever lost in the process, as Wordsworth seems to say. The "humanised" conscience, unlike conscience as tribunal, can seek a healthier involvement in the world than that reflected by guilt and dread. Its power of sympathy can free one from self-incarceration. Conscience, on the other side of nightmare, must be vitalized by imagination.

For now, it is enough to say that in his writings on conscience and consciousness, Coleridge has in effect revised the Cartesian maxim to read "I ought, therefore I am." It is not epistemological or biological or religious truth that most pointedly defines us as human; rather it is moral awareness. The problem he poses is to develop moral awareness without forever condemning the self to divisive guilt and dread. He knows all too well that alienation may be so intense that the self may recoil, the growth beyond alienation be arrested, the imagination be slain. In spite of this threat, one must not cure a bad conscience by blunting consciousness itself. The choice is posed unequivocally: "O let me be awake, my God!" cries the Mariner, "Or let me sleep alway."

Duty and Inclination

Whether conscience be thought of as an internal tribunal or as a finer form of consciousness, its relationship to moral principle or to moral situation in Coleridge's own life is, most often, one of ironic antagonism. The greater his sense of obligation, the less likely his performance of duty. Obligation is, to him, a "narcotic," not a "stimulant." Of a period during which his opium suffering had been especially acute, he writes, with obvious echoes of his Mariner, that "tho' there was no prospect, no gleam of Light before, an indefinite indescribable Terror as with a scourge of ever restless, ever coiling and uncoiling Serpents, drove me on from behind.— The worst was, that in *exact proportion* to the *importance* and *urgency* of any Duty was it, as of a fatal necessity, sure to be neglected: because it added to the Terror above described."[75] The incapacity predates the addiction, and Coleridge thinks it may have its source in a basic and common psychological resistance to the call of duty. "*Now*, all Duty is felt as a *command*," and commands by the law of association remind us of "pains endured from Parents, Schoolmasters."[76] A command, apart from any unpleasant associations it may spark, is inherently unpleasant because it "acts as Disruption." Those who are most immersed in private reflection, who are "most reverie-ish & streamy," like Coleridge and his son Hartley, are most likely to respond to commands with resentment. (He is probably confessing to a virtue here.) The commands of duty, then, by constricting and interrupting the freedom of the mental life, subvert their own ends. The hereditary weakness of the Coleridges is a richness of consciousness that resents such intrusions.

The cure of guilt and dread, Coleridge discovers, requires a respect for psychological health. This discovery may not seem at all astounding, but it is a hard-earned one for him. It entails the difficulty of defining the relationship of morality and psychology. If moral questions are resolved in a formal way by appeals to principle and if one's acquiescence to principle is itself rational, then psychology—one's emotional,

75. CL, III, 489.
76. N, I, 1833.

attitudinal, and motivational makeup—is irrelevant. But Coleridge learns painfully that personal psychology can be ignored only with the gravest moral consequences.

If his criticism of contemporary British philosophies is that they are debased forms of Epicureanism, his own philosophy not infrequently strikes a Stoic note, but it is usually a false one because it abrogates psychology for principle. In 1805, while in Malta, he writes, "Let us do our *Duty:* all else is a Dream, Life and Death alike a Dream/this short sentence would comprize, I believe, the sum of all profound Philosophy, of ethics and metaphysics conjointly, from Plato to Fichte."[77] This cry is prompted by the death of Wordsworth's brother John, whose last words, before going down with his ship, were reportedly, "I have done my Duty! let her go!" The heroics of duty appeal to someone who dwells so much on his own infirmities. Though he would not "willingly kill even a flower," Coleridge announces that he would destroy a city if it were his duty. "I would give the order, & then in awe listen to the uproar, even as to a Thunder-storm/the awe as tranquil, the submission to the inevitable, to the Unconnected with my own Self, as profound/It should be as if the Lightning of Heaven passed along my Sword, & destroyed a man—."[78] The avowal is perhaps not so forbidding as it seems; *if* it is one's duty, it is, after all, one's duty. But this is clearly Coleridge pretending to a kind of moral thunder he cannot gracefully accommodate. Like Hamlet, he would waste "in the efforts of resolving[,] the energies of action."

In looking back at his early mistakes, he sees that he had falsely assumed his duty to be just about anything he did not *wish* to do. Guilt had often led him to act against his inclination, and ironically it had worked against the best interests of those persons for whom he had made a sacrifice. For example, the 1795 letter to Southey on the breakup of the

77. *N*, II, 2537.
78. *N*, II, 2551.

Pantisocracy scheme shows a high-minded young Coleridge excoriating Southey for backing out. "You are *lost* to *me*, because you are lost to Virtue," he cries. Pantisocracy was to have resulted in a "*moral sameness*," but Southey had wished to keep his servant and private property, and had "pleaded with increased pertinacity for the Wisdom of making Self an undiverging Center." Self-interest should have been secondary to the principles of Pantisocracy, even if this meant disregarding "father and mother and wife and children and brethren and sisters, yea, and his own Life also." Coleridge had himself given up "friends, and every prospect & every certainty, and the Woman [Mary Evans] whom I loved to an excess." Southey's complaint about him had been his "indolence," but if this complaint had been true, Southey should have said openly, "that much as I love Him, I love Pantisocracy more: and if in a certain time I do not see this disqualifying propensity subdued, I must and will reject him." Indeed, Southey had been seduced by pride, "a Harlot that buckrams herself up in Virtue only that she may fetch a higher Price—."[79]

Coleridge's marriage to Sarah Fricker prompts some of the same moral rigidity, partly comic, partly ruthless. The lofty renunciation of Mary Evans ("Far distant, and never more to behold or hear of her, I shall sojourn in the Vale of Men sad and in loneliness, yet not unhappy. He cannot be long wretched who dares be actively virtuous") may, as Beverly Fields suggests, be a self-serving gesture, since Coleridge is frightened by sexuality in those women he would prefer to think pure. (She argues that he would rather marry the

79. *CL*, I, 163–173. Beverly Fields, in *Reality's Dark Dream: Dejection in Coleridge* (Kent, Ohio: Kent State University Press, 1967), pp. 15–17, suggests that the real motive behind the high moral tone is not principled indignation but jealousy over Coleridge's imminent loss of his inamorato Southey to Edith Fricker in marriage. This seems plausible, though it need not lessen our interest in the moral categories to which Coleridge makes reference.

shrewish Sarah Fricker, a kind of "bad mother" who can, without compunction, be sexually abused.)[80] Prior to the marriage he tells Southey that although he does not love Sarah, he will marry her anyway, since it "still remains for me to be externally Just though my Heart is withered within me." He knows that to marry a woman he does not love is "to degrade her . . . by making her the Instrument of low Desire," but despite this, "Mark you, Southey!—*I will do my Duty*."[81] And a few days later, "Wherein when roused to the recollection of my Duty have I shrunk from the performance of it?—I hold my Life & my feebler feelings as ready sacrifices to Justice—."[82] In later years he sees the cheerless marriage as the penalty for his mistaken conviction that duty and inclination must be mutually exclusive.

Wordsworth's "Ode to Duty" (1805), a poem Coleridge probably takes with him in manuscript to Malta, treats inclination and duty as to a degree reconcilable, though it is inclination that must be prepared to give way. Duty is the "stern Daughter of the Voice of God," a rod "to check the erring, and reprove," an "awful Power" to whom the poet would become "Bondman" in a "spirit of self-sacrifice." The poet, tired of "unchartered freedom" and the "weight of chance-desires," longs for the control, the repose that the "stern Lawgiver" offers. The formal rhetoric of the ode intensifies the sense of willing servitude. The poet, however, wishes to qualify the forbidding aspect of Duty, who wears the "Godhead's most benignant grace" and even manages a smile. The published text of 1807 contains a stanza, omitted later when Wordsworth's thought takes on a more stoic cast, that would be to Coleridge's liking in his more tolerant vein:

> Yet not the less would I throughout
> Still act according to the voice
> Of my own wish; and feel past doubt

80. *Reality's Dark Dream*, pp. 47–56; CL, I, 145.
81. CL, I, 132, 145.
82. CL, I, 149.

That my submissiveness was choice:
Not seeking in the school of pride
For "precepts over dignified",
Denial and restraint I prize
No farther than they breed a second Will more wise.[83]

While in Malta Coleridge, prompted in part by Wordsworth's poem, speculates on his own paradoxical relationship to duty. His "sense of Duty, [his] hauntings of conscience from any stain of Thought or Action" increase proportionately to a decrease in his eagerness to promote the happiness of mankind. He had explained this in a letter to Wordsworth, "in consequence of his Ode to Duty," as the "effect of *Selfness* in a mind incapable of gross Self-interest—decrease of Hope and Joy, the Soul in its round & round flight forming narrower circles, till at every Gyre its wings beat against the *personal Self*."[84]

The sense of duty defeats its own purpose, then, if it produces this claustrophobic pressure. Instead of providing a sense of relatedness to a moral universe beyond the private self, it may trap one as the "Starling self-incaged," and moral effort then becomes self-directed scrupulosity. "Hope and Joy," the energies that sustain the moral imagination, are needed to reach beyond the confines of self, but scrupulosity has taken hold of him in concrete ways. He worries that he cannot endure a speck of dirt on his person; he now washes his "body all over 20 times, where 8 or 9 years I washed half of it once."[85] Wordsworth's "Ode to Duty" has not adequately taken into account the likelihood that the "stern Lawgiver" perverts its own function if it suppresses too harshly the "unchartered freedom" and "chance desires" that the poet has

83. *The Poetical Works of William Wordsworth*, ed. Ernest de Selincourt and Helen Darbishire, IV (Oxford: Clarendon Press, 1947), 83–86. The editors note that the quotation in the stanza is from Milton's *The Doctrine and Discipline of Divorce* (1643): "to enslave the dignity of Man, to put a garrison upon his neck of empty and over-dignified precepts."
84. *N*, II, 2531.
85. Ibid.

tired of. Coleridge projects, as a corrective to Wordsworth's poem, an "Ode to Pleasure—not sought for herself, but as the conditio sine qua non of virtuous activity—."[86]

He debates the issue of duty and inclination within the philosophical framework that Kant provides and tries to develop, in opposition to Kant, a theoretical basis for a moral orientation that embraces emotional as well as rational powers. His objections to this aspect of Kant's thought take much the same form as Schiller's, Friedrich Schlegel's, and other post-Kantians'. Notebook entries for December, 1803, quote, translate, paraphrase, and criticize portions of Kant's *Grundlegung zur Metaphysik der Sitten*. After Kant writes that "it is not enough that we act in conformity to the Law of moral Reason—we must likewise FOR THE SAKE of that law," Coleridge interpolates, "It must not only be our Guide, but likewise our Impulse—Like a strong current, it must make a visible Road on the Sea, & drive us along that road." Like many readers of Kant, Coleridge is bewildered by the statement that personal inclinations are irrelevant to an act's moral worth, which for Kant is assessed solely by one's willingness to obey the categorical imperative for its own sake. Coleridge thinks the emotional life bound up in the ethical: "Will not a pure will generate a feeling of Sympathy/Does even the sense of Duty rest satisfied with mere *Actions*, in the vulgar sense, does it not demand, & therefore may produce, Sympathy itself as an Action/?—This I think very important/—."[87] He objects to Kant's identification of the love commanded by the Golden Rule with benevolence. Kant writes that we are commanded to have a "*practical* love, and not *pathological*—a love which is seated in the will, and not in the propensions of sense—in principles of action and not of tender sympathy; and it is this love alone which can be commanded."[88] Coleridge knows this

86. *N*, II, 2091.
87. *N*, I, 1705.
88. *Fundamental Principles of the Metaphysic of Morals*, p. 17.

is a strong argument; how indeed can we be commanded to love "pathologically"? Can "Sympathy itself" be considered an "Action," and therefore obligatory in the same way?

He tends, whatever the theoretical difficulties and even personal repercussions, to enlarge the sphere of moral responsibility to include the content of the emotional life. He is not, as he may seem to be, replacing austerity with sentimentalism in asserting that we have a duty to have certain emotions; indeed, he increases in theory one's potential for guilt by expanding those areas directly accountable to moral judgment. We have a duty, also, to have proper feeling, feeling itself as an obligatory activity of the self. "The Feelings, that oppose a right act, must be wrong Feelings," he writes.[89] The point he is making is not the anti-intellectual one that feelings are superior to reason, and he is certainly not so naive as to think that all feelings are somehow good. There are wrong feelings. Rather he wishes to be comprehensive and to align morality with psychological reality. He thinks Kant has defined as irrelevant to morality too many aspects of human consciousness that do enter—and that indeed should enter—into the decisions we make. Psychological health for Coleridge is not naively to be equated with happiness or always feeling good. It is, instead, the state of the organism in which all elements of the psyche—instincts, emotions, reason—are permitted to play their role. Moral situations call on one to exercise more than a single power. Moral failure may be indicated by a lack of personal suffering when administering to the suffering of others, and Coleridge dreads the self-recrimination that should rightfully attend a failure to feel. What is needed, then, is integration and cooperation of the various powers one with another.

In relation to this point, he questions one of the most problematic elements of Kant's moral philosophy, that of *Achtung*, the feeling of respect or reverence for the moral law. He

89. *AR*, pp. 91–92.

writes in the 1803 notebook that reverence for the moral law is, according to Kant, a "feeling, but says Kant it is a self-created, not a received passive Feeling—it is the Consciousness of the Subordination of the Will [to a Law]." He then raises what becomes his perennial objection to Kant. "Examine this: for in Psychology Kant is but suspicious Authority." *Achtung* as an "imposed Necessity" would be "Fear or an Analogon of Fear," but if it is "a Necessity imposed on us by our own Will it is a species of Inclination."[90] Coleridge thinks that Kant, too, has attempted to find a principle of integration: does not the rational feeling, *Achtung*, presuppose a harmony of duty and inclination on some level? Kant's concept of *Achtung* has often been objected to on similar grounds.[91] Coleridge thinks

90. *N, I,* 1710.
91. See H. J. Paton, *The Categorical Imperative: A Study in Kant's Moral Philosophy* (London: Hutchinson, 1947), pp. 63–68. Coleridge's mention of Schiller (*N,* I, 1705) suggests that the concept of the *schöne Seele* is a possible influence in his initial questioning of Kant's *Grundlegung zur Metaphysik der Sitten.* In his essay *Über Anmut und Würde* (1793) Schiller objects to Kant's idea of duty, which is "proposed with a harshness enough to ruffle the Graces, and one which could easily tempt a feeble mind to seek for moral perfection in the sombre paths of an ascetic and monastic life" (*The Works of Schiller,* trans. anon [New York: Harvard Publishing, 1895], p. 206). Kant's theory may have been, Schiller writes, a needed corrective to sensualist maxims, but this was no reason to suspect all inclinations. The harshness of the imperative would in itself, by emphasizing our fragility, prompt us to disobey it. Because nature has given us both a sensuous and a rational capacity, it would be contrary to nature to deny the former in developing the latter. The possessor of the *schöne Seele* combines the two, performs his duty at the same time that he abandons himself to his inclinations. Kant answers Schiller in a footnote to his essay, "On the Radical Evil in Human Nature." He admits that he does not associate "pleasantness" with moral obligation. Rather one approaches obligation with the kind of awe and respect due its dignity, indeed the very dignity Schiller thinks so essential. One pursues one's duty with a "cheerful spirit, without which one is never certain that he has *taken a liking* to good, that is to say, adopted it into his maxim." Self-denial, yes, but Kant denies that self-mortification is implicit in his theory (p. 330n; see also the *Critique of Practical Reason,* pp. 168–173, and *The Doctrine of Virtue,* pp. 158–160).

that if Kant had recognized the affective component of *Achtung* sufficiently, he would not have divided so clinically the claims of inclination and duty. Coleridge does not adopt *Achtung*, so reinterpreted, as his own principle of integration, but it is implicit in his insistence that feelings be rational, that rationality be felt.

In the Opus Maximum he calls Kant the "great restorer of the Stoic Moral Philosophy."[92] His objections to Stoicism generally are stated as early as the *Lectures 1795*. "To be totally unaffected by external objects, to feel neither Love or Pity, was their first Precept, their middle, and their last. They held it right to abstain from Vices not because their fellow Creatures would be injured, but because Vice was beneath them."[93] Godwin practices this gloomy ethic; he is, according to Coleridge, a "severe Moralist!" who declaims against filial love. The Stoic, Coleridge writes three decades later in *Aids to Reflection*, attaches highest honor to one who acts virtuously in spite of his feelings, whereas Christianity's aim is to "moralize the affections."[94] And in 1817 he writes:

I reject Kant's *stoic* principle, as false, unnatural, and even immoral, where in his Critik der Practischen Vernun[f]t he treats the affections as indifferent (ἀδιάφορα) in ethics, and would persuade us that a man who disliking, and without any feeling of Love for, Virtue yet *acted* virtuously, because and only because it was his *Duty*, is more worthy of our esteem, than the man whose *affections* were aidant to, and congruous with, his Conscience.[95]

Kant declares the affections irrelevant to ethics, Coleridge continues, because his entire system would be subverted if any elements not derived from the rational will, such as affections, "were yet indispensable to it's due practical direction."

92. OM, B₂, f. 63.
93. *Lectures 1795*, p. 157.
94. *AR*, pp. 91–92.
95. *CL*, IV, 791–792.

Kant's purpose, he has to admit, was not to give "a full *Sittenlehre*, or system of practical material morality, but the *a priori* form—*Ethice formalis:* which was then a most necessary work and the only mode of quelling at once both Necessitarians and Meritmongers, and the idol common to both, Eudæmonism."[96] He recognizes that Kant attempts to define the a priori basis of morality, not the data of sensibility that is logically posterior to it, on his terms. If psychology is defined as irrelevant, can Kant be faulted for not demonstrating psychological expertise? He is laying the groundwork of a moral theory and is not attempting to describe the total experience of the moral life. Much of this Coleridge admits, but he still argues that Kant's moral philosophy is self-contradictory and limited.

His commentary on it has taken two tacks: first, the *Ethice formalis* is defective internally, both because our respect for the moral law is itself a kind of inclination, indicating a coincidence of duty and inclination even in the abstract, and because our feelings, given this linkage, must themselves be considered moral acts; and second, this type of moral system is inadequate in its totality, however successful it may have been in its limited aims. Kant's philosophy has vanquished the necessitarians, meritmongers, and eudaemonists, but must now be itself supplanted by a moral perspective more inclusive of moral life. To Southey, Coleridge writes of metaphysicians, whom Southey, for a moment excelling himself, terms "Metapothecaries": "There does not exist an instance of a *deep* metaphysician who was not led by his speculations to an austere system of morals—. What can be more austere than the Ethics of Aristotle—than the systems of Zeno, St. Paul, Spinoza (in the Ethical Books of his Ethics), Hartley, Kant, and Fichte?"[97] He himself feels the temptation to create such a

96. *Notes and Lectures upon Shakspeare,* ed. Sara Coleridge, in *The Complete Works* (Shedd ed.), IV, 401–402.
97. *CL,* II, 768.

system, but the kinds of exclusion upon which it would be based are disquieting. This is especially true of Fichte, who "in his moral system is but a caricature of Kant: or rather he is a Zeno with the Cowl, Rope, and Sackcloth of a Carthusian Monk."[98] He demands "an ascetic, and almost monkish, mortification of the natural passions and desires."[99] Coleridge declaims against the "monkish-Cell of Fichtean pan-egoistic Idealism."[100]

As a result, he sets out to humanize the imperatives, to rescue morality from its "Procrustean Bed of Kantean Formalism."[101] In his early poem, "Reflections on Having Left a Place of Retirement," he had suggested the form that his objection to Kant was to take. One should pity the fallen person one is aiding, but

> . . . he that works me good with unmov'd face,
> Does it but half: he chills me while he aids,
> My benefactor, not my brother man!

There must be a harmony of inner life and the gesture which represents it. "That system of morality is alone true and suited to human nature, which unites the intention and the motive, the warmth and the light, in one and the same act of mind. This alone is worthy to be called a moral principle."[102]

98. *CL*, IV, 792.
99. *BL*, I, 102.
100. MS Notebook 29, f. 121ᵛ. Fichte gives a lecture as an appendix to *Das System der Sittenlehre* (1798) in which he argues that "the moment man elevates himself to consciousness, he tears himself loose from the chain of natural mechanism and organism: that which he does thereafter he must do altogether himself. Man as such, *i.e.,* as free, as consciousness, has no natural inclinations, affections, or passions at all. He depends altogether on his freedom. An important proposition!" ("Ascetism, or Practical Moral Culture," *The Science of Ethics,* trans. A. E. Kroeger [London: Kegan Paul, 1897], p. 389). Coleridge probably has this kind of comment in mind. It should be added that he conceals perhaps even from himself an indebtedness to Fichte in issues of morality.
101. *PL*, p. 428.
102. *F*, I, 325.

In a significant notebook entry Coleridge describes both music and "Poetry in its grand sense" as "Passion and order aton'd! Imperative Power in Obedience!" He asks what the "first and divinest Strain of Music" is, and answers:

In the Intellect—"Be able to *will*, that thy maxims (rules of individual conduct) should be the Law of all intelligent Being."
In the Heart—or Practical Reason—Do unto others, as thou would'st be done by.[103]

That music or poetry and the sensibility of the truly moral person both manifest "passion and order aton'd" suggests another connection between moral and aesthetic categories, at least by analogy. The discussion of poetic meter in the *Biographia Literaria* is dressed in the language of morality. In poetic meter one discovers "an interpenetration of passion and of will, of *spontaneous* impulse and of *voluntary* purpose."[104] Just as the poet ideally "brings the whole soul of man into activity," so the moral agent ideally responds to the situations that confront him with the whole soul. He is propelled by a creative tension, articulated elsewhere most pointedly by Schiller, between passion and order, inclination and duty. In Blake's terms, he would embody the creative opposition of "contraries" instead of the strife of "negation." As Coleridge says, through an act of imagination the poet "*fuses*, each into each," all powers in a "balance or reconciliation of opposite or

103. *N*, II, 3231. This alternative way of construing the categorical imperative is repeated in *The Philosophical Lectures*, though Coleridge had written earlier that the Golden Rule "is the Maxim of a good man—but it is not a *Law*, nor was taught as a Law" (*N*, I, 1722). Likewise, Kant writes that the common *quod tibi non vis fieri* cannot be a universal law. It does not really command benevolence, "for many a one would gladly consent that others should not benefit him, provided only that he might be excused from showing benevolence to them" (*Fundamental Principles of the Metaphysic of Morals*, p. 47n). (Note, incidentally, that Kant casts the Golden Rule in negative form.) But Coleridge deliberately ignores the subtlety in this entry. He would emphasize his intuition of what constitutes the moral person over any precise articulation of a moral theory.
104. *BL*, II, 49–50.

discordant qualities."[105] In denying that such a balance should be achieved in the moral life, the austere moralists produce the strife of negation that paralyzes the agent. The victory of reason over emotion is then Pyrrhic at best.

The sensibility of the moral person must be "musical," therefore, but one should remember that music embraces the tragic perspectives of Bach and Beethoven as well as the "delicious melodies of Purcell or Cimarosa." Coleridge's talk of reconciliation does not necessarily imply happiness.

It is just a bit disheartening to watch an older Coleridge forsake reconciliation altogether as he creeps back into the Kantian fold. A notebook entry of 1828 finds him regretting that he had publicly denounced "the ascetic or in the phrase of the day *Monk*-Morality." It would have been wiser to have "allowed some small demur and pause of judgment (There was Silence in Heaven for the space of half an hour!)." He thinks the "essentials of the Ascetic Morality" may "follow inevitably from my own views of Nature [is contrary to] God, and Man like the Moon flown off, but still reclaimed by the Sun & rolling a serpentine orbit—as the attractive force of the general or the partial center predominates." The attack should not have been directed against asceticism in theory, he concludes, but merely against "the Monkish Faquirish misapplications of the Ascetic Principle in the detail of practice, the superstitious Self-tormentings, too often only a grisly sort of Sensuality—."[106]

The older Coleridge has apparently given up on the ideal of wholeness and reconciliation, and has come full circle on the question of inclination and duty. In the early 1790s he had uneasily assumed that his duty was, more likely than not, what he did not at all wish to do. He soon realized that a sense of duty could work perversely if it did not answer to inclination in some way; this reflection led to the provocative

105. *BL*, II, 12.
106. MS Notebook 37 (1828), ff. 22^V–23.

comments we have pursued here and that one would call most "Coleridgean." An older Coleridge once again assumes that there should be antagonism of a mutually exclusive character between inclination and duty.

Nevertheless, one would not call him stoical or resigned or austere in his later years. When he is not holding forth with celebrated vigor to his disciples at Highgate, he continues to complain of his health, the obtuseness of his critics, the injustice of Oxford's treatment of his son, Hartley. Renunciation or asceticism has never been his practice. He is too much a would-be participant, too gregarious, and never sufficiently in control of his own life for that. The man continues to be found out. We now know that, far from renouncing his addiction, he talks one of James Gillman's servants into making visits to the apothecary for the opium the doctor is denying him. We know, too, that he leaves Highgate for extended periods with Mrs. Gillman. They vacation together at Ramsgate and evidently enjoy each other's company so much that they occasion some rumors. And one might recall that this is the man whose favorite breakfast is reportedly a pint of laudanum and six fried eggs.

It is clear, in conclusion, that Coleridge does give some justification for the common reading of him as apostle of the absolute, the rather un-English bearer of the transcendent light of reason and principle to an age whose spirit is succumbing to the lesser powers of understanding and prudence, with their offspring materialism and sensuality. As Pater says, Coleridge thirsts after absolutes and they get him into trouble. But certainly he is aware of the problem of the absolute in morals as well as in other branches of his thought. Olympian assertion is quickly qualified, or even withdrawn, as he attempts to find a moral orientation more suitable to psychological health and self-development—and one less likely to encourage the ruthlessness and pride of the "conscientious Persecutors." He discovers that the awesome sense of duty which had seemed one way of dealing with infirmity of spirit only compounds his paralysis. The commands of duty seem to come from without as constraints and do not take into account the idiosyncratic needs and strengths of Samuel Taylor Coleridge, who cannot and should not, he feels, be called upon to fulfill the conventional expectations of a husband and family man, poet and philosopher, and friend. Behind his criticisms of formalism is his concept of the organic whole, his own absolute truth, perhaps. Just as organisms live, so must morality be a living "process" that adapts to circumstance and the individual life while it promotes personal growth within the social whole.

The Ancient Mariner knows that something is required of him, but he has no idea what. Even the love that gushes from his heart at the sight of the water-snakes is, inexplicably, insufficient. No human response, no merely moral gesture, finally satisfies the inscrutable hostile power that persecutes him. The moral sphere of human reason, motive, value, and action is powerless before it. The moral act, Kierkegaard says, may exist as temptation, ironically the temptation of an Abraham *not* to kill Isaac.[107] Coleridge seems to suggest that if a moral gesture may not appease divine authority anyway, or, as Kierkegaard suggests, may even give offense, it would be redundant and pointlessly cruel to establish within the moral sphere itself an analogous authoritarianism. The moral sphere must have a liberality and coherence that protect one from absurdity and cosmic injustice. In removing duty from its dominant role, Coleridge hopes to gain this liberality without diluting moral awareness. There are, he will say, means of assuaging the guilt that strikes at the very heart of morality. One must strive to transcend the state of the Mariner, for whom alienation from the Absolute is futilely compounded by the self-alienation that is guilt.

107. *Fear and Trembling*, trans. Walter Lowrie (Princeton: Princeton University Press, 1970), pp. 64–91.

3 | The Evolution of the Self

A New Focus

Coleridge writes that everyone has the "instinct and necessity of *declaring* his particular existence, and thus of *singling* or singularizing himself."[1] There is a limitation and potential harm, he has argued, in a morality based on too restrictive a sense of duty. Instead of declaring his particular existence, a person may inhibit personal freedom and development in his anxiety to conform to a command conceived of as external. Many of Coleridge's writings develop a conception of the moral life that is in large part dissociated from conscience as tribunal. The moral goal is instead the highest development of the self's potential. Kant describes self-realization as an "imperfect," "contingent," or "meritorious" duty—it is one that cannot be categorically commanded. "There are in humanity capacities of greater perfection which belong to the end that nature has in view in regard to humanity in ourselves as the subject; to neglect these might perhaps be consistent with the *maintenance* of humanity as an end in itself,

1. MS Notebook 29, f. 110ᵛ.

but not with the *advancement* of this end."[2] The meritorious duty exists as opportunity, not command. Coleridge's writings on education, method, language, friendship, and love describe the process of "educing" the self, of realizing these "capacities of greater perfection." Of course it must be said that he feels acute guilt for his failures here as in everything else; his theory points the way to the freedom that is never to be his own.

Brief mention of a traditional schema of moral theories will provide a context for assessing the total movement of Coleridge's moral thought. The two broadest categories are teleological theories, such as Bentham's utilitarianism, and deontological theories, such as Kantian formalism. Teleological theories assert that an act is to be judged by the degree to which it promotes some end, usually the happiness of an individual or of society; deontological theories assert that factors other than consequences, usually the intrinsic rightness or wrongness of an act, must enter into moral judgments and decisions. Self-realization theories—whether the classical ethic of Plato and Aristotle, Nietzschean egoism, or the Coleridgean variety we are about to explore—would mostly fall into the category "teleological," because they argue that morality addresses itself to an end or consequence, the realization of the self in whatever form this is prescribed. But it will be proper here to think of self-realization, relative to formalism and utilitarianism, as a third possibility, a new departure fundamentally different in spirit from them. If not superior to these other theories, self-realization is decidedly more congenial to the Romantic temper.

We have already seen Coleridge's critique of Kantian formalism, of the theory that the moral worth of an action is determined by the consistency of the motive or private maxim with a universal or categorical imperative. The worth

2. *Fundamental Principles of the Metaphysic of Morals*, p. 47. See also *The Doctrine of Virtue*, pp. 110–112.

of the act according to Kant does not depend on personal inclination or the act's consequences. Coleridge thinks Kantian formalism is limited because it does not adequately embrace the real concerns of the moral life—the importance of consequences, the need for psychological health. In reaction against formalism, however, he does not argue for utilitarianism, and in Chapter 4 I will present his case against it. The utilitarians judge the value of an act not by the quality of the agent's motive but by the extent to which the act promotes some end, usually the happiness of the greatest number of people. Coleridge's attack on the theory, we shall see, is comparable in its vigor to his attack on formalism, though he does admire some of the concerns of each. He admires formalism's concern with the inner disposition of the moral agent and utilitarianism's concern with promoting the good of mankind through beneficent acts. But, characteristically, he thinks each excludes what is good about the other, and he seeks an approach that might embody aspects of each, a "tertium aliquid." The result is a morality whose emphasis is clearly self-realization.

Coleridge's moral position is not precisely a balanced "synthesis" of German formalism and British utilitarianism, however. His self-realization theories develop more in coordination with tendencies in German thought and in reaction against those in his native tradition. His critical response to Kant parallels and, at certain points, may be derived from that of Schiller, Fichte, and Schelling. We have seen that like Schiller he thinks duty and inclination should be harmonized within the self, at least as an ideal. The development of the self requires the meritorious exercise of all its powers. At the same time he emphasizes, like Fichte, that the self develops through striving, striving to achieve freedom over all the obstacles that represent the alien or not-self. That one must strive in pursuit of harmony is no contradiction in theory but simply a contradiction in our moral predicament. Though

Schiller, Fichte, Schelling, and others have some influence here, the concrete content and expression of Coleridge's self-realization theories are, in the main, his own and cannot be wholly attributed to any intellectual tradition. It is difficult to avoid personalistic criticism here: the basic sensibility of the man accounts for much of his intellectual exploration. From his earliest years he is preoccupied with the meaning of the self and the idea of wholeness. Many of his criticisms of the British moral tradition presuppose his view of the self's enlarged potential. Consequently I will develop this view first, so that we will then be familiar with the moral criteria against which his compatriots are found to be so lacking.

Coleridge himself would seem to have coined the term "self-realization." I find its use, for example, in an interpretive paraphrase of Fichte's *Das System der Sittenlehre* (1798), written sometime during 1813–1815, and in the Opus Maximum.[3] The *OED* gives the first use to F. H. Bradley in 1876. Though Coleridge does not adopt it in moral discussion, the term best describes the kind of moral theory he is developing.

Self-realization theories are usually said to have begun with the Greeks. Aristotle in the *Nicomachean Ethics* gives less attention to judgment of the rightness and wrongness of human action than to the various "virtues" the human being may develop through discipline and moderation. No single formula is offered; Aristotle graciously suggests that one

3. "However, we yet do distinguish our Self from the Object, tho' not in the primary Intuition—Visio visa—now this is impossible without an act of abstraction—we abstract from our own product—the Spirit snatches it (self) loose from its own self-immersion, and self-actualizing distinguishes itself from its Self-realization—But this is absolutely impossible otherwise than by a free Act—" (*N*, III, 4186); "If then personeity, by which term I mean the source of personality, be necessarily contained in the idea of the perfect Will, how is it possible that personality should not be an essential attribute of this Will, contemplated as self-realized?" (OM, B$_3$, f. 243). Another example can be found in the Huntington Library MS "On the Divine Ideas," f. 73, though as in the latter instance the context is more theological than moral.

should not hope for more certainty than the subject matter can afford. Intellectual virtues, such as knowledge, wisdom, and skill, contribute to the harmonious development of the whole person and cannot be excluded from moral discussion. Plato argues in *The Republic* that in the just society the cobbler pursues his special skill and does not usurp the role of the carpenter or musician or statesman; by analogy, the just soul is harmonious because its various elements are permitted their proper function, "like the three chief notes of a scale." Harmony and excellence are the desiderata of most self-realization theories, which argue that to develop "capacities of greater perfection" is inevitably to promote many of the values of the formalists and utilitarians without legislating them. Moral theories that limit themselves to the rightness and wrongness of actions slight the role of the complex human character.

Coleridge does not focus on "virtues" as such, though his discussion of use of the word is pertinent here. The full title of his late work is *Aids to Reflection, in the Formation of a Manly Character*. He uses the perhaps all too revealing "manly" in a brief critique of Shaftesbury and the "modern Pagans," in which he defines both *arete* and virtue as *"manly energy."* He rejects Shaftesbury's use of the word "virtue" in the "high, comprehensive, and *notional* sense in which it was used by the ancient Stoics."[4] Shaftesbury sees virtue as the exclusive property of the civilized and discerning moral judge; anyone who cannot "attain the speculation or science of what is morally good or ill" is not virtuous.[5] Coleridge, on the other hand, thinks of virtue as "energy," an energy which is the self-affirming excellence of the moral agent, not of the moral judge. Whereas duty reminds one of deficiency and evil, virtue is ideally a power of affirmation that is not so

4. *AR*, pp. 7, 188.
5. Lord Shaftesbury, *An Inquiry concerning Virtue, or Merit*, in *British Moralists*, ed. D. D. Raphael, 2 vols. (Oxford: Clarendon Press, 1969), I, 173.

intimately linked with its negation, even though Coleridge speaks of it as "correlative" to vice.[6]

Predictably, he does not discuss virtues in any systematic way and would not, in any event, approve of such inventories. The many fragments fall together, however, to describe the complex process of discovering and channeling the "manly energy" of the self. There will be in some of his writings quasi-existential formulations to describe this process: one must will what one is to be, in a context in which value is not gratuitously presented and human nature not predetermined. On this point he will waver, since he more often speaks of "educing" powers that are somehow already there, simply waiting to be led out of mere potentiality into full growth. Such ambivalence is common in self-realization theories. He postulates, in the metaphor which pervades his writings, an organic unity of self as the major goal of the fully realized human being. This is an ideal so familiar to us now that we may miss the innovative character in Britain of Coleridge's formulations. Blake's myth seems to imply something like it, but Blake provides no theoretical description of the process of self-realization outside the mythic grammar itself. And the process of self-realization is for him not so much a consistent growth and development of the whole organism, root stem and flower, as it is the sudden illumination of one aspect of the union which thereby illuminates the others. In Coleridge, the idea of organic growth is applied to human personality in a more radical and aggressive way than in any other British moralist. Joseph Butler speaks of a "system" of human powers, but the idea of self as "organism" is Coleridgean. Bradley, in *Ethical Studies* (1876), proposes very explicitly a moral theory of "self-realization" in which wholeness of self is the moral goal, but it is without Coleridge's metaphoric richness and, with its Hegelian method and its even greater emphasis on one's duty as determined by station and function

6. *CL*, IV, 960.

in society, it does not attempt to offer anything like Coleridge's dramatic account of the theory's implications for the individual moral agent.

The Unconjugated Self

Coleridge is especially upset by his son Hartley's deficiencies because they parody his own. He agrees that Hartley is guilty of many things, but not the pride and insolence he has been accused of. He has lost his Oriel fellowship for alleged drunkenness and has accepted the invitation of the Rev. John Dawes to teach in a school at Ambleside, although Wordsworth and others, sensing disaster both to Hartley and to his students, attempt to block the appointment. Anticipating Hartley's misdemeanors at Ambleside, Coleridge writes a letter to Dawes in which he justifies his methods of child-rearing.

He had never disciplined Hartley by "forcing him to *sit still*, and *inventing* occasions of trying his obedience." He had never interrupted his enjoyments to "sting him into a will of resistance to my will" in order that he might then crush it. It might appear that "Self-will" has been the result, and Coleridge almost wishes it had been, "for then I should have more Hope. But alas! it is the absence of a Self, it is the want or torpor of Will, that is the mortal Sickness of Hartley's Being, and has been, for good & evil, his character—his moral *Idiocy*—from his earliest Childhood." Coleridge then asks, significantly, what the greater evil is, "*morally* considered, I mean: the selfishness from the want or defect of a manly Self-love, or the selfishness that springs out of the excess of a worldly Self-interest." The latter, which Hartley has none of, is worse—that "narrow proud Egotism, with neither Thou or They except as it's Instruments or Involutes." But without "manly self-love," one becomes like Hartley the "relationless, unconjugated, and intransitive Verb

Impersonal with neither Subject nor Object, neither governed or governing."[7] Coleridge earlier judged that Hartley is "absent to the present." His "seeming entire suspension of all distinct Consciousness" means he literally does not know what he is doing when, for example, he imbibes glass after glass of wine. Hartley's early absorption in nature and unteachable good will have been vitiated by his failure ever to connect self with circumstance. His dreamy periods of forgetfulness indicate both a potentially poetic spirit and a dissipation of energy. Coleridge wishes Hartley "could but promise himself to be a *Self* and to construct a circle by the circumvolving line—."[8]

There is perhaps a surplus of current books featuring this strange entity, the self, but one has a special prerogative here because of Coleridge's own absorption. He uses the word "self" as a substantive in this philosophical sense more insistently than any previous major writer. By "self" he means the organic unity of human powers, conscious and unconscious, that evolves through time and changing circumstance. Ultimately incomprehensible, it is fragile and often empty, easily threatened by the usurping "phantom self" and other forms of dislocation. That one must promise oneself "to be a *Self*" could stand, I suggest, as Coleridge's quintessential precept. And he fears that he fulfills it little more than Hartley. There is pith instead of solid wood at his center. He is a "Ghost" and is not "*consubstantial*" with other human beings.[9] His past life seems like a dream to him, "a feverish dream! all one gloomy huddle of strange actions, & dim-discovered motives."[10] He complains that he has "no rooted thorough thro' feeling—& never exist[s] wholly present to any Sight, to any Sound, to any Emotion, to any series of

7. *CL*, V, 228-233.
8. *CL*, VI, 551.
9. *N*, III, 3324.
10. *CL*, I, 184.

Thoughts received or produced/always a feeling of yearning, that at times passes into Sickness of Heart."[11] He is "whirled about without a center—as in a nightmare—no gravity—a vortex without a center."[12] To echo Beckett's phrase in *Watt*, he fears that he may vanish behind the farce of his properties. As if preempting Carlyle's portrait of him several decades later, he writes in 1796 that "my face, unless when animated by immediate eloquence, expresses great Sloth, & great, indeed almost ideotic, good nature. 'Tis a mere carcase of a face: fat, flabby, & expressive chiefly of inexpression.—"[13] A pencil sketch of him by the German artist Kayser in 1833 dismays him. It is "a Likeness, certainly; but with such unhappy Density of the Nose & ideotic Drooping of the Lip, with a certain pervading Woodenness of the whole Countenance."[14] His body with its awkward gait seems to mock his genius, energy, capacity for love, just as his public person lends itself to caricature. Clearly some program of self-development other than the lax if ingratiating one the Coleridges have pursued is needed to draw that circumvolving line.

To identify the "I" with the objectification of self in the world, the "me," is the quickest way of losing identity altogether. One can give over to that fat vacuity of face and become it. Sarah Coleridge's vagueness and lack of reality derive from her creating "her own self in a field of Vision & Hearing, at a distance, by her own ears & eyes—& hence [she] becomes the willing Slave of the Ears & Eyes of others."[15] This kind of alienation is best described as the yielding of the true self to the "phantom self" or "representative image." This image, which is of cardinal importance to

11. *N*, II, 2000.
12. *N*, III, 3999.
13. *CL*, I, 259.
14. *CL*, VI, 974.
15. *N*, I, 979.

Coleridge's moral thought and is possibly adapted from discussions in Fichte and Schelling on the structure of consciousness, is one's sense of the public, physical self "as the one object constantly recurring amid the flux of experience." It is the "complex cycle of images, or wheel of act and sensation that by its constant presence and rapidity becomes a stationary *Unity*, a whole of indistinguishable parts, and is the perpetual *representative* of our Individuum, and hence by all unreflecting Minds confounded and identified with it."[16] If the sense of individuality remains strong, the representative image can be manipulated as a persona, but just as often it is an alter ego that impoverishes and usurps the ego. To constitute the representative image as the "centre, the proper unity of all else" is to objectify the self and, literally, to alienate ourselves from our *selves*. Objectified in our own consciousness, we become a thing to ourselves and lose a sense of the interior self altogether.

This threatening mechanism operates even in infancy and is implicit in the very structure of human consciousness. Children innocently pass outside themselves and exist in the being of mother or siblings, "As if their whole vocation / Were endless imitation." Though the child's instinctive absorption of self into that of another is analogous to the sympathetic imagination, it is also a vulnerability. The oceanic vision of the child, which does not distinguish between self and other, can lead him to accept whatever self-definition circumstance provides. If parental affection is insufficient or if the child is surrounded with playthings instead of playmates, he may borrow "a sort of unnatural outwardness," an emptiness of self ironically represented by selfishness. Or worse, with no core of self one is vulnerable to "a usurping *Self* in the disguise of what the German Pathologists call a

16. *IS*, pp. 68–69. My reading of the passage in MS Notebook 47 differs slightly from Kathleen Coburn's. Cf. *N*, II, 2793.

fixed Idea." The self must not be subject to a "ruling *Eddy.*"[17]
Integrity of self depends, then, on a conception of the "I"
distinct from the "not-I." The articulation of self by self-
image, the "me," must be seen only as a manifestation of the
I, not the I itself.

As we might expect from Coleridge's connection of consciousness with conscience, the sense of self develops as one
becomes more and more conscious of one's participation in a
wider social world. An 1825 letter to James Gillman on the
subject of Gillman's twelve-year-old son Henry explains the
boy's problem in such terms. Coleridge has diligently tried
to tutor the inattentive Henry in Greek and Latin and has
arranged for his admission to Eton. But Henry is having
trouble adjusting to Eton's rigors (he eventually is withdrawn at the school's request). Coleridge responds to Henry's
difficulties with almost as much anguish as he does to those of
Hartley and tries to diagnose his case. Part of Henry's problem has been his too solicitous upbringing and his resultant
dependency on others, "his Idleness, the absence or great
deficiency of *initiative* power, of *setting* himself off on the
skaits, no momentum from within, and even when this had
been supplied from without, yet no fulcrum to renew it
from—." Other problems—his "combination of intenacity with
unimpressibility," his intellectual feebleness in spite of able
intelligence—arise because Henry lacks the power of perceiving himself in relation to other selves and objects. Coleridge
echoes the argument in the Opus Maximum and Notebook
26 for the close relationship between consciousness and conscience. If one were not aware of the relatedness of the self
to others, the self would lack definition; one would be a
somnambulist amid a delirium of surrounding objects.

It is only, I say, by the habit of referring a number and variety
of passing objects to the same abiding *Subject*, that the *flux* of the

17. Ibid.

former can be arrested, and the latter made a nucleus for them to chrystallize round. But again it is only by the habit of referring & comparing the Subject to and with the Objects, that it can be consciously known as the *same* & *abiding*—and before it can be *compared*, it must have been distinguished, thought of separately, and singly for itself—. There must be Reflection—a turning in of the Mind on itself.[18]

The self turns inward at some discernible moment in time; the moral life begins then and not at birth. Coleridge translates from Fichte's *Das System der Sittenlehre:* "The moral Law referred to the empirical human being, or Man the φαινομενον [as contradistinguished from] Homo Νουμενον, has a determinate *commencement* (punctum incipiens) of its career, viz. the definite sphere or circumscription in which the Individual finds himself at the time he first finds himself, i.e. at the first exertion of reflective Self-consciousness—."[19] The paradox of conscience, we remember, is that its investigation of the inner self connects that self with others, "for Self is Definition; but all Boundary implies Neighbourhood." One cannot truly turn the mind inward without awareness of one's relatedness to other moral beings. One knows oneself "by means of knowing another," and the moral act is therefore an act of self-definition. The self is defined not by some "romantic" pursuit and inflation of private consciousness, but by social awareness that locates the self within a community of other selves, the greater organism of the society.

How does the developing personality find in "Neighbourhood" a sphere of free agency and not a prison? Coleridge envisions a struggle in which man's power to create his world anew has a slight edge over the force of circumstance. "The individuality of Man, how wonderful. No one merely man,

18. *CL,* V, 515–518.
19. *N,* III, 3673. That the passage is a translation of Fichte escaped the editor's notice. See *Werke,* II (Leipzig: Fritz Eckardt, 1908), 560, and *The Science of Ethics,* p. 176

as every Tyger is simply Tyger—little more than numerically distinguishable—but this man, with *these* faculties, *these* tendencies, this peculiar character—His Wishes, Hopes, Actions, Fortunes, spring out of his own nature—." He admits that "this very nature appears conditioned & determined by an outward Nature, that comprehends his own—What each individual *turns out*, (Homo Phainomenon) depends, as it seems, on the narrow Circumstances & Inclosure of his Infancy, Childhood, & Youth—& afterwards on the larger Hedge-girdle of the State, in which he is a Citizen born—." His charged description of this "outward Nature" illustrates well the manner in which he absorbs and vivifies the concepts of German philosophy. Instead of an analytic disquisition on subject and object, the noumenal and phenomenal, the I and the not-I, he continues in his rich rhetorical vein with the admission that each human being is

influenced & determined (caused to be what he is, qualis sit = qualified, *bethinged*) by Universal Nature, its elements & relations.—Beyond this ring-fence he cannot stray, of these circummurations he can seldom overleap the lowest & innermost, and the outermost is his apparent horizon, & insurmountable—from this Skein of necessities he cannot disentangle himself, which surrounds with subtlest intertwine the slenderest fibres of his Being, while it binds the whole frame with chains of adamant.

But to pursue this meditation is to see that "this conspiration of influences is no mere outward nor contingent Thing, that rather this necessity *is* himself, that that without which or divided from which his Being can not be even *thought*, must therefore in all its directions and labyrinthine folds belong to his Being, and evolve out of his essences." With his informal and probably illegitimate adaptation of a Kantian conception of the priority of mind, Coleridge argues that the human being can become the playwright of his own drama. His powers themselves determine the character of his surroundings: "the stimulability determines the existence & character of the Stimulus, the Organ the object, the Instincts, or the germinal Anticipations in the Swell of nascent evolution, the dark yet ⟨pregnant⟩ prophecies of the Future in the Present[,] bud or blossom forth in the Organs, and the Volitions beget the instruments of Action—the temptability constitutes the temptation, and the Man the Motives."[20] Recognition of the centrality of human mind empowers us to "beget each in himself a new man."

The mind cannot turn in on itself without what could be described as a component of egotism, but that need not be the "narrow proud Egotism, with neither Thou or They except as it's Instruments or Involutes." Freed from moral narrowness, egotism is the self's vitality. Great persons are often accused of it, but "it is scarcely possible for a man to meet with continued personal abuse on account of his superior talents, without associating more and more the sense of the value of his discoveries or detections with his own person."[21] Among the great egotists Coleridge mentions are Paracelsus, Bruno, Wolff, and Milton. Milton's egotism is a "revelation of spirit."[22] The defense of egotism begins early with the Preface to *Poems on Various Subjects* (1796), where he writes that egotism in poetry is to be condemned only when it violates decorum or "would reduce the feelings of others to an identity with our own."[23]

Throughout his life Coleridge develops the idea that a sense of our own powers is vital to the continuance and growth of the self and, in the moral sphere, is the meaning of "fidelity to our Being." It is a central tenet of his moral thought that one works through and beyond what we commonly call "Romantic individualism" to a sense of community; not only

20. *N*, III, 4109.
21. "Contributions to Southey's *Omniana*," in *Table Talk and Omniana* (London: Oxford University Press, 1917), p. 336.
22. *Table Talk*, p. 479.
23. *Poetical Works*, II, 1135–1136.

does he see no necessary contradiction between these, but in fact the one is necessary for the other. Not everything that derives *from* the self is necessarily directed *to* the self. It is this kind of nourishing egotism Hartley and Henry lack. Hartley's free expression and movement reveal the absence of conventional restraints that characterized his upbringing, but they do not represent a spirit truly free. Lacking a sense of power and purpose, he has in a very basic way no attachments. This lack of attachments is revealed in a failure to absorb experience. His weakness of self is paradoxically shown in that Hartley always remains the Hartley we already know.

Coleridge's failure is not exactly Hartley's, since, with the exception of some notable blind spots and studied avoidances, he absorbs enormously and undergoes many palpable transformations (though all conspire somehow to misrepresent him): from Pantisocrat to Unitarian minister to poet to philosopher to Alexander Ball's secretary at Malta to political observer and theorist, to literary critic to Sage of Highgate to theologian, with much overlapping of these roles. Hartley's and Coleridge's failures are contrary manifestations of the same dilemma of finding an enduring, growing, and creditable identity. Hartley seems to avoid the search altogether by a metaphoric and often literal absenteeism, but Coleridge does not. He feels his failure all the more acutely because he has himself urged that the evolution of personal identity is the most inclusive moral goal. In part, that whirling vortex without a center is brought about by too great a sense of possibility—where does the encyclopedist begin, and how is he to limit his goals? He fears, too, that the center he lacks and seeks may, in any event, be a fiction, and that perhaps the interior self must always be the associative delirium that David Hartley's model of mind, interpreted loosely, implies.

More important, Coleridge does not free himself from the restrictive framework of moral evaluation I described in the preceding chapter. One can speak only of his efforts to do so. The very experimentalism in discovering and creating the self suggests, from the standpoint of duty's austerities, a remiss indulgence. Duty restricts his sense of play and opportunity, his youthful desire to be all things. The result is the extraordinary discrepancies we see in his life as a whole. Contrast the Coleridge of the exuberant early letters, for example, with the Coleridge of the lugubrious *Lay Sermons* twenty years later. Play and opportunity have somehow been coerced into these dreary performances, which one feels are not at all what Coleridge had in mind. We applaud the young man when he realizes—with an assist from the Wedgwoods' philanthropy—that the ministry is not his calling. We know it already, and we watch him discover it too. Unhappily, little of his life has this marriage of good fortune and self-mastery. Either he takes on tasks that are not suitable for him, or he falls into the lethargy for which he is famous. The pity of it is all the greater for his having described in detail the process of self-realization that would free him. He describes the growth of the germ of self into *homo liberalis*, the thinking and loving human being who senses that restrictive duty and decisive action are not coterminous with the broad expanse of the moral life. With an ideal self mocking the combination of false role and lethargy that makes up so much of his life, there is little surprise that this inquiring spirit should feel himself without a center.

The Perplexity of Growth

Coleridge has argued that one must turn the mind in on itself, become self-conscious, as the first step in the process of self-realization. At the same time he emphasizes that there is a limit to the reach of self-exploration as it confronts one's own unknown ground. The dynamics of growth reside precisely in the tension between the strong impulse to know and the limit to knowing. Growth of personality is nourished by the deep perplexity and sublime feeling that arise when the self senses its own obscure powers within. In this emphasis Coleridge differs from Wordsworth, Schiller, and most other practitioners and theorists of the sublime, for whom sublime feeling is more often a quality of subjective response to the powers of the external world. Coleridge thinks the growth of personality requires a creative linkage between consciousness and the inscrutable will, between knowledge and power. We investigated the destructive conflict between them in Chapter 1. Now we shall see Coleridge responding to that dilemma by, among other things, arguing for the moral uses of the sublime.

That something more is required for the development of moral vision than clear-headed notions of right and wrong, good and evil, is obvious enough to the lucid and tormented Coleridge. Unlike knowledge as "information," virtue cannot be given by one person to another. His critique in *The Philosophical Lectures* of Socrates' doctrine that virtue can be taught suggests the idle role of the moral preceptor. He ponders two different interpretations of Socrates' doctrine. If it means that people will not commit crimes upon learning that the ultimate bad effects will be disproportionate to immediate gratification, then it is simply incorrect. Coleridge, undoubtedly thinking of his opium habit, says that one can be perfectly aware of the effects and yet commit the act "to get rid of the pain arising from the want of it. . . . Not a single ray of pleasure beforehand, but the daily round of habit from behind, *that* presses on the human mind."[24] We call someone a criminal only *if* he knows the wrongness of the act; ignorance argues for acquittal.

If, on the other hand, Socrates' doctrine means that "vice [is] not possible, [is] not compatible with the clear perfect insight into the very nature of the action of the soul," then it

24. *PL*, pp. 150–151.

is correct. That he has this latter idea in mind is indicated by his using the "word *apatheia*, not *ignoria* [*sic*], for ignorance." But Coleridge notes that the use of *apatheia* concedes the argument—there must be something attached to knowledge that is not knowledge itself, that "is necessary to make this knowledge efficacious or influential."[25] And this, he says, is found in the more basic principle of will.

In his considerations of knowledge and virtue, Coleridge may have in mind not only Socrates but also such thinkers as Godwin, who assumes people will desire what they judge to be desirable, or Hazlitt, who writes that people sin for not knowing better, or Spinoza, who (according to Coleridge) "saw so clearly the *folly* and *absurdity* of Wickedness, and felt so weakly & languidly the passions tempting to it, that he concluded nothing was wanting to a course of well-doing but clear conceptions and the fortitudo intellectualis/."[26] But if virtue cannot be taught, Coleridge fears a dispassionate and clear-headed moralist is ineffectual, for he may be "talking the language of sight to those who do not possess the sense of seeing." The question then becomes how moral ideas are learned. How does one fasten them to will, which is not after all susceptible of "knowledge"?

A partial answer, at least, comes from analysis of the kinds of ideas or conceptions we do in fact respond to. Coleridge, like theorists from Burke and Kant to Freud and Jung, argues that totally clear conceptions lack the power over human behavior that dim ones have. An indistinct conception may have a greater hold on the emotions and therefore be both more sublime and more dangerous. The exaltation of a Göttingen crowd upon seeing the Queen of Prussia prompts him to exclaim, "Spread but the mist of obscure feeling over any form, and even a woman incapable of blessing or of injury to thee shall be welcomed with an intensity of emotion

25. Ibid. See *N*, II, 2032 on the futility of moral advice.
26. *N*, III, 3869.

adequate to the reception of the Redeemer of the world!"[27]
Indistinct conceptions can easily lead to fanaticism, "intense
sensation with confused or dim conceptions. Hence the fanatic
can exist only in a crowd, from inward weakness anxious
for outward confirmation."[28] The indistinct and the sublime
lend themselves to political tyranny. "It is by the agency of
indistinct conceptions, as the counterfeits of the Ideal and
Transcendent, that evil and vanity exercise their tyranny on
the feelings of man."[29] Why would we purchase a wreath of
diamonds, the expense of which will result in ruined health
and honor, yet refuse poisoned wine however great our
thirst? "Evidently because the conceptions are indistinct in
the one case [diamonds], and vivid in the other [wine]; because all confused conceptions render us restless; and because
restlessness can drive us to vices that promise no enjoyment,
no not even the cessation of that restlessness."[30]

Still this truth does not make Coleridge a partisan of the
clarity that casts out mystery, dimness, the sublime. One
should have "clear, distinct, and adequate conceptions concerning all things that are the possible objects of clear conceptions," but not everything *is* such an object. There are
ideas in themselves obscure, and all the more profound for
their obscurity. His argument is ultimately directed against
Descartes, who argues in *Discours de la méthode* (1637) and
Meditationes de prima philosophia (1641) that the clarity
and distinctness with which we can conceive an idea are the
measure of its truth. Coleridge, echoing Kant, thinks that
"deep feelings" align themselves with "obscure ideas," and
that indeed "one should reserve these feelings . . . for objects, which their very sublimity renders indefinite, no less
than their indefiniteness renders them sublime: namely, to

27. *F*, I, 36.
28. *IS*, p. 103.
29. *F*, I, 37.
30. *F*, I, 105.

the Ideas of Being, Form, Life, the Reason, the Law of Conscience, Freedom, Immortality, God!"[31] The significance of these and other exclusions from the requirement of distinctness should not be underestimated. The restlessness, passion, and sense of dimness that Coleridge condemns in other contexts are essential to all profound experience and human growth. The same "deep feelings" that are components of fanaticism and fetishism when directed to improper objects are, properly directed, the components of enriched personality.

Works of art, for example, can properly occasion indistinct, sublime, enriching feeling. In a famous and debated passage, Coleridge writes that "Poetry gives most pleasure when only generally & not perfectly understood." He seems to assert that the French language, because of its exceptional clarity, is "wholly unfit for Poetry." Indeed, "the elder Languages [were] fitter for Poetry because they expressed only prominent ideas with clearness, others but darkly—."[32] Elsewhere, he wonders "whether or no the too great definiteness of Terms in any language may not consume too much of the vital & idea-creating force in distinct, clear, full made Images & so prevent originality—."[33] Coleridge is proposing a double standard. Ideas that are capable of clarity should be so expressed, but ideas in themselves obscure should not be rendered too definite. He is not, of course, justifying lack of poetic form. The most tightly structured work of art can properly give rise to obscure feeling. As he says in the *Biographia Literaria*, poetry has, even in the "wildest odes . . . a logic of its own, as severe as that of science; and more difficult, because more subtle, more complex, and dependent

31. *F,* I, 106.
32. *N,* I, 383. See J. A. Appleyard, *Coleridge's Philosophy of Literature* (Cambridge, Mass.: Harvard University Press, 1965), pp. 86–93, for a cogent discussion of this passage.
33. *N,* I, 1016.

on more, and more fugitive causes."[34] Poetry must mediate obscurity by its own imaginative logic.

A moral idea, like a work of art, must retain a fundamental obscurity the power of which penetrates the fabric of the personality, entwining "Thought with the living Substance." Paradoxically, this is an obscurity that nourishes the "form" of the personality. It is the curse of the age, Coleridge argues, that ideas are becoming inert "conceptions" that do not have power over our imagination, that do not result in growth. A telling notebook entry of 1805 describes his vexation at asking a Paleyan or Priestleyan to answer to "my *mist*, my delving & difficulty"—his difficulty, that is, in solving some moral problem. The Paleyan would reply "in a set of parrot words, quite satisfied, clear as a pike-staff,—nothing *before* & *nothing behind*—a stupid piece of mock-knowlege, having no *root* for then it would have feelings of dimness from *growth*, having no buds or twigs, for then it would have yearnings & strivings of obscurity from *growing*."[35] Instead of sympathy with the intellectual difficulty, "with this delving, this feeling of a wonder," the Paleyan would offer up "a dry stick of Licorish, sweet tho' mawkish to the palate of self-adulation." It is precisely this perplexed sense of impinging meaning— not yet clear but struggling from dimness toward distinct consciousness—that is requisite for moral and intellectual growth. It is only in the active appropriation of an idea sought out by this "delving" curiosity and perplexity that the self *adds* to itself organically. Otherwise the self is the dead receptacle of mere "notions" or "conceptions." Education should make "unindicable notions" intelligible but only in its "*latter* stages." "I say, *latter*, because I believe, nothing more unfavorable to intellectual progression, than a too early habit of rendering all our ideas distinct & indicable."[36]

34. *BL*, I, 4.
35. *N*, II, 2509.
36. *N*, I, 902.

In a familiar passage of *The Prelude*, Wordsworth makes a similar connection between obscurity and growth:

> I deem not profitless those fleeting moods
> Of shadowy exultation: not for this,
> That they are kindred to our purer mind
> And intellectual life; but that the soul,
> Remembering how she felt, but what she felt
> Remembering not, retains an obscure sense
> Of possible sublimity, to which,
> With growing faculties she doth aspire,
> With faculties still growing, feeling still
> That whatsoever point they gain, they still
> Have something to pursue.[37]

Though Wordsworth's response derives from memory and the "ghostly language of the ancient earth," the connection he makes between the sublime and growth is much like Coleridge's.

Coleridge's emphasis is that sublime feeling results when the self turns inward and confronts the ghostly language of its own ground. The self delves both into the world and into its own act of reflecting. It gains an intensity of feeling at the same time that the objects and ideas it pursues lose their facile clarity. This perplexed sense of an idea's rootedness in the self's own ground is, for him, essential to the growth of personal identity. Through this perplexity, one attaches oneself to the world. The process of delving into the self produces perplexity in the knower and dimness in the thing known, but the enlarged sense of self that can arise from this obscurity will be the product of effort and appropriation instead of the inert accumulation of information that has "nothing *before* & *nothing behind*," that does not attach to personality.[38] Coleridge would have to admit the idea he is

37. II.331–341 (1805 ed.).

38. In a notebook entry of 1801 Coleridge quotes from "Tintern Abbey" the lines that speak of "the eye made quiet" by the power of harmony and joy

pursuing here is itself obscure, however pivotal. He is on the frontier of discussion of the unconscious and is already attempting to describe a creative relationship of ego with it. The process of bringing the indistinct into distinct consciousness is a never completed one of giving form to the chaotic energies of the unconscious will. The growth of personality (or we might say the enrichment and structuring of the ego) occurs when these life-giving and chaotic energies are claimed by consciousness. One must be in touch with those energies, recognizing both that they give the self "initiative power" and that they can, if uncontrolled, produce the fanatic. To give in to them altogether, to dissolve ego structures into the unconscious, is the insane abrogation of humanity.

Coleridge has presented three major possibilities, then, in structuring the relationship between consciousness or reason and the unconscious will. The first is dissociation, the state described in Chapter 1, with its dual consequence of paralysis and lack of control. There is a perverse justification in existing in a negative relationship to the will, since the will is evil, the ground of selfhood and pride, but Coleridge knows this is an unhealthy posture. The struggle between consciousness and the unconscious results in a living nightmare. The state of dissociation brings with it ironically all the guilt and dread that should accompany active wrongdoing. The individuality that results is, he knows too well, subject to the kinds of weakness seen in one who believes himself less than real and who seeks substantiation by farming out his identity

---

that enables us to "see into the life of things." In a passage that G. N. G. Orsini has attempted to link to Fichte, he then writes: "By deep feeling we make our *Ideas dim*—& this is what we mean by our Life—ourselves. I think of the Wall—it is before me, a distinct Image—here. I necessarily think of the *Idea* & the Thinking I as two distinct & opposite Things. Now (let me) think of *myself*—of the thinking Being—the Idea becomes dim whatever it be—so dim that I know not what it is—but the Feeling is deep & steady—and this I call *I*—identifying the Percipient & the Perceived—" (*N*, I, 921; see *Coleridge and German Idealism*, pp. 178-183).

to that of others. Coleridge cries in agony that his friends are his soul.

More pernicious is the second, contrary relationship, in which the will overpowers and absorbs consciousness. This state is the romance of the will, the prideful worship of selfhood seen in the Satanic personalities of Napoleon, Iago, and, when he shoots the Albatross, the Mariner. The individuality that results, and thus the apostasy from God's will, is illusory, as Coleridge points out in his quasi-Kantian analysis of fanaticism. The worship of will, or energized selfhood, is most contagious in crowds, and leads to the collective barbarity of fanaticism. The fanatic who seeks power over others, such as Napoleon or Iago, uses his intelligence as one uses a tool; it merely directs the evil will to its ends and does not result in what Coleridge would call self-consciousness. Iago has great intellection but no self-consciousness, as his motive-mongering demonstrates.

Since neither dissociation from will nor giving way altogether to will results in real individuality or sense of self, Coleridge describes the third relationship—one that provides the framework of his self-realization theory, and one I will gingerly call "Romantic humanism," the *"tertium aliquid."* Here the will and consciousness, though remaining contraries, work creatively toward fully energized, individuated consciousness. The unconscious is the ground of individuality and source of life, which must be given form, directed by a reflective consciousness that is fully aware of the chaotic sea of energy beneath it. Coleridge writes that "consciousness is the *form* of the personal *Individuality*."[39] In living form, unlike static "shape," "all is energy."[40] As we have seen, consciousness that is not informed by will is inert, witnessed in the inert ideas of a Paleyan, the person of too easy comprehension who does not recognize that all true knowledge

39. MS Notebook 26, quoted by Boulger, p. 232.
40. OM, B_3, ff. 114–118.

must be appropriated by an act of will. The point of inter-section between will and consciousness, the indistinct or sublime, is the point at which the growth of the self origi-nates. Here inert conceptions are transformed into sublime ideas. This activated consciousness is conscience cleansed of guilt and claustrophobic self-involution. Instead of succumbing to the sickening and divisive guilt that comes from static recognition of the will's depravity, the moral agent delves into the self and works toward a productive relationship with will. He does not deny its evil potential, but seeks ways to turn its energy into form.

Of the many dialectics "Kubla Khan" expresses, this one seems to me most suggestive of Coleridge's thought else-where. The logic of the imagery tells us that the poet wishes he could achieve a series of transformations. He would transform "huge fragments" that vault from the "deep romantic chasm" into the "sunny pleasure-dome"; he would transform the wailing of the woman for her demon-lover into the "symphony and song" of the Abyssinian maid. The aboriginal chasm that shoots forth the mighty river is analogous to the unconscious will: it runs "through caverns measureless to man" and though it impregnates the scene with "ceaseless turmoil seething," it also leads "down to a sunless sea." The civilized pleasure-dome contains the fertile ground that is measured precisely and "girdled round" with "walls and towers." The dome is fertile, pleasurable, con-trolled, creatively formed; it is analogous to the kind of consciousness the poet would develop. To build it, I have said, is presumptuous and illusory, for the poet envisions himself as demonic artificer alien to "all who heard." But his is a demonism that would emerge creatively—its destructive and chaotic power appropriated by an act of conscious shap-ing into a civilized and pleasurable, though unstable, con-struct. Terror and savagery would be transformed into delight and order. The instrument of these transformations would be "music," which, we remember, Coleridge has called "passion and order aton'd."

The poet within the world of the poem can only dream of these transformations as correlative to his sense of failure and vexation. Coleridge, looking at the poem from outside, could not believe that he had in a sense achieved these transformations when he wrote the great poem itself.

Method and the Germinating Powers

Coleridge's theory of education, the procedure for "educing" the self, shares some features with that implicit in Rousseau's *Emile* (1762): the goal is not to funnel information into one's head but to develop the personality. It is perhaps the most progressive aspect of his thought. But the procedure of liberal development he proposes lacks Rousseau's very careful tutorial manipulation; instead it is closer to that which Wordsworth propounds in Book V of *The Prelude*. I think it probable that Wordsworth's thinking on this subject derives more directly from Coleridge, a theoretician of education who enters into the public debate on the subject, than it does from Rousseau, as is sometimes proposed.

M. H. Abrams illustrates in *The Mirror and the Lamp* (1953) that one encounters organic and vegetative metaphors everywhere in Coleridge's works.[41] These metaphors are nowhere so rife as in his educational theory, I find. The self is the caterpillar that must develop into the butterfly, the germ that must develop into the plant; the body of knowledge is a gigantic tree with many branches and a common trunk. Just as ideas have a "root" and an initiative power that suggest the living plant, so the human personality commences with an inchoate, indeterminate, and energized

41. *The Mirror and the Lamp* (1953; rpt. New York: W. W. Norton, 1958), pp. 68–69, 114–124, 167–183, 218–225.

"germ" of self that seeks to grow. Coleridge's use of organic metaphors is somewhat awkward in terms of the idea of human freedom. Is not the end product of this educing process, the whole person, implicit in the "germ," and is not growth in accordance with the germ's properties a denial of freedom? Can we shape our personalities any more than broccoli can shape itself? Indeed, Coleridge speculates that if there was no "fault in the Germ," perhaps Henry Gillman's problem was "some nipping Frost or Blight in early Spring." He seems now to lack a "*specific* sensibility, having it's seat and source in some special energy of the organic and organific Life."[42] Henry is something of a special case, however; he has lamentably been nipped in the bud and stunted. Coleridge is sensitive to the vulnerability of children and to the difficulty of diagnosing the sources of neurosis. The human organism otherwise eludes any too literal extension of the organic vegetative metaphor, since its powers can be both educed and newly created through active and deliberate human effort. The human being is an unusual vegetable, because it can, to a large extent, consciously direct its own growth, unless irreparable harm has been done in early years.

In a commentary on Plato's educational system, Coleridge argues that education should not "fill, bucket by bucket, the leaden cistern" but should awaken the "principle and *method* of self-development." It is not information stored in the passive mind, "as if the human soul were a mere repository or banqueting-room"; rather education must place the mind "in such relations of circumstance as should gradually excite the germinal power that craves no knowledge but what it can take up into itself, what it can appropriate, and re-produce in fruits of its own."[43] He thinks, oddly, that Rousseau's system depends too much on giving children intellectual and moral convictions preparatory to action. Rather he would

42. *CL*, V, 517-518.
43. *F*, I, 472-473.

emphasize with Aristotle the importance of developing proper habits, of gradually *"training up."* A liberal education is "that which *draws* forth, and trains up the germ of free-agency in the Individual—Educatio, quae *liberum* facit: and the man, who has mastered all the conditions of *freedom*, is *Homo Liberalis*—."[44] Freedom, so considered, is paradoxically a matter of habit. The enervation of an opium habit has an ironic analogue in "the increase almost indefinite of *Power* by Practice in a vital Being—the muscular motions of a capital Performress on the Piano Forte."[45] This metaphoric use of music is once again significant. The greater freedom is not that offered by vitality alone, but vitality that has been "trained up" into constructive form, until the form itself becomes second nature or habitual. The will is then raised into free will.

The antecedence of conscience to consciousness, Coleridge has argued, is structural, not temporal; obviously a child absorbs experience before he converts it into moral awareness. If a parent hears his child mistakenly call a round leaf "long," he should fetch him a long leaf, thereby making "words conformable with ideas." With this habit of accuracy, "the child would have the *habit* of truth before he had any *notion* or *thought* of *moral* truth. . . . Stimulate the heart to love and the mind to be early accurate, and all other virtues will rise of their own accord, and all vices will be thrown out."[46] He is especially opposed to teaching morality by precept, which teaches vanity instead of virtue, "goodiness" and not goodness. "The lesson to be inculcated should be, let the child be good and know it not."[47] This is similar to his remark to Emerson that it is preferable to be

---

44. *CL*, VI, 629.
45. *N*, III, 3361.
46. *Notes and Lectures upon Shakspeare*, p. 222. The passage is taken from accounts of lectures Coleridge delivered in 1808.
47. Ibid., p. 223.

purposefully dedicated to the true than to the good—for the sake, ultimately, of the good.[48] In *The Friend* and elsewhere, he dwells on the redemptive power in the act of thinking itself. The "deficiency of good, which everywhere surrounds us, originate[s] in the general unfitness and aversion of men to the process of thought, that is, to continuous reasoning."[49]

Because Coleridge thinks "virtuous habits" are formed by the way in which knowledge is communicated, he proposes several innovations in teaching methods. In most schools teachers, not students, are the dunces. Students should be allowed to teach one another and progress at their own rate. They should be permitted to indulge in free play and not be pressured into learning what cannot yet be absorbed. "Touch a door a little ajar, or half open, and it will yield to the push of your finger. Fire a cannon-ball at it, and the Door stirs not an inch: you make a hole thro' it, the door is spoilt for ever, but not *moved*. Apply this to moral Education."[50] Coleridge thinks his habitual procrastination originated in his having been allowed three hours at school for what he could have accomplished in fifteen minutes; "the present moment was neglected, because the future was considered as sufficient." Students should be given a minimum of punishment and should in matters of discipline judge one another, so that they will not come to treat justice contemptuously as something administered by those with arbitrary power. Instead of treatises on how to speak and act, students should be given Jack the Giant-Killer or the Seven Champions, the imaginative literature Rousseau prohibits, inasmuch as these do not foster a premature and prideful concern with self.[51]

If one teaches by strict discipline and rote memorization and in effect makes "knowledge" and not "education" the

48. *Coleridge the Talker*, p. 209.
49. *F*, I, 62.
50. *IS*, p. 81.
51. *IS*, pp. 83–87.

end of instruction, one may indeed produce prodigies, and "prodigies with a vengeance have I known thus produced! Prodigies of self-conceit, shallowness, arrogance, and infidelity!"[52] At the same time, Coleridge is opposed to total unregulated freedom and makes more of a point of this than Wordsworth does. He is fond of a debate he once had with John Thelwall, who was advocating total freedom in education. Coleridge's reductio ad absurdum was to take Thelwall to a weed patch and tell him that it was his botanical garden. The unsuspecting Thelwall replied that it was no garden because it was covered with weeds. "Oh," Coleridge replied, "*that* is only because it has not yet come to its age of discretion and choice. The weeds, you see, have taken the liberty to grow, and I thought it unfair in me to prejudice the soil towards roses and strawberries."[53] Coleridge later fears that his rearing of Hartley has been too lax and that Hartley has indeed turned into something of a weed. Though one cannot be *forced* to be free, as Rousseau believed one could, one should be given the proper means of working out the "germ of free agency." Some directions must be pointed out.

The content or field of knowledge should be radically altered to accord with mind as germinal spirit instead of mind as receptacle, the implicit metaphor at work in most contemporary educational theory. A letter to James Gillman, Jr., in 1826 seems to me to be as cogent a presentation of the content and purpose of a liberal education as John Henry Newman and Matthew Arnold offer later in the century. The different departments of literature and science used to be thought of as separate plants, he writes, for which one either had a "*Turn,* or *Taste,*" or not. But the philosopher considers the various disciplines "as springing from one Root, and rising into one common Trunk, from the summit of which it diverges into the different Branches, and ramifies

52. *BL*, I, 7.
53. *IS*, p. 75.

without losing it's original unity into the minutest Twigs and Sprays of practical application." All professional people, whether physicians, clergymen, or military officers, must possess the "Trunk of the Tree of Knowledge" if they are not to be "hacks," or "a sapless *Stick.*" This "trunk" of knowledge that we should all share is comprised of the principles that "become the mind itself and are living and constituent parts of it." All knowledge "that enlightens and liberalizes, is a form and a means of Self-knowlege, whether it be grammar, or geometry, logical or classical." Euclidian geometry, for instance, is "but a History and graphic Exposition of the powers and processes of the Intuitive Faculty—." "We learn to *construe* our own perceptive power, while we *educe* into distinct consciousness it's inexhaustible *constructive* energies." Mere memory is vulnerable to accident and decay, but knowledge of principles is not, once it has fastened to personality. Memory works with "insulated knowleges, seen each for itself without it's relations and dependencies, the recollections stick together like the Dots in Frog-spawn by accidents of Place, Time, and Circumstance." The mind, therefore, that directs itself outward in accordance with memory and a utilitarian motive is not only less knowing but more vulnerable, indeed less utilitarian. Coleridge claims to have a deficient "passive or spontaneous Memory," but when he sets his "Logic-engine and spinning jennies a going," it is another matter.[54] He recognizes the fact of nonspecific transfer of learning. "Learn but *one* thing *fundamentally*, so as to *know* what you know, and the habit will be formed which will at length leaven all your other pursuits."[55]

One might imagine Coleridge's wistfulness in contemplating the product of his ideal education. The "Essay on Method" in the 1818 revision of *The Friend* describes the

54. *CL*, VI, 628–633.
55. *CL*, V, 298.

truly educated person as one in control of time, circumstance, and the form his life takes. The control over time is the distinguishing mark, and one Coleridge could hardly lay claim to himself. The methodical person is like a clock in that both "divide and announce the silent and otherwise indistinguishable lapse of time." But only the methodical person "realizes its ideal divisions, and gives a character and individuality to its moments." The moving passage which follows contains echoes, I think, of Schiller's *Briefe über die ästhetische Erziehung des Menschen* (1794–1795):

If the idle are described as killing time, [the methodical person] may be justly said to call it into life and moral being, while he makes it the distinct object not only of the consciousness, but of the conscience. He organizes the hours, and gives them a soul: and that, the very essence of which is to fleet away, and evermore *to have been,* he takes up into his own permanence, and communicates to it the imperishableness of a spiritual nature. Of the good and faithful servant, whose energies, thus directed, are thus methodized, it is less truly affirmed, that He lives in time, than that Time lives in him.[56]

Schiller writes that since everything ruled by time "exists as succession," one moment excludes another, creating "the highest degree of limitation." If we are ruled by time, we are nothing but "a unit of quantity, an occupied moment of time" and all personality is "suspended." But our rational nature or "formal drive" attempts to affirm the personality, to make limitations disappear, to enlarge our being. Schiller writes that during "this operation we are no longer in time; time, with its whole never-ending succession, is in us."[57]

Coleridge's own sense of time is, bluntly, that of a wasted past, a fleeting present, and a menacing future. The bulk of his list of projected works is proportionate to his felt poverty of accomplishment. Memory for him is not Wordsworthian

56. *F*, I, 450.
57. *On the Aesthetic Education of Man*, pp. 78–83.

enrichment but a "wan misery-Eyed Female" promising "a hideous phantom of her own visage," a numbering, irrepressible power both shadowy and palpable, that works through "subconsciousness."[58] For Wordsworth, a sense of continuity of self in time is the stuff of lyrical poetry. For Coleridge, the past is ghostly and returns to haunt the sinner; continuity of self is the perpetuation of guilt. He has a chronic fear of opening letters, and, typically, does not know the correct date of his birthday. Nothing affects him at the moment it happens, "It either stupifies me, and I perhaps look at a merry-make & dance the hay of Flies, or listen entirely to the loud Click of the great Clock/or I am simply indifferent, not without some sense of philosophic Self-complacency."[59] Most lives are "fractional," lives "symbolized in the thread of Sand thro' the orifice of the Hour-glass, in which the sequence of Grains only *counterfeits* a continuity."[60] He would like to make life as "continuous as possible, by linking on the Present to the Past," but he knows the truth of the chemist Humphry Davy's comment that he would always be "the victim of want of order, precision, regularity."

If he does have "method," it is like that of Hamlet, with whom he contrasts Mrs. Quickly. She has no method at all and is completely tyrannized, in her narratives, by mere sequence with no principle of organization. Hamlet, however, is so meditative that even though his profound reflections and seeming discontinuities are methodical in their essence, they lack the "form" of method and can degenerate into the grotesque and fantastical. Hamlet's excessive reflectiveness leads to procrastination and to reflections on the noble dust of Alexander stopping a bunghole.[61]

The apposite piece of self-analysis by Coleridge is a con-

58. *N*, II, 2915.
59. *N*, I, 1597.
60. *CL*, V, 266.
61. *F*, I, 450–457.

trast of himself with the earnest plodding Southey. Southey has called Coleridge a greyhound who noses every nettle along the hedge while Southey himself is like a greyhound that would straightaway get the hare. Coleridge replies he does not "care two pence for the *Hare*," but he does by the way find a hare in every nettle.[62] By indirection he finds directions out. This might answer to Hazlitt's famous observation that Coleridge "continually crossed me on the way by shifting from one side of the foot-path to the other," an abnormality which Hazlitt eventually interpreted as "instability of purpose or involuntary change of principle."[63] His may be a mazy walk, but he is on his feet and finding many objects of wonder along the way. His metaphysical excursions—all that talk of "sum-m-mjects and om-m-mjects" that Carlyle derides—have a method in their madness. But at the same time he knows the form of true method results from a "due mean or balance" between external stimuli and internal meditation that he and Hamlet lack.

Significantly, the person Coleridge describes as exhibiting such form is Wordsworth. What he says about Wordsworth is perhaps tinged with animus; he is a "happy man,"

> because he knows the intrinsic value of the Different objects of human Pursuit, and regulates his Wishes in Subordination to that Knowlege—because he feels . . . that we can do but one thing well, & that therefore we must make a choice—he has made that choice from his early youth, has pursued & is pursuing it—and certainly no small part of his happiness is owing to this Unity of Interest, & that Homogeneity of character which is the natural consequence of it—.[64]

"Unity of Interest" and "Homogeneity of character" and, in fact, "happiness" itself suggest a certain limitation and

62. *IS*, pp. 143–144; cf. *CL*, VI, 634.
63. *My First Acquaintance with Poets*, in *Works*, ed. P. P. Howe (London: J. M. Dent, 1933), XVII, 113.
64. *CL*, II, 1033.

lack of depth, in keeping with Coleridge's not infrequent indulgence in backhanded compliments. But the point is made. The methodical person has a purposefulness and concentration of energy, he works with a "leading thought" or "initiative" that results in a "unity with progression." Coleridge points out that "method," etymologically, signifies "a way or path of transit." In scientific concerns, the "initiative"—a word he borrows from Bacon's *De augmentis scientiarum* (1623)—is one's intuitive grasp in germ of the organization of an entire system, opposed to dead arrangement as in an alphabet.[65] More important here, initiative is also the power within the person to order his life in time and space. The imperatives are internalized, and instead of following principles one's life *becomes* a principle, as it were. The traditional "virtue" closest to it would be, I suppose, "self-government." "The necessity for external government to man is in an inverse ratio to the vigor of his self-government. Where the last is most complete, the first is least wanted. Hence, the more virtue the more liberty."[66] The term lacks the sense of creative interaction with the not-self, however—the sense that all experience is "a modification of our own being."

In Coleridge, then, one finds an early proponent of a liberal education which emphasizes not knowledge, thought of as information, but self-knowledge: moral awareness and the development of personality. Yet he does not limit the field of profitable inquiry only to that which contains overt humanistic content. He is an encyclopedist. There is nothing he would confess not wishing to know, nothing that does not potentially attach itself to personality, if only one is receptive and inquisitive. His impulse to know is a moral one. He hopes that the immense learning will somehow deepen his sense of self, entwine itself "with the living Substance." But he begins

65. *F*, I, 455–457.
66. *Table Talk*, p. 458.

to be suspicious of his own scholarly enterprise, thinks it a delaying action and a substitute for the real task of moral regeneration. The mind discovers relationships, finds the east out (he is fond of the root meaning of "orientation"), and fills more than sixty notebooks in the hope that they will talk him into something. The more he writes, the more he fears his writing may, after all, be only a subtle acquiescence in the form his self has already taken, or more dismally, in a certain formlessness as the self gives way on all sides the way a sponge does. Those who have method or self-government commit a useful kind of oversimplification. Wordsworth's "Unity of Interest" or his feeling that "we must make a choice" exhibits limitation at the same time that it results in a productivity and self-definition that Coleridge, who wishes to expand in all directions at once, cannot attain. There is nothing vulgar or misconceived in Wordsworth's sense of vocation and purpose. It is based on genuine power and an audience to which he communicates it. Perhaps it is Coleridge's inability to "subordinate" that makes him feel at times as if he is not the purposeful humanist but rather an all-encompassing receptacle, himself the eddy without progression. He perceives all relationships, charts out all courses of action, and ultimately can only commit himself, weakly, to all of them at once.

He gives us the best idea of what he means by method or self-government in a character analysis, much admired by Hazlitt, of someone who has only the simulacrum of it: William Pitt, the Younger. The brilliant portrait, printed March 19, 1800, in the *Morning Post*, was supposed to have been followed by one of Napoleon, but this did not appear. Pitt does not have Napoleon's fiendishness, nor even the failings of the natural man. His is finally, and Coleridge so construes it, a banal evil deriving more from a deficient habit of mind than from malign will. Pitt lacks sensibility, proper education, and indeed a sense of reality. Instead of permitting him as a child to determine his own pursuits, his father Lord Chatham forced him to declaim before company. "His father's rank, fame, political connections, and parental ambition were his mould;—he was cast, rather than grew." All free agency and individuality were thwarted, "and that, which he *might have been,* was compelled into that, which he *was to be.*" He was a plant in a "hot house," who was "regulated by the thermometer of previous purpose." His puritanical temperament developed not from unity of purpose but from vanity, love of power, and dissociation from human fellowship—in fact a bit of debauchery might have done him some good. His relationship to time became one of total unpreparedness. He had always lived "amid objects of futurity," but these objects were merely the "*projected*" familiar objects already given him. With no principle of progression he was unprepared for the French Revolution and did not know what attitude to take toward it, half favoring, half condemning.

The most telling symptom, however, is Pitt's use of language. For Coleridge the primary evil of language is not its power of tempting Eve, telling lies, or making accusations, but its power of shielding one from experience. Language can shield one from facts of human suffering and from one's own consciousness. To wield inert language is already to be in bad faith. Pitt's verbal facility has produced something like eloquence, yet he gives "an endless repetition of the same *general phrases.*" If his boasts of national prosperity are met in the face with facts of real social and economic suffering, he declares this too is owing to prosperity, a declaration "unenforced by one *single image,* one *single fact* of real national amelioration."[67] The abstraction of language is both cause and symptom of his entire orientation toward reality— his lack of close friendships or response to beauty. For Coleridge, true perception, moral and intellectual, requires an

67. *EOT,* II, 319–329.

eye sensitive to particularity, to all the elements making *a* situation *that* one. His own style thus reveals a moral purpose in its profusion of image and metaphor. That the symbol is "consubstantial" with the thing represented suggests that language still alive with image and accurate detail puts one in touch with the objects of consciousness. Language should be a tool of exploration that commits the interior self to its world.

Love

Wordsworth's "Unity of Interest" and mastery over time, reflected both in his life and poetry, are, to the irregular and sometimes envious Coleridge, strengths correlative to a weakness that no amount of training up could mend. He is "by nature incapable of being in Love, tho' no man more tenderly attached—."[68] In a fit of jealousy Coleridge imagines that Wordsworth has supplanted him in Sara Hutchinson's affection. He is "greater, better, manlier, more dear, by nature, to Woman, than I," but "he does not love, he *would* not love, it is not the voice, not the duty of *his* nature, to love *any* being as I love you."[69] Coleridge, we have seen, tends to parade his capacity for love, so much so that, as in his verse epistle to Sara, we may begin to doubt it. What he lacks in self-government or methodical fulfillment of duties toward others, whether in letter writing or repayment of debts, he thinks he makes up in degree and constancy of love. Wordsworth's preoccupation is continuity of self in time; Coleridge's, reciprocity of self with other selves. He sees in Wordsworth his own complementary opposite—together they would make up one whole person, a partnership in human personality as well as in literary manifestos.

As Coleridge describes it, love takes something of the

68. *CL*, III, 305.
69. *N*, II, 3148,

reverse direction, in a metaphoric sense, from the process we have been examining of educing or leading out the self's unconscious powers into consciousness. Love is rather a craving to *return* to the substance of the self, though in full consciousness. It promises to redress the evil tendency of will to establish an independent base and, in so doing, would free the moral eye of its "film."

Perhaps it seems we have taken a long time in arriving at everybody's cure for everything. But Coleridge would say of love what Joseph Butler says of benevolence: it is not the whole of virtue and does not preempt all other moral discussion. Coleridge would add that it is also not an all-powerful force, because, as a symbolic act, it is subject to the limitations of all symbolism.

M. H. Abrams remarks in *Natural Supernaturalism* (1971) that the paradigmatic form of love for Coleridge is friendship, and sexual love is "an especially intense kind of confraternity."[70] This is certainly true, though Coleridge does not for that reason make friendship the more inclusive concept. Indeed I find his writings explicitly on friendship disappointing to expectations raised by his friendships with Wordsworth, Poole, Southey, and Lamb, which are as noteworthy as his love affair with Sara Hutchinson. The conversation poems are more companionable than they are amorous; the name of his enterprising periodical is *The Friend*. He sees himself as one who, like the companionable Albatross, would bring succor, and who hopes to be met hospitably. But in explicit discussions of friendship and love, he downgrades the companionable or hospitable, while he exaggerates the potential of marital bliss, almost out of spite, it would seem, for having been so improvident in his own marriage. Perhaps his fear of a homoerotic element in his closest friendships prevents him from probing them too analytically. I would suggest, however, that we have already examined at

70. *Natural Supernaturalism* (New York: W. W. Norton, 1971), p. 297.

least the theoretical basis of friendship. It is implicit in his account of the conscience that through self-exploration paradoxically achieves a sense of human community, and in his use of the Kantian distinction between persons and things. Friendship evolves out of the total recognition of the "thou" as "other," yet as equally conscious and worthy.

The difference between friendship and love is that the latter seeks to deny that the "thou" *is* "other." Contradicting Sir Thomas Browne's comment that he could more easily give true affection to a male friend than to a woman, Coleridge says that love includes friendship but differs radically from it. Indeed the distinction between tender attachment and love is absolute. Love occurs instantaneously as an act of will. There may be a "dawning" period of several years during which the loved object has been merely a "habitual attachment," but "between the brightest Hues of the Dawn and the first Rim of the Sun itself there is a *chasm* . . . a chasm of Kind in a continuity of Time." "All in a moment *Love* starts up or leaps in, and *takes place* of Liking." Wordsworth, according to Coleridge, errs in thinking love no more than "a compound of Lust with Esteem & Friendship, confined to one object," but one who has not experienced it cannot be expected to know what it is. Coleridge's image for love is "two hearts, like two correspondent concave mirrors, having a common focus, while each reflects and magnifies the other, and in the other itself, is an endless reduplication, by sweet Thoughts & Sympathies."[71] The image suggests that the solipsism of "Dejection: An Ode" is remedied not simply by escape from the prison of private consciousness into the consciousness of another, but by return to the self *by way of* the other. Love and self-love are exercised in the same moral act.

We find in Coleridge elements of the familiar Romantic conception of love—developed by Schiller, Hegel, Shelley,

71. *CL*, III, 303–305.

Keats, all of whom are adding footnotes to Plato's *Symposium* and *Phaedrus*—as the force that brings the fragmentary back to unity. The aim of love is to be perfect, to be made whole. Our sense of "self-insufficingness," of being "but *half* of a compleat Being," extends to the "Understanding, to the Affections, as well as to it's animal organization—."[72] In another person we see the "supplement and completion" of our own being. Love is the "yearning of the whole Being to be united with some one other Being."[73] The metaphor of union is complicated by the fact that in love there exists a "sort of antipathy, or opposing passion" as each strives to be the other and "both together make up one whole"[74]—a comment which may remind one of the comic pathos of Aristophanes' myth in the *Symposium*.

Coleridge does not exclude sensibility from love, which presupposes a "tenderness of nature; a constitutional communicativeness and *utterancy* of heart and soul; a delight in the detail of sympathy, in the outward and visible signs of the sacrament within—."[75] Physical and psychological process can contribute to love:

> All thoughts, all passions, all delights,
> Whatever stirs this mortal frame,
> All are but ministers of Love,
> And feed his sacred flame.[76]

But sensibility is not its ground. He objects to Sterne's glorification of "irresistible Feelings, the too tender Sensibility." Love is "an act of the will—and that too one of the *primary* & therefore unbewusst, & ineffable Acts." It is not a "romantic Hum, a mere connection of Desire with a form appropriated to that form by accident or the mere repetition

---

72. MS Notebook 60, ff. 9ᵛ–10.
73. MS Essay on Love, Victoria University Library; cf. *N*, III, 3514.
74. *Table Talk*, p. 348.
75. "The Improvisatore" (1827), *Poetical Works*, I, 464.
76. "Love" (1799).

of a Day-dream—."[77] By grounding love in will, not sensibility, Coleridge is objecting not only to eighteenth-century British sentimentalism but also, as we have seen, to Kant's assertion that "*Love* is a matter of *feeling*, not of *will*, and I cannot love because I *will* to, still less because I *ought* to (*i.e.* I cannot be necessitated to love). So a *duty to love* is logically impossible."[78] Coleridge writes that Kant himself admits that Adam's choosing of evil is an "ineffable act of the will which is underneath or within the consciousness tho' incarnate in the conscience." Love, likewise, "must be conceived as taking place in the Homo Νουμενον not the Homo ϑαινομενον," a concept of love he attributes to Petrarch.[79] Coleridge sees love as the extraordinary and mysterious struggle of the will to subvert its own evil drive toward separation, a struggle that must ultimately fail in this world.

An elliptical notebook entry of 1807 attempts to connect love with duty, and both of these with a sense of reality. The old conflict between duty and inclination ceases, while both are enriched, in love. To understand his argument we must keep in mind his expressed need of confirmation of his own powers, indeed of his own reality, through the testimony of reflecting mirrors, the reciprocal gesture from the objective world. He writes of the "necessary tendency of true Love to generate a feeling of Duty by increasing the sense of reality, & vice versâ feeling of Duty to generate true Love." A sense of duty, if refined beyond what he has called "selfness" or reflexive scrupulosity, increases a sense of reality when it registers one's place in a total environment and the demands that environment makes. The more we know what our situation is, the more we know what is fitting. Love is the most intense form of knowing, and it entails the enrichment of one's sense of reality by means of the felt reality of another.

77. *N*, III, 3562.
78. *The Doctrine of Virtue*, p. 62.
79. *N*, III, 3562n.

The more we know another human being through love, the more we know our obligation toward him or her, and, simultaneously, the more we feel inclined to do and be what is fitting. Ideally, guilt decreases as love increases, because our duty and our inclination in loving are one and the same. In love we witness the "Incarnation & Transfiguration of Duty as Inclination."[80]

Conscience, we recall, is the recognition of the "thou," the consciousness of a self not our own yet equally worthy and real. The 1807 notebook entry suggests love is a "craving" to get beyond the mere "shadow" or phenomenal representation of another and of oneself, and to appropriate the substance of both. Conscience develops with recognition of the limits of self and its relatedness to the "sphere of free agency" of others, but love is the effort to transcend *relationship* altogether. One might say it is an exertion of the sympathetic conscience that has got out of bounds. We remember that "the lowest depth that the light of our Consciousness can visit even with a doubtful Glimmering, is still at an unknown distance from the Ground." Love is the effort to explore that distance. The "Phaenomenon Self is a Shadow" that senses its own shadowiness and realizes that it "ought to belong to a Substance/." The "Substance" of the self, unlike its phenomenal manifestation, has "no marks, no discriminating Characters, no hic est, ille non est/it is simply substance—."[81] The effort to reach beyond the phaenomenon self does not, however, dismiss that self, which is valued *as* the representative image of the true self. In love, the image is reconstituted as symbol; it becomes the translucent medium through which we get a glimmering of the substance of true self. Love seeks an ultimate identity in substance beneath the psychic and physical traits that define us as this or that person or sex. "Were there not an Identity in the Substance,

80. *N*, II, 3026; cf. *N*, III, 3989.
81. Ibid.

man & woman might *join*, but they could never *unify*."[82]
Love is this craving for the substance of another: "Love a
sense of Substance/Being seeking to be self-conscious, 1. of
itself in a Symbol. 2. of the Symbol as not being itself. 3. of
the Symbol as being nothing but in relation to itself—&
necessitating a return to the first state, Scientia absoluta."[83]
The pattern is an example of the "circuitous journey" that
M. H. Abrams has demonstrated to be the structural myth of
much Romantic literature. The self journeys outward to a
symbol of the self of another, and returns through the mediation of that symbol to itself, now felt as substance, not
shadow. Through the act of imagination that is love, one
comes home to where one has never been.

Coleridge elsewhere relates these perceptions more directly
to personal context and sees that love must remain a "craving," not a consummation, just as grief, he says, is a craving.
The separateness of individual wills finally mocks the tendency of love to seek an "Identity in the Substance." An
1801 notebook entry describes an embrace of, one assumes,
Sara Hutchinson by candlelight:

> Prest to my bosom & felt there—it was quite dark. I looked in-
> tensely toward her face—& sometimes I *saw* it—so vivid was the
> spectrum, that it had almost all its natural sense of *distance* & *out-
> ness*—except indeed that, feeling & all, I felt her as *part* of my
> being—twas all spectral—But when I could not absolutely *see* her,
> no effort of fancy could bring out even the least resemblance of
> her face.[84]

The tension between otherness and union is articulated by
the image. That it is by turns spectral and vivid, distant and
consubstantial, suggests its role of ironic mediation.

His love for Sara works toward a coalescence of the "real"
and "symbolical," "and the more because I love her as being

82. *CL*, III, 305.
83. *N*, II, 3026; cf. *N*, III, 3996.
84. *N*, I, 985.

capable of being glorified by me & as the means & instrument of my own glorification/In loving her thus I love two Souls as one, as compleat."[85] The symbol, he stresses, "always partakes of the Reality which it renders intelligible; and while it enunciates the whole, abides itself as a living part in that Unity, of which it is the representative."[86] Love accordingly assumes in the moral sphere a function analogous to imagination in the aesthetic; it is itself an act of imagination. The artist coalesces the multitudinous data of perception into the translucent symbol. The lover apprehends the loved object in the totality of his or her physical presence, moods, gestures, and actions, which collectively become the symbol of that person. The symbol hints at the substance, and in appropriating it the lover hopes, as Blake puts it, to "seize the inmost form." The craving of love is to transcend the symbol to the substance itself. That Coleridge is not loved by the Wordsworths comes from their "Ignorance of the Deep place of my Being—."[87] The loved one must be "one who is & is not myself—not myself, & yet so much more my Sense of Being. . . . Self in me derives its sense of Being from having this one absolute Object [Sara], including all others that but for it would be thoughts, notions, irrelevant fancies—yea, my own Self would be—utterly deprived of all connection with her—only more than a thought, because it would be a Burthen—a haunting of the dæmon, Suicide."[88] His fear that Wordsworth has stolen Sara's love threatens the stability and even the reality of his self.

Pervading much of Coleridge's work is the agony that love, at least for him, can never in the first place transcend the symbol to the substance. The symbol, whether in language, art, or love, is an imaginative projection that answers

85. *N*, II, 2530.
86. *Lay Sermons*, p. 30.
87. *N*, II, 3146.
88. *N*, II, 3148.

to one's sense of "Halfness." It is the symbol's very property of vivid *"Outness"* that promises to gratify the interior emptiness. But the symbol does not feed that emptiness fully, "for the utmost is only an approximation to that absolute *Union*, which the soul sensible of its imperfection in itself, of its *Halfness*, yearns after."[89] A love embrace is but a metaphor of union that promises so much but gives so little, just as the eye does with its spectral images. Faced with an inevitable failure of reciprocity, brought on by the fact that there is always something alien in the other, love may die. He quotes Claudius' "There lives within the very flame of Love, '/ A kind of wick or Snuff, that will abate it," and cries, "Merciful Wonder-making Heaven! What a man was this Shakespear!"[90]

Several of Coleridge's late poems, such as "Love's Apparition and Evanishment" (1833) and "Love's Burial-Place" (1828), portray the death of love. Two untitled quatrains of 1828 are pointed and bitter:

> Though veiled in spires of myrtle-wreath,
> Love is a sword which cuts its sheath,
> And through the clefts itself has made,
> We spy the flashes of the blade!

> But through the clefts itself has made
> We likewise see Love's flashing blade,
> By rust consumed, or snapt in twain;
> And only hilt and stump remain.[91]

Unreciprocated love is a kind of spiritual emasculation. A notebook entry of 1825 employs once again the image of two looking glasses confronting each other and then speaks of the loss of love with age. "How often do we become more and more loveless, as Love, which can outlive all change save a

89. *N*, III, 3325.
90. *N*, III, 3285.
91. *Poetical Works*, I, 450–451.

change with regard to itself, and all loss save the loss of its *Reflex*, is more needed to sooth us & alone is able so to do!"[92] A stanza excluded from the poem "Work without Hope" (1825) finds the poet lamenting that his "Sister Mirror" hiding the "dreary wall" of the world has broken, and he has lost his "Object." Love requires reciprocity, but Coleridge doubts that there has ever been an instance of complete reciprocity or constancy, "where the Affection endures in the same intensity, with the same increased tenderness & *nearness—*."[93] He entertains no Romantic myth of the triumph of human love, which he calls "evanescent."

Love, then, is an effort to transcend human alienation by denying that the "thou" is unconditionally "other." With reference to Coleridge's analysis of human bondage, it is the power that would soften the look of the loveless observer and that would awaken one from the solipsistic nightmare through its transitiveness—it would connect the self to reality in a creative way. The sense of self would be activated in seeking the substance or interior self of another. It is an act of will that, extraordinarily, would subvert the will's own drive toward separateness. It would reconcile will and consciousness in the maximum development of both. Considered in contrast with the remarks on reverencing the individuality and sphere of free agency of one's friend, this analysis explains why Coleridge thinks the distinction between friendship and love is so absolute. Love, after all, attempts to appropriate the sphere of another and is therefore a kind of usurpation. Resistance to love may have its source in a fear of usurpation; and Coleridge discovers that his impassioned overtures are sometimes treated as threats. Perhaps Wordsworth's offer of tender attachment with sexual interest superadded is more attractive to women. Coleridge exclaims in his notebooks that no one loves Sara as he does and that she

92. MS Notebook 29, f. 82^V.
93. MS Notebook 26, f. 159; *CL*, V, 414–416.

still does not, if we are to believe him, fully accept that love. The antidote to human alienation may actually intensify alienation, or such, at least, is Coleridge's reading of his own experience with love's bitter mystery. His failures in love are more disheartening to him than those in vocation, because they strike at the one aspect of the ideal personality that he wishes to think he possesses fully and that extenuates his failures elsewhere. In 1822 he reflects sadly on his deepest friendship and on his only relationship that might have been called a love affair. Alienation from Wordsworth "spread a wider gloom over the world around me," but alienation from Sara Hutchinson "left a darkness deeper within my-self— . . . the latter had more of Self in it's character; but of a Self emptied—a gourd of Jonas—and is *this* it, under which I hoped to have prophesied?"[94]

Irony and the Coleridgean Personality

In the Opus Maximum Coleridge writes that human personality should not be predicated on limitation or deficiency. The reductio ad absurdum of thinking otherwise would be that

the wiser a man became, the greater his power of self determination, with so much less propriety could he be spoken of as a person; and vice versâ the more exclusive the limits & the smaller the sphere enclosed, in short the less Will he possessed, the more a person, till at length his personality would be at its maximum when he bordered on the mere animal or the ideot i.e. when according to all use of language he ceased to be a *person* at all.[95]

Personality is "a thing of degrees," which is acquired gradually through intensification of consciousness. One draws the "circumvolving line" with the greatest perimeter, yet the

94. *CL,* V, 250. See Jonah 4.
95. OM, B$_3$, ff. 173–174.

area encompassed must somehow be a unity well-defined. As we have seen, the most encompassing moral endeavor is not so much the performance of right acts as it is the greatest development of the self—its germinal powers and its capacity for love. In *The Friend* he writes, "The nurture and evolution of humanity is the final aim."[96]

The distinction he makes between true form that develops *ab intra* and mere shape that is superimposed *ab extra* is applicable to morals as well as to aesthetics. In his search for proper authority he intermittently adopts a moral view emphasizing duty for duty's sake, but in a combination of personal and theoretical qualifications he fears that duty is a divisive voice that too often comes from without, even when it issues from one's own accusing conscience. Love and the kind of self-government he has described are both characteristics of a moral consciousness that has developed from within; they contribute to wholeness of self. Through them duty loses its punitive character and is transfigured as inclination. Coleridge's is a theory of self-realization based on the idea that the self is an organism with the latent power of growth, growth that must be directed mostly by the organism itself. One's actions over a period of time express the self by leading it out, educing it from the germ, as its organic offshoots.

For as the Will or Spirit, the Source and Substance of Moral Good, is one, and all in every part: so must it be the Totality, the whole articulated Series of Single Acts, taken as Unity, that can alone, in the severity of Science, be recognized as the proper Counterpart and adequate Representative of a good Will. Is it in this or that limb, or not rather in the whole body, the entire Organismus, that the Law of Life reflects itself? Much less then can the Law of the Spirit work in fragments.[97]

96. *F*, I, 508.

97. *AR*, pp. 289–290. Similarly, Schiller writes that "the destiny of man is not to accomplish isolated moral acts, but to be a moral being." The possessor of the *schöne Seele* reveals that "it is not this or that particular action, it is the entire character which is moral" (*Works*, p. 206).

The metaphors of expanding consciousness and organic growth might legitimately raise the question of whether Coleridge exhibits or leaves room in theory for the flexibility and play of mind, the freedom to choose *not* to be all things, that would insure that the Coleridgean personality has not expanded beyond human dimensions altogether, and become turgid, humorless, even inanimate. Carlyle thought Coleridge "deficient in laughter; or indeed in sympathy for concrete human things either on the sunny or on the stormy side." What he needed was "one right peal of concrete laughter at some convicted flesh-and-blood absurdity, one burst of noble indignation at some injustice or depravity, rubbing elbows with us on this solid Earth."[98] This "deficiency" may indeed have been a character trait, though Carlyle himself admits to "touches of prickly sarcasm" in Coleridge.

A contrast between the two on this point is instructive. Carlyle's criticism can be extended to suggest that Coleridge is no ironist, while irony is of course Carlyle's specialty. An ironist confronted with incompatibles or absurdities is not likely to seek some principle of reconciliation but instead rests uneasily with fractured perception. Absurdity energizes protective wit, acerbity, or, as such figures as Pascal and Kierkegaard remind us, religiosity. The ironist's play of mind is itself the protective distance between self and the matter of perception. To become what one beholds would be, for the ironist, to dissolve the boundaries of the self, to abandon the hard-earned personality, and to submit to heteronomy. The ironist's integrity often depends upon remaining in the uneasy realm of perception deprived of power rather than risking all in participation or commitment. If there is commitment, it is not without, as in Carlyle and Nietzsche, a lingering sense of its absurdity. Carlyle's fierce rhetorical grappling with the subject at hand is what Coleridge might call a "species of Histrionism"— one that, in a complex way, plays back and forth between committing "representative

98. *Coleridge the Talker*, p. 117.

image" and "interior self." The play is so constant that image and self are inseparable and mutually protective; rage becomes the representation of rage without becoming any the less genuine for it.

Coleridge does not practice, and is probably incapable of, the willful play of perspective that irony implies. His habit of mind is to seek greater and greater inclusiveness, to circle around the object of consciousness in ever widening gyres just as his periodic prose does. His metaphors are of absorption, vegetative growth, or widening circumferences. In response to suffering and alienation, he does not often employ irony or humor. Instead he tries to accommodate the suffering through some broader perspective, to see some way of growing from it, or, more simply, to suffer it. He tries not to be the Underground Man and postulates the integrated personality as the end of human effort.

He fears, however, that alienation may be an essential constituent of human growth. In language that exactly anticipates existential formulations, he writes that

the moment, when the Soul begins to be sufficiently self-conscious, to ask concerning itself, & its relations, is the first moment of its *intellectual* arrival into the World—Its *Being*—enigmatic as it must seem—is posterior to its *Existence*—. Suppose the shipwrecked man stunned, & for many weeks in a state of Ideotcy or utter loss of Thought & Memory—& then gradually awakened/.[99]

His use of shipwreck is evidence of his tendency to see self-realization issuing from the other side of alienation or disaster. It is only when one has suffered alienation fully that the self encounters its own profundity. Deprived of all inherited moral truths, the shipwrecked man would have to pursue the more arduous task of self-discovery in the search for "relations." Through intense reflectivity, not through acquiescence to received truths, the self begins to awaken and become a

99. *N*, III, 3593.

moral being. How the self grows is a matter of choosing. In this very pointed anticipation of Sartre, Coleridge has argued that one's "Being," or personal identity, is "posterior" to one's "Existence," or the bewildering state of finding oneself in the world. Sartre writes that "I am condemned to exist forever beyond my essence," and that "freedom is precisely the nothingness which *is made-to-be* at the heart of man and which forces human-reality *to make itself* instead of *to be*."[100] Though he finds more than nothingness at the heart, Coleridge certainly rubs elbows with the rest of us on this solid earth in his recognition that alienation, whether for good or ill, is the central fact of modern moral consciousness. The ideal Coleridgean personality is not found in some joyful transcendent consciousness so distended and undiscriminating that it lacks personal texture or "sympathy for concrete human things."

His response to alienation, paradox, absurdity, I have said, is not humor or irony but an often painful and bewildered receptivity. He is, of course, perplexed, even dumbfounded, by the paradoxical quality of what he perceives. The death of love is not just and eludes rational explanation. But irony and paradox are not his ways of dealing with paradox. I think one could say his habit of mind is thus in radical opposition to the matter of his perception. He exists in what he sees to be an ironic world, but he is not the ironist. Without the protective play of irony, he is in theory more vulnerable than the ironist to the painfulness of his own vision—and Coleridge can at times excel in suffering. He does have, as everyone knows, another response to potential suffering: the blind spot. He will not acknowledge, for example, female sexuality, the brutality of the upper classes, or the extent of his plagiarisms, aggressions, or religious doubts, which suggests tactics of evasion less forthright than irony. Spinoza has long ago said,

100. *Being and Nothingness*, pp. 415–416.

though, that "all things excellent are as difficult as they are rare."

Coleridge's life is an effort to transcend the ironic suffering state of the Mariner, to survive shipwreck, and to become the free personality that he has himself described so well. This personality has not expanded beyond human dimensions; the integration and growth one achieves are, he knows, won through struggle and they can always be subverted. There is little glib talk of mystical transcendence in Coleridge. The Mariner still wanders within him. On his deathbed he is the "undischarged Debtor" who is "hopeless of recovery, yet without prospect of a speedy removal." He can only hope God "will *deliver* me from the Evil One."[101] To be human is to be afflicted indeed, and Coleridge never puts off the affliction. What he has suggested in his theory of self-realization is not that suffering in this life will cease, but that through intelligence and love the self-contradiction can be eased, the pain in some measure transmuted into the "nurture and evolution of humanity."

101. *CL*, VI, 990.

4 | Coleridge and the British Moral Tradition

Coleridge was in many ways the seminal mind John Stuart Mill took him to be, but his specifically moral writings, most of them unpublished, were not put into the assimilable form that might have created a school of moral thought in Britain. The British Idealists of the late nineteenth century—Thomas Hill Green, F. H. Bradley, and Bernard Bosanquet—looked back to Hegel, not to their compatriot Coleridge. Hegel's brilliance notwithstanding, this was a loss, because the writings that I have collected are different in kind, in my judgment, from those of any other British moralist.

Coleridge's significant immediate influence as moralist is discovered less in his contemporaries' responses to his scattered formal writings in *The Friend, Aids to Reflection,* and elsewhere, than in the diverse comment his life provoked—comment that, I have said, he himself initiated by self-characterization in conversation, letters, lectures, and poems. Here was a person so arresting and contradictory, and one who told portions of his tale so publicly, that others, from Lamb and Hazlitt to De Quincey and Keats, had obviously to awaken sadder and wiser for his example. The Victorians tried to come to terms with him in some of their finest essays, as those by Carlyle, Mill, F. J. A. Hort, and Pater attest. These writers, and others such as Julius Hare, Thomas Arnold, Newman, and Disraeli, were not so appalled by the cripple that they did not try to listen. Mill treated him as a significant figure in the history of ideas, while Carlyle and Pater, each in his own way, dwelt on the moral riddle of his life. Perhaps the most tenacious moralist to study Coleridge was Emerson, whose connection with him has to date been explored mostly in terms of the reason/understanding distinction. Since Emerson was a better moralist than epistemologist and since Coleridge has been rarely studied as a moralist, the most intriguing aspect of a direct influence is yet to be fully elucidated.

My purpose here, beyond these few suggestions, is not to chart Coleridge's influence but to construct his commentary on those British moralists who in some way influenced *him*. We will find, once again, the argument of a passionate, inquiring, distinctive mind, better equipped than any other of the period to undertake a critical evaluation of British moralism.

His distinctiveness as moralist resulted in part, as we have seen, from his own response to and use of German moral philosophy. Kant was to Coleridge what Hegel was to Green and Bradley later in the century. Coleridge's discussions of freedom, duty, and self-realization reveal that he read, in addition to Kant, such thinkers as Friedrich Jacobi, Schiller, Fichte, Friedrich Schlegel, and Schelling. He was also distinctive for his complex critical response to his native moral tradition, in which he was well read; he studied the British moralists closely, if not with the expectancy he felt when he turned to the Germans. His self-realization theory, though it was a form of humanism without exact precedent in Britain, built on the debates between humanists and skeptics of the sixteenth and seventeenth centuries. But his most rigorous moral argument was directed against theories still very much alive in his own day—hedonism, and the "mechanico-corpuscular" notions of egoism and utilitarianism that he regarded as having descended from Hobbes. His critique of these dominant British moral schools has never been amply presented and examined; many of the pertinent writings, found in greatest concentration in the Opus Maximum manuscript, have remained unpublished. I wish to present these writings, to show how they relate to the argument we have developed in previous chapters, and to assess in the broadest possible terms Coleridge's position in the great debates of British moralism up to his day.

The Young Moralist

Coleridge develops precociously the vocabulary of existential guilt. Two school essays written for his schoolmaster Rev. James Boyer's "Liber Aureus" dwell on *la condition humaine* with august periodicity. "In the beginning of Life Error and Folly wear their most alluring dress. They have then all the charms of Novelty to recommend them, and the inexperience, credulity, and rashness of the youthful mind to combat on their side. That they too often obtain the conquest therefore produces rather Pity, than Wonder, in the candid mind." Youth is to be treated indulgently, but if evil habits persist into adulthood, that is another matter:

To sacrifice then all, that is truly advantageous & honourable in life to the pursuit of useless pleasures implies a disposition so congenial with Vice, that well may the conduct, w̄ch was pitied in Youth, now be punished by the neglect and contempt of others, and by the remorse of our own breasts. For the very pleasures, which influenced us, are fled! If awoke from a pleasing dream we will lay Reason and Shame asleep, that we may again enjoy the delightful vision. Alas! far different scenes must succeed—darkness, and haunts obscene and frightful, with all the gloomy offspring of a diseased fancy.[1]

Though this is a school exercise there are hints of a personal nature in these incriminating dreams.

The other essay, on habit, ends on a note even more prophetic of Coleridge in his prime:

Alas! at the moment we contract a habit we forego our free agency. The remainder of our life will be spent in making resolutions in the hour of dejection and breaking them in the hour of Passion. As if we were in some great sea-vortex, every moment we perceive our ruin more clearly, every moment we are impelled towards it with greater force. What is the event? Too trite to mention—We cut the knot, which we cannot untye.[2]

These vivid images are otherwise lost in a sea of conventional moralizings, very much intended to please the adult world. The "two Coleridges" of which Stephen Potter writes (though why stop at two?) are already visible—the reflexive, exploratory Coleridge on the one hand, the public, declamatory STC on the other.[3]

His moral writings during the 1790s are important partly because they tell us of his interests prior to his reading German philosophy. According to Gillman, Coleridge first got started in philosophy in his teens by reading the discussions of freedom and necessity in *Cato's Letters* (1724), a philosophical treatment of contemporary political issues employing a Lockean epistemology and arguing for necessity over

1. "Nec Lusisse Pudet, Sed Non Incidere Ludum" (1790), Victoria University Library. The text is printed in Lawrence Hanson, *The Life of S. T. Coleridge* (1938; rpt. New York: Russell & Russell, 1962), pp. 424–425, though with a serious error in transcription. See also the early poem, "Progress of Vice" (1790).

2. "Quis Fas, Atque Nefas, Tandem Incipiunt Sentire Criminibus" (1791), Victoria University Library. Hanson, pp. 425–426.

3. *Coleridge and S. T. C.* (New York: Russell & Russell, 1935; rpt. 1965), pp. 11–21.

free will.[4] Even before studying Paley, Hartley, Priestley, and Godwin, he exhibits a strongly moral cast of mind, though surely much of this is attributable to his being the son of an Anglican vicar. The letters and notebook entries through 1794, by which time he was reading these British moralists, are rich in moral vocabulary—"egotism," "pleasure," "happiness," "will," "benevolence," "virtue," "vice," "habit," "morality," "prudence," "sensibility," "conscience," "agent," "motives," and especially "duty." His borrowings from the Bristol Library during 1795 included works with moral implications, such as Ralph Cudworth's *The True Intellectual System of the Universe*, John Balguy's *Divine Benevolence*, Paley's *Evidences of Christianity*, Thomas Clarkson's *An Essay on the Impolicy of the African Slave Trade*. Borrowings for 1796 included Richard Cumberland's *The Observer* and George Berkeley's *Works*.[5] By 1798 at the latest he had read a figure with whom he has some significant affinities, Joseph Butler.

According to Hazlitt in *My First Acquaintance with Poets* (1823), Coleridge thought Butler was "a true philosopher, a profound and conscientious thinker, a genuine reader of nature and of his own mind. He did not speak of his *Analogy*, but of his *Sermons at the Rolls' Chapel*, of which I had never heard. Coleridge somehow always contrived to prefer the *unknown* to the *known*."[6] The point Hazlitt was discuss-

4. This treatise was written mostly by John Trenchard (1662–1723). See Orsini, p. 17.

5. The list of books borrowed from the Bristol Library by Coleridge and Southey has been compiled by George Whalley and published in *The Library*, Transactions of the Bibliographical Society, 5th Ser., 4 (2 Sept. 1949), 114–132.

6. *My First Acquaintance with Poets*, p. 113. F. J. A. Hort in his essay on Coleridge in *Cambridge Essays* (1856) thinks it difficult to believe that Coleridge could have known Butler "without placing him habitually among his chosen friends of all ages" (p. 336). But there is no evidence, he says, that he did know Butler. Muirhead comments on "Coleridge's apparent entire ignorance of Butler," an especially woeful ignorance since there is so

ing with Coleridge early in 1798 was "disinterestedness." We will see that Coleridge's own refutation of psychological egoism in the Opus Maximum is at some points similar to Butler's. In a letter of 1801 to Josiah Wedgwood, he identifies Butler, Berkeley, and Hartley as the three greatest and indeed only metaphysicians which England has produced.[7] That he rarely mentions Butler in moral discussion might suggest an "anxiety of influence" in the philosophical as well as the poetic sphere. When dealing with eighteenth-century moralists, he turns instead to those with whom he disagrees— Hartley, Paley, Godwin—and says little about those with whom he would have some agreement—Richard Price, Berkeley, and Butler. An orthodox explanation would be that his interest in and affinities with the seventeenth-century Cambridge Platonists make the eighteenth-century rational intuitionists seem dry and superfluous. Butler would be, however, a better propaedeutic to Kant than the Platonists in moral matters; as C. D. Broad points out, Butler and Kant have much in common.[8] In addition to the refutation of psychological egoism, Coleridge shares Butler's insight into the nature of the constitutional balance between the principles of self-love and benevolence, a balance that is produced by the conscience. When Coleridge, refusing the Wedgwood annuity in January, 1798, writes, "An enlightened Selfishness

---

much affinity in doctrine. To assert that Coleridge does not know such and such an author is dangerous business. He thinks highly enough of Butler to propose to his Unitarian friend, John Prior Estlin, that they collaborate in 1798 on an edition of the *Analogy* (1736) complete with notes and a refutation of Hume's system of causation (or "non-causation") (*CL*, I, 385–386). Though his interest in Butler here appears to be his refutation of Deism, he is, as Hazlitt says, even more interested in Butler's ethical *Fifteen Sermons* (1726). As I will show later in this chapter, I have discovered one direct borrowing from this work. See McFarland, *Coleridge and the Pantheist Tradition*, p. 360n43, for a discussion of Coleridge and Butler.

7. *CL*, II, 703.

8. *Five Types of Ethical Theory* (New York: Harcourt, Brace, 1930), p. 53.

was in this case the only species of Benevolence left to me," he is echoing Butler, who sees no necessary conflict between the two.[9] Butler is an unseen presence in Coleridge's articulation of moral problems.

He has a basic disagreement with Butler, though—and with most British moralists—on the subject of evil. Shaftesbury, Butler, Hartley, Price, Priestley, Paley, and Godwin are at best concerned with the wet sinner, who tries but fails from weakness; the malignancy of the dry sinner, who actively wills evil, is beyond the ken of all of them. There is a certain lack of dignity in Coleridge's stooping to tangle with the likes of Paley, the complacent divine. The school essays we have just seen suggest that even at age eighteen he is out of Paley's league, and an early notebook entry voices disapproval of Paley's views on the pleasures of poverty.[10] Coleridge's treatment of depravity rebukes eighteenth-century sentimentalism and links him in substance with the Augustans, though his reflections on the problem of evil have greater philosophical depth than theirs.

The very style, stance, and vocabulary of British moral writing sit uneasily with him. What would the Ancient Mariner do with Butler's "cool self-love"? "Benevolence," if it is but a generalized quasi-aesthetic response, is an instance of the same self-serving detachment that Coleridge aligns with moral corruption.

In the early *Lectures 1795*, however, Coleridge's indebtedness to late eighteenth-century moralists is so strong that he presents evil as a quite manageable problem. It is either something brought about by foul physical circumstances and insensitive governments (Godwin, Rousseau), or it is a disharmony essential to a divine plan we cannot fully comprehend (Hartley, Priestley). In either case, as the editors point

9. *CL*, *I*, 367.
10. *N*, I, 75.

out, evil is contingent and not an absolute principle emanating from the corrupt will.[11]

This brief flirtation with religious and political optimism has its internal inconsistencies brought about by his failure to coordinate conflicting sources. It is also inconsistent both with Coleridge's later thought and, I would say, with his own attitudes *of the time*, at least as they are elsewhere expressed. While enlisted as Silas Tomkyn Comberbache in the King's Dragoons after running away from debts at Cambridge in 1794, he writes to George that he had responded to his tutor's bill gloomily and turbulently. "Instead of manfully disclosing the disease, I concealed it with a shameful Cowardice of sensibility, till it cankered my very Heart." "Where Vice has not annihilated Sensibility, there is little need of a Hell!" Perhaps he confesses more sins to his brother than he has committed, but there is evidence that he visits prostitutes during this period. "Repentance may bestow that tranquillity, which will enable man to pursue a course of undeviating harmlessness, but it can not restore to the mind that inward sense of Dignity, which is the parent of every kindling Energy!—I am not, what I was:—*Disgust*—I *feel*, as if it had—jaundiced all my Faculties."[12] There is posturing here, of course, but it is a posturing closer (and therefore

11. *Lectures 1795*, p. 107n.
12. *CL*, I, 67–68. In 1801 Coleridge writes to Humphry Davy, albeit the context is facetious, that he has searched "as far as memory served, thro' all the loose women I had known, from my 19th to my 22nd year, that being the period that comprizes my Unchastities," without being able to come up with the name of a woman in question (*CL*, II, 734); in 1805 he speaks of "a short-lived Fit of Fears from sex" at some unspecified time before the "horror of DUNS" at Cambridge (*N*, II, 2398); and in 1814 he had "begun to suspect a Source of Disease in myself anterior to, & even more serious than the OPIUM; & which had been from it's constitutional effects the *cause* of my resorting to that Drug: tho' from never having had any 'Complaint' in my whole Life, and having since my twenty second year never had any illicit connection, I did not till lately even *suspect* it—" (*CL*, III, 514–515).

truer) to the Coleridge who is soon to write *The Ancient Mariner* than is the pompous and optimistic pastiche from Hartley and Priestley that one finds in most of his first public sallies into philosophy and religion.

Although the British moralists are lacking in tragic perspective, and though their "schemes" are misdirected, sentimental, and often morally dangerous, Coleridge learns much from them that he does not learn from the Germans. It remains true, to be sure, that he learns mostly in response to what he perceives to be their insufficiencies and errors.

Romantic Humanism

One idea Coleridge develops largely in response to the British tradition is the role of sensibility. His approach to this question reminds one that his position on many matters is difficult to define because he enjoys outflanking his opponents. He attacks Sterne for giving priority in moral concerns to sensibility over reason. But since he himself questions the adequacy of reason alone to direct the moral life, he does not wish to underestimate the importance of an active sensibility. It is simply insufficient. It may be the "ornament and becoming Attire of Virtue," and he writes, conscious of the pun, that "it may almost be said to *become* Virtue." Yet sensibility, "a keen sense of the gratifications that accompany social intercourse, mutual endearments, and reciprocal preferences," is "no sure pledge of a GOOD HEART." It is a "quality of the nerves, and a result of individual bodily temperament" that may or may not be based on accurate perception of a moral situation.[13]

In *Aids to Reflection* he repeats what he had written some thirty years earlier in *The Watchman* (1796). In a "nervous" and "over-stimulated" age, people make an outcry only

13. *AR*, pp. 51–53.

about those injustices that disturb their own serenity. "Provided the dunghill is not before their parlour window, they are well contented to know that it exists, and perhaps as the hotbed on which their own luxuries are reared."[14] Sentimental distortion of moral perception allows the slave trade to flourish. Coleridge denounces the subterfuge in a 1795 Bristol lecture later printed in *The Watchman:* "The merchant finds no argument against it in his ledger: the citizen at the crouded feast is not nauseated by the stench and filth of the slave-vessel—the fine lady's nerves are not shattered by the shrieks! She sips a beverage sweetened with human blood, even while she is weeping over the refined sorrows of Werter or of Clementina."[15] What is needed is "truth-painting imagination" that would put us in touch with the horror of the slave ship. "Would you choose to be sold? to have the hot iron hiss upon your breasts, after having been crammed into the hold of a Ship with so many fellow-victims, that the heat and stench, arising from your diseased bodies, should rot the very planks?"[16] The lecture given less than two years before composition of *The Ancient Mariner* suggests, as Empson points out, that Coleridge's horror at the idea of a slave ship provides many of the images and motifs of that poem.[17]

The proper response to slavery is outrage that prompts the agent to act in some way. There is "one criterion by which we may always distinguish benevolence from mere sensibility—Benevolence impels to action, and is accompanied by self-denial."[18] In *Aids to Reflection* he quotes from his early poem, "Reflections on Having Left a Place of Retirement." Even worse than Godwinian "*cold* beneficence," he

14. *AR*, p. 52.
15. *The Watchman*, ed. Lewis Patton (Princeton: Princeton University Press, 1970), p. 139.
16. Ibid., p. 138.
17. *Coleridge's Verse*, pp. 28–31.
18. *The Watchman*, p. 140.

had written, is the response of "sluggard Pity's vision-weaving Tribe,"

> Who sigh for Wretchedness yet shun the wretched,
> Nursing in some delicious Solitude
> Their Slothful Loves and dainty Sympathies.

Sentimental response or "bastard Sensibility" is a form of *moral* bombast: feeling inappropriate to its object. It is hypocritical because it arises "only in *parts* and *fragments* of our nature." Coleridge writes huffily that the same natural sympathy that would prompt someone to free a friend from prison might also prompt him to seduce his friend's wife.[19]

He connects the rise of a cult of sensibility with the "sentimental Novelists," who spread their disease to the "English Philosophers." Of Sterne he writes that there is a danger, "in respect of pure morality," in seeing that "all follies not selfish are pardoned or palliated."[20]

All the evil achieved by Hobbes and the whole School of Materialists will appear inconsiderable if it be compared with the mischief effected and occasioned by the sentimental Philosophy of STERNE, and his numerous Imitators. The vilest appetites and the most remorseless inconstancy towards their objects, acquired the titles of *the Heart, the irresistible Feelings, the too tender Sensibility:* and if the Frosts of Prudence, the icy chains of Human Law thawed and vanished at the genial warmth of Human Nature, who *could help it?* It was an amiable Weakness![21]

England and the Continent have been swept over by the plague of sensibility, which has confounded love with sentiment. Coleridge objects to the effeminacy of this substitution of "shapeless feelings, sentiments, impulses" for the "distinguishing Characters of Humanity," which are "Reason,

19. *AR*, pp. 52–53.
20. *Miscellanies, Aesthetic and Literary*, ed. Thomas Ashe (London: George Bell, 1892), p. 124.
21. *AR*, pp. 53–54.

Discrimination, Law, and deliberate Choice." And he repeats the idea that love is "an inward FIAT of the Will, by a completing and sealing Act of Moral Election, and lays claim to permanence only under the form of DUTY."[22]

In thus objecting to the idea that we have natural sympathy running in our veins, Coleridge takes a role analogous to that of John Balguy, who objects to Francis Hutcheson's account of natural affections. Balguy writes the affections are more expertly practiced by animals, who "pursue the instincts and impulses of nature, more steadily and regularly than men; they show affection to their respective kinds, and a strong degree of love and tenderness towards their offspring."[23] Our natural impulses, writes Coleridge, "differ from the vital workings in the brute animals" only if they are connected with moral awareness. It is "a painful, a mortifying, but even therefore a *necessary* business, to make strict inquisition into the amiable tendencies of the comparatively best-natured Individuals, as soon as they are loose from the leading-strings of the Universal Reason." He thinks his own "craving for sympathy" may be only a surreptitious form of "Selfishness: that is, the Self is not only the starting-point *from*, but the Goal, *to*—which the Soul is working in such moments—."[24] A praiseworthy emotion such as pity may, if undisciplined, "co-operate to deprave us."[25]

But with characteristic balance, Coleridge does not intend to remove the "temperamental *pro*-virtues" from morality. Following the attack on Sterne he says morality has "Twin Sources" in "the Affections and the Conscience."[26] His rejection of Stoicism, we have seen, is based on its undervaluation of these "Affections," which need not be merely passive

22. *AR*, pp. 55–56.
23. *A Collection of Tracts Moral and Theological* (1734), in *British Moralists*, I, 391.
24. MS Notebook 46 (1830), ff. 21–21^v.
25. *CL*, II, 711.
26. *AR*, p. 57,

responses to actions but which can have an active mental component. Analogous to the debate between Schiller and Kant is the one he sets up, tacitly, between Hartley and Godwin, though the deductions he makes have to do more with familiar aspects of social conduct than with self-realization of the *schöne Seele*. His objection to Godwin from his first encounter with *Political Justice* (1793) is an overestimation of the role of reason in the moral life and a dismissal of emotion. (Godwin does make something of a concession to emotion when he says the just society would not necessarily preclude some passion between the sexes.)

Coleridge attacks Godwin in letters to Thelwall and in the *Lectures 1795* with much declaiming against a morality "that teaches us that filial Love is a Folly, Gratitude criminal, Marriage Injustice, and a promiscuous Intercourse of the Sexes our wisdom and our duty."[27] Less blustering are his objections to Godwin's idea that benevolence derives from loyalty to country over and against loyalty to private acquaintances and family. Patriotism itself, Coleridge insists, must instead begin and end in private attachments. He might have Plotinus' argument against the Gnostics in mind: one must love those nearest before one can develop eros toward the world. More directly the idea comes from David Hartley, who argues that attachments to larger entities such as the state are based on psychological associations created by immediate personal experience with family and peers. Arguing for this kind of transference, Coleridge writes that the "intensity of private attachments encourages, not prevents, universal Benevolence."[28] I find the most vivid expression of the idea in a letter to Southey: "Philanthropy (and indeed every other Virtue) is a thing of *Concretion*—Some home-born Feeling is the *center* of the Ball, that, rolling on thro' Life collects and assimilates every congenial Affection."[29]

27. *Lectures 1795*, p. 164.
28. Ibid., p. 46.
29. *CL*, I, 86.

Coleridge's sour marriage prompts him to write several tracts on finding a spouse with "natural sensibility." "O that you could feel the wretchedness of having your heart *starved* by selfishness and frost-bitten by moral frigidity!" A letter of 1819 describes two women, probably Edith Southey and Godwin's second wife, Mary Jane Clairmont, who have equal and opposite infirmities. The one, Edith Southey, does "*attach, retain,* and *proportion* her natural sensibility and affection to it's proper objects in their proper order," but she has so little sensibility that it is stillborn. "It is but attachment participated between the Face before, and the Image in the Looking-glass of Self-love." Godwin's wife, on the other hand, has an "overflowing sensibility" but is "a wholly uncentering Being." She lacks "inward legislation & secret *police* of the Will & Affections," with the result that every new acquaintance is instantly a "delightful creature," her "*very* dear, Mr. FUSS-*about*," while her husband "is an old piece of House furniture in the Lumber room, or Dormitory of her attachments."[30] Natural sensibility, then, must be intense enough to transcend the sterile reflex of self-regard, and it must be proportioned to its object in a fitting and unsentimental way. The affections give structure and meaning in that they are directional and transitive; they are, in a most emphatic sense, attachments. Coleridge objects to the "shapeless" and sentimental feelings and passion of "Sterne and his imitators," not to feeling appropriate to its object.

It is not unlike Coleridge to attack excessive sensibility with appeals to rationality, and excessive rationality with appeals to sensibility. When the "whole soul" is engaged, after all, there is a "balance or reconciliation of opposite or discordant qualities." Perhaps there is something less than intellectually engaging in bald summaries of such amalgamations. One's interest may be directed more to the rhetorical

30. *CL,* IV, 905–906. The *OED* lists no use of "centering" or "uncentering" in this modern psychological sense.

verve with which the argument is presented and to the concrete illustrations of it. One should keep in mind, however, the entire portrait of human nature Coleridge envisions. Within the context of British intellectual history, one of the fathers of conservative compromise is adding an exciting chapter to the progress of liberalism. Human nature is an organism in which many powers seek to be realized. The moral task is to direct their realization and to permit no destructive imbalances through constriction of one power for the sake of another.

This liberal concept comes to Coleridge most directly, among British moralists, by way of Joseph Butler. In an unpublished and never delivered sermon of 1799, Coleridge employs Butler's argument in an attack on Godwinian rationalism. In this highly rhetorical but instructive sermon, I detect the unacknowledged use of Butler's *Fifteen Sermons* (1726). In his Preface Butler writes that there are "two ways in which the subject of morals may be treated. One begins from inquiring into the abstract relations of things: the other from a matter of fact, namely, what the particular nature of man is." Butler and Coleridge would both ask the latter question first, but Coleridge, updating the context, thinks Godwinians, instead of "considering that as moral truth, which is suited to the system of our nature would fain suit the system of our nature to that which *they* consider as moral truth." Butler notes that the "ancient moralists" (Stoics) asserted that virtue "consists in following nature," and that William Wollaston in *The Religion of Nature Delineated* (1722) called this a loose way of talk. To understand the imperative to follow nature the Stoics properly had in mind, we must, says Butler, state "exactly the idea of a system, economy or constitution of any particular nature" and thereupon find that "it is an one or a whole, made up of several parts; but yet, that the several parts even considered as a whole, do not complete the idea, unless in the notion of a whole, you include the relations and respects, which those parts have to each other. Every work both of nature and of art is a system." Similarly, Coleridge writes that the "opinion of the wisest ancients that virtue consists in following nature is safe and well-founded, if by the word nature be understood not any single appetite, affection, passion, or quality, but the *system* of our nature: that is those relations and correspondencies which these several parts bear, each to all, and all to each."

Butler compares the system of human nature to a watch, which mechanism makes sense only when the parts are considered in their relation first to each other and then to the whole. "Appetites, passions, affections, and the principle of reflection, considered merely as the several parts of our inward nature, do not at all give us an idea of the system or constitution of this nature." These must be considered in their relation to one another and, more important, to the "supremacy of reflection or conscience." Similarly, Coleridge writes that the Godwinians in emphasizing reason would do away with all other constituents of human nature, its "appetites," "passions," and "affections." He writes, "To repair a faulty time-piece they would disembowel it of its springs, weights and wheel-works, and leave only the regulator remaining."[31]

His assertions, in *The Friend, Aids to Reflection,* and elsewhere, that morality must be suited to human nature in its highest form take on added significance with this direct linkage to Joseph Butler, with whom he recognizes his affinities and to whom he has paid the compliment of plagiarism in a sermon. Butler's conception of a "system" of human nature is itself taken from Shaftesbury, who in turn had taken over the humanistic concerns of the Cambridge Platonists in his own efforts to disprove Hobbesian psychological

---

31. Literary Transcript 29, Victoria University Library; *Fifteen Sermons,* in *British Moralists,* I, 325–330.

egoism. Both Shaftesbury and Butler think the rationalists Richard Cumberland, Samuel Clarke, and William Wollaston have not adequately refuted Hobbes when they describe morality purely in terms of reason. The rationalists have given no role to affect or motivation or will, and have therefore not described how or why one goes about *being* moral. Shaftesbury and Butler take a different tack, believing Hobbes is simply mistaken in his assertion that self-interest is the only possible motive of all human action. Shaftesbury asserts that we are directed by natural social affections as well as by "self-affections," Butler that we are directed by the principle of benevolence as well as by that of self-love. Unlike Clarke and Wollaston, they base their refutations of Hobbes not on immutable rational truths but on empirical fact as they perceive it.

In Butler's view, the conscience, confronted with a plurality of self-love, benevolence, and particular passions, appetites, and affections, can seek to harmonize the conflicting powers into a system, to regulate and not suppress them. Conscience works toward a harmony within the self, not self-division. Coleridge would find Butler's position attractive, because it suggests a liberality toward the emotional component of human nature and yet puts a reasoning faculty, conscience, at the center. Man is neither Hobbes's egoistic beast, nor Clarke's and Wollaston's moral geometrician, nor Hutcheson's sentimental cherub. Rather he is a complicated being capable of reason, of emotional warmth, of bestiality. Even more than Butler, Coleridge recommends a liberal morality, one that would in theory unleash the full powers of self. He is opposed to all reductive and coercive systems, and conceives of the self as an organism containing many powers. He does not normally use Butler's word "system" (except when he is plagiarizing Butler); rather "organism" is the appropriate word. It suggests the vitality of the living thing, not the mechanism of the timepiece.

Stylistically and temperamentally Coleridge has less in common with Butler than with the seventeenth-century Cambridge Platonists. His fondness for Ralph Cudworth and
Henry More is based on the unified sensibility they seem to
possess. The Newtonian rationalists, Clarke and Wollaston,
were to align morality strictly with sciential reason, but
Cudworth and More developed a liberalism that combines,
as John Herman Randall, Jr., remarks, nous and eros in a
"warm intellectualism." Randall notes that the Cambridge
Platonists give birth to both the eighteenth-century rationalists and the competing moral sense school of Shaftesbury,
which emphasizes the affections and a nonrational moral
faculty.[32] Coleridge, then, by identifying in spirit with the
Cambridge Platonists is, in effect, returning to the original
Platonic egg prior to the split. His relationship with them has
been much discussed, mostly in relation to his distinction
between reason and understanding.[33] Though they may have
some influence on his general moral orientation, I have found
their influence on the specific content of his moral writings
to be minimal. Cudworth does not really devote much space
in *The True Intellectual System of the Universe* (1678) and
Eternal and Immutable Morality (1731; written before 1688)
to moral theory apart from his theory of mind, and Coleridge most likely did not know his *Treatise on Free Will,*

32. *The Career of Philosophy*, 2 vols. (New York: Columbia University
Press, 1962), I, 743. For comprehensive discussions of these episodes in intellectual history, see especially pp. 460–497, 709–773.

33. Some Anglophiles, including Coleridge himself, seem eager to prove
that he develops the distinction between reason and understanding from
his native tradition before reading Kant. Orsini and others have argued, to
me persuasively, against this reading. See Orsini's *Coleridge and German
Idealism*, pp. 144–148. An early monograph by Claud Howard, *Coleridge's
Idealism: A Study of its Relationship to Kant and to the Cambridge
Platonists* (Folcroft, Pa.: Folcroft Press, 1924; rpt. 1969), pp. 70–86, attempts
to demonstrate a direct influence of the Cambridge Platonists on Coleridge's
moral thought. It would be safer, in my estimation, to speak of "affinity"
than of "influence" here.

not published until 1838. More's *Enchiridion Ethicum* (1667), while it explicitly provides a recipe for living well, with its emphasis on happiness and the "boniform faculty" and with its opposition to Stoicism, is not to my knowledge directly echoed in Coleridge's moral discussion. Their high estimation of human powers, however, and especially of intellectual intuition, is an influence on the young Coleridge.

His own assessment of his position in intellectual history, with regard to the estimation of human powers, is not totally in accordance with what I have been calling, variously, his liberalism or his humanism—and the difference is crucial. With some arrogance he writes of the meeting of "four Roads," of which only one (his own) is "the right road." He opposes first the Hobbesian view that "motives act on the Will, as bodies act on bodies" and that mind is absorbed into body. Hobbes is an "anti-moralist" who does away altogether with the idea of moral responsibility. The road opposite Hobbes is that of "the Disciples of Shaftesbury" and "the Misinterpreters of Plato" whose pious Deism is too confident of innate human virtue.[34]

And, finally, he opposes those who differ from him "in exaggerating the diseased *weakness* of the Will into an absolute privation of all Freedom," the modern Calvinists such as Edward Williams. These "gloomy Doctors" retain the idea of moral responsibility even as they deprive the human being of all moral power. In opposition to the "splendid but delusory Tenets" of Shaftesbury, he does profess a "deep conviction that Man was and is a *fallen* Creature, not by accidents of bodily constitution, or any other cause, which *human* Wisdom in a course of ages might be supposed capable of removing; but diseased in his *Will*, in that Will which is the true and only strict synonime of the Word, I, or the intelligent Self."[35] He thinks Calvin and Luther, rightly in-

34. *AR*, pp. 135–139.
35. *AR*, p. 137.

terpreted, deny *free* will only because to assert otherwise would be prideful; but a will, to be a will, must be capable of originating its own acts. As we have seen in Chapter 1, he thinks the will is evil, free, and perversely powerful.

His "right road" is, therefore, Lutheran and Calvinist doctrine as he interprets it. The point I wish to emphasize is that he sides here mostly with the archenemies of humanism, the "counter-Renaissance" forces that emphasize the evil human will. Is this simply inconsistent with the liberalism I see him professing in his moral writings?

I would suggest that we are getting at the heart of Coleridge when we see that he retains both concepts—the liberal humanism and the depravity of will—whatever the philosophical improbability implied by the established traditions that treat them as mutually exclusive. The humanism that emerges is unstable, since the evolution of human powers I have traced in Chapter 3 both derives from and is vulnerable to the will's evil potential. Hence the challenge is to harness the will's powers constructively, to take the risk of living with great intensity, and not to succumb to resignation. The joining of these incompatibles of humanism and the infamy of man—of "Frost at Midnight" and *The Ancient Mariner*— is Coleridge's perennial task.

His position relative to the great Renaissance debate on human powers is an extraordinary embrace of opposing factions. The moral autonomy of mankind implied in the Stoical concept of *recta ratio*, as reinterpreted by the early Christian humanists of the English Renaissance and the later Cambridge Platonists, carries more than a hint of the Pelagian heresy: the human being possesses powers of will and intellect not undone by Adam's curse, powers that should be used, not debased. George Chapman, Samuel Daniel, More, and Cudworth ignore the warnings of St. Paul, St. Bernard, and Cornelius Agrippa against intellectual pride and curious learning. Coleridge and Butler likewise accept the Stoic imperative to "follow nature," though only so long as what is thought worthy of development in human nature includes the emotional life as well as the "regulator," reason. Coleridge thinks morality must be suited to a comprehensive view of human nature, and he develops a liberal morality with that in mind.

But he senses deficiencies in liberalism as well. It lends itself to a complacent conception of human nature, to sentimentality and unfounded optimism, to myths of moral and social progress, to materialism, to overconfidence in mankind's ability to dissolve mystery. With reference to the Renaissance debate between skepticism and humanism, he would agree with the skeptics that mankind is diseased in its will.

At this point in Coleridge's thinking, the old conflict between skeptics and humanists is superseded, because he believes paradoxically it is the diseased will that is the source of our humanity. In its drive for independence, the will makes possible the development of human powers that comprise the moral self. In addition, Coleridge flatly denies the skeptics' position that reason has itself been so severely dimmed by the fall of man. The human being retains a mind with powers of consciousness that should be developed freely and fully, a mind capable of "reason," not merely "understanding." Somewhere between will and reason is the emotional life, and here Coleridge's argument is that the emotions must be developed freely for the sake of reason. Calvinists and Lutherans hold that man is diseased in will, mind, and emotion, but Coleridge argues, with the humanists, for the potential soundness and worth of mind and emotion. At the same time, the central theme of his greatest works is the will's inherent sinfulness. He develops a morality notable for its liberality, yet he surprisingly retains an Augustinian sense of the depravity of will.

The human being embodies, therefore, the extreme con-

traries of expansive reason and enormous potential for sin,
contraries which resist any easy reconciliation. These contraries in themselves suggest why the "good" conscience can
so readily become "bad." The good conscience, like the right
reason of the Cambridge Platonists or the regulator of Butler,
promotes a healthy psychological balance. But Coleridge,
unlike either the Cambridge Platonists or Butler, dwells on
man's evil potential. To maximize reason or consciousness is
for him to maximize the capacity for dread and remorse. The
Calvinist position that we are weak in both will and mind is
less disquieting; the limitation of consciousness the Calvinist
posits would be, at least in theory, a limitation to the sense of
sin.

In Coleridge, sensitivity to inner depravity is not a ritualistic self-debasement but a newly developing existential
awareness that the growth of consciousness produces, as one
of its components, a disgust at one's own presumption in
daring to be. The self is realized through alienation and
strives to reach beyond the plight of the Mariner, forever
doomed to work off the curse. The free development of
human powers can never altogether absorb the will's evil.
Coleridge's humanism is the development of the good conscience—of civilizing constructive consciousness—but he
knows that civilization is a fragile vessel on a sea of chaos
and death.

What Coleridge brings to the British philosophical and
literary tradition is the elaboration of this paradox. There
are analogues in Milton, whose "Christian humanism" and
"Puritanism," as everybody knows, are locked in mortal
combat. It is probably Milton with whom Coleridge has
closest kinship. One might say that Milton construes the
problem as one of choosing. The recognition of the fallen
will ultimately seems to make necessary the casting out of
classicism in *Paradise Regained*. The pathos derives from
attachment to what must be renounced. But renunciation is

not a mode of the Coleridgean dialectic, which strives toward "reconciliation of opposites," a reconciliation that would result in a "tertium aliquid." As we have seen, the evil will can emerge as an essential egotism that is life's intensity; it gives one the persistence to be a self. Its energies can be transformed into humane consciousness. Through love, it works mysteriously to subvert its own prideful independence. It provides the impetus for the artist who emulates the work of God in creating his own world. Samuel Johnson offers another instructive contrast: his strong sense of human depravity leads him to seek not the dynamic unity of human powers but at best the sanity maintained by a precarious reign of reason over imagination and desire. While Coleridge's thought is not evolutionary with regard to human nature or society, it *is* evolutionary with regard to the human individual—and Johnson would pronounce this a vanity. Rather than self-realization, one should pursue duty for duty's sake, reason weakly pointing the way, without the Stoic's assurance that, in so doing, one frees oneself of misery, victimization, and madness. Dignity, not transcendence, is the moral hope.

We may conclude that Coleridge has performed two major "reconciliations" with respect to the British moral traditions we have examined thus far. In neither case is he a compromiser; his more comprehensive vision is, he would say, something other than a larger aggregate. The eighteenth-century debate between rationalism and sensibility, already somewhat arbitrated in theory by Joseph Butler, is more pointedly addressed by Coleridge, who, in the spirit of the Cambridge Platonists, argues that thought and feeling are reconcilable. One can feel a thought and think a feeling. Perhaps he has still been insufficiently acknowledged to have developed in Britain the ideal of the unified sensibility at the same time that he has described most analytically the state of dissociation.

The more fundamental issue, however, is whether human nature is so corrupt that the debate between rationalism and sensibility would be in any event academic. What role is to be salvaged for humanistic development if Calvin and Luther are correct in their assessment of the will's depravity? The humanistic ideal is fought for against great odds. Coleridge does not pave the way for it by brushing aside the will's evil potential as earlier humanists were likely to do. His liberal humanism avoids sentimentalism and optimism. The will must be claimed by and for consciousness, its drive toward independence directed into the evolution of the self. Like the power at the summit of Shelley's Mont Blanc, the will is mute but energizing. Mont Blanc's indifference to human constructs is seen in the destructiveness of its glaciers. Coleridge's will, also potentially destructive, must be channeled into civilizing constructs. Even the speaker of "Frost at Midnight" hints of the alien and demonic, but he uses their pressures to invest the moment with creative perplexity and prophetic love.

Hedonists, Egoists, Utilitarians

A construction of Coleridge's analyses of hedonism, egoism, and utilitarianism will demonstrate that his response to the dominant moral traditions of contemporary Britain is more than a poet's response to their lack of poetry, though this is part of it. I would argue that his critique, in Britain at least, is the most thorough and penetrating of its day. Considering that John Stuart Mill says, and everyone after him reiterates, that Coleridge and Bentham are the two great seminal minds of the contrary traditions of nineteenth-century British thought, it is surprising that Coleridge's moral critique of his opposition has not yet been constructed and examined comprehensively.

The most important source of these arguments is the unpublished Opus Maximum manuscript, the second volume of which is the closest Coleridge comes to writing a treatise on moral philosophy.[36] The critique's tone, vocabulary, and method of argument are more philosophically rigorous, and to students of literature probably drier, than his moral writings elsewhere. But underlying it is his very personal commitment to an enlarged conception of human potentiality which is simply not satisfied in the monistic theories of Bentham and Paley.

His argument can most lucidly be constructed by extracting, first, his commentary on the self-contradictions of the hedonists, who put forward a simplistic view of pleasure and happiness and then contradict that view by their own use of language. Coleridge has his own enlarged view of pleasure and happiness, which is pluralistic and susceptible of qualitative as well as quantitative distinctions.

Second, his analysis of psychological egoism, from Hobbes to Paley, will show that Hobbes's mechanistic model of mind is factually wrong. As we have seen, motives are themselves demonstrably powered by the deeper principle of will. The will in conjunction with moral consciousness can determine whether the personal self or another self is to be the object of its actions. But even action undertaken to benefit the self is not necessarily selfish. Echoing Joseph Butler's critique of psychological egoism, he thinks the doctrine is based on a shoddy, self-contradictory notion of the psychological nature of desire itself. The egoist may argue something even more dubious when he attempts to base a social ethic such as utilitarianism on private interest; Coleridge will attempt to show the errors in logic here, the invalid syllogisms implicitly at work.

The egoist's argument more than the hedonist's, therefore, leads Coleridge to a consideration of utilitarianism, the re-

36. Muirhead has published portions of this material in *Coleridge as Philosopher*, pp. 136–161.

cipient of his third major attack on contemporary moralism. Utilitarianism is a theory that is self-defeating because it is based on mere conjectures about probable consequences. The utilitarians in pursuing conjectures would sacrifice an immediate response to concrete moral situations. Coleridge's surprising counterthrust is thus to defeat them on their own terms: the dreamy airy idealist accuses the utilitarians of concocting imaginary schemes that float above the immediately perceived contexts of human experience.

Coleridge writes, perhaps exaggerating, that "one may best judge of men by their Pleasures." A dutiful servant of society during daylight hours may turn into a reckless debauchee at night. Dutifulness can be a "trick learnt by heart—for we may even learn the power of extemporaneous elocution & instant action, as an automatic Trick/—but a man's Pleasures—children, Books, Friends, Nature, the Muse/—O these deceive not!"[37] Happiness and virtue are, ideally, mutually supportive, though Coleridge, as we have seen throughout, distrusts facile alignments: we are often punished for our virtue, just as we pay for our happiness. But while neither is sufficient for the other, each may promote the other. "Our usefulness, & to a great extent even our virtue depend on our happiness, by which word I understand such a general pleasurable state of our Temper, Thoughts, Feelings and Sensations, as is requisite for inward tranquillity and the power of cheerful and active attention to the objects without us." From this principle he deduces "that whoever wilfully puts to risk his own happiness by a step which once taken is irretrievable, wilfully exposes to a fearful hazard his future usefulness and his own moral Being. He acts *dishonestly*."[38] The dishonesty is in thinking that one is not oneself part of

37. *N*, I, 1600.
38. *CL*, IV, 903.

any moral equation and that one can injure oneself alone. "*Love yourself* as your Neighbor, is no less true & no less imperative than the converse."[39]

These and many other comments suggest Coleridge is not entirely unsympathetic to some of the values of hedonism and, by extension, the utilitarianism of his day. Much of what he says about happiness and utility would not give offense to these schools of thought. His quarrel is not with the idea that pleasure and happiness are values but that they are or should be ultimate ends. In addition, he sees limitations and contradictions in contemporary analyses of the *nature* of pleasure and happiness.

He protests the "absolute Duumvirate, & twin Despotism of Pain & Pleasure!" Though they are "great Springs of human conduct," they are not the only ones, as the hedonist claims.[40] Coleridge's method of desynonymization serves him well as he tackles this problem with the kind of thinking characteristic of twentieth-century moral philosophers. He writes that the "sum total of Moral philosophy is found in this one question—Is 'good' a superfluous word?—or lazy synonime for the pleasurable, and its causes? at least, a mere modification to express degree & comparative duration ⟨of pleasure?⟩–/–Therefore we may more unanswerably state the question—Is 'good' superfluous as a word exponent of a *Kind?*"[41]

That the question can be answered "no" is seen by his analysis of how we actually use language. He recalls a conversation he had in Keswick with some hedonist ("a man of great notoriety in the present day as a critic," who Kathleen Coburn surmises must have been Hazlitt, though we might note that the views imputed are certainly not those he was

39. *CL*, IV, 909.
40. *N*, II, 2058.
41. *N*, III, 3938.

to express in his *Essay on Human Action*). His supposed interlocutor had been conflating the pleasure of a good conscience with the pleasure of a good brandy. His assumption was that "pleasure is a general term, in short the *genus generalissimum* of whatever is desirable for our nature." Coleridge has some significant objections. The first is that we already have a term to express this *genus generalissimum* in "good"; "pleasure" then becomes a "lazy synonym, whereas it is the business of the philosopher to desynonymize words originally equivalent."[42] In fact the word "good" obviously does much more work, covers more territory than "pleasure." "If I say pleasure is a good and pain an evil, will it be pretended that I convey the same impression and am talking as childishly as if I had said black is black & white is white[?] Shall I not be as intelligible to all men, as when I say, that green is a colour and an octave a sound?"[43] The hedonist's persistence in using the word "good," which on his own argument should be stricken from the language, betrays that he too senses it is a more inclusive term than "pleasure." Indeed the hedonist guards against uttering the truism that there is "no pleasure but pleasure and no pain but pain."[44] Obviously the substitution of "pleasure" for "good" changes the meaning of most sentences—pleasure is only *a* good.

Coleridge appears here to have anticipated the method of G. E. Moore's famous "open-question argument," which is directed against "naturalistic ethics" (an ethics that makes fallacious leaps from "is" to "ought" statements and defines morality in terms of scientific or psychological truth, as do the psychological hedonists). Moore writes, employing an "argument from trivialization" exactly echoing Coleridge's, that when the naturalists "say 'Pleasure is good,' we cannot believe that they merely mean 'Pleasure is pleasure' and noth-

42. *PL*, p. 152.
43. OM, B$_2$, ff. 61–62.
44. OM, B$_2$, f. 62.

ing more than that."[45] Indeed no predicate can be found to substitute for "good" about which one could not sensibly ask the question, "Is that good?" (Moore attempts, as Coleridge does not, to prove that "good" is no more definable than "yellow" and that any attempt to define it in terms of psychological or scientific fact will be necessarily invalid.) A. N. Prior writes that Shaftesbury, Hutcheson, and Price anticipate Moore, but none of their arguments, it seems to me, comes so close as Coleridge's.[46]

He continues his own attack against naturalistic ethics. When the hedonist says that "good" defined as "pleasure" is "whatever is desirable for our nature," he is begging the question. "For *desirable* means either that which actually I do desire, or that which I know I ought to desire, though perhaps I am not virtuous enough actually to will it." The hedonist assumes "*Good* is nothing more than a reflex idea of the mind after a survey and calculation of agreeable or delightful sensations included within any given time, the whole of our life for instance." This reflex idea may offer no moral guide at all, for it is obviously wrong to "call that good which I feel I desire, instead of endeavouring to desire that only which I know to be *good*."[47]

Precisely this conflation of the desirable with the desired appears to many scholars to be a stumbling block for Mill in *Utilitarianism* (1861).[48] "Good" or the "desirable" is some-

45. *Principia Ethica* (Cambridge: Cambridge University Press, 1903; rpt. 1959), pp. 1–21.

46. *Logic and the Basis of Ethics* (Oxford: Clarendon Press, 1949), pp. 95–107.

47. *PL*, p. 153.

48. Frankena and others have argued that Mill makes no logical leap from "is" to "ought" but simply asserts that, as Frankena puts it, "if human nature is so constituted as always to aim at pleasure, then it is absurd or unreasonable to deny that pleasure is the good. . ." (*Ethics*, p. 70). For Frankena's more extended treatment of Mill's argument, see "The Naturalistic Fallacy," *Mind*, 48 (1939), rpt. in *Readings in Ethical Theory*, ed. Wilfrid Sellars and John Hospers (New York: Appleton-Century-Crofts, 1952), pp. 103–114. For another treatment, see W. D. Hudson, *Modern Moral Philosophy* (New York: Doubleday, 1970), pp. 248–264.

thing more than what people happen to desire. Since "good" is, according to Coleridge, not so much an "indefinable" as it is a *genus generalissimum* under which "many sorts are subordinated: it follows, that each of these sorts must be good or evil in different senses, that each must have its characterising mark by which it is distinguished from others of the same class." There are relative and conditional goods, things good in themselves, and finally the Good, which Coleridge dutifully identifies with God, though at this point in the Opus Maximum he is leading up to his translation, the first in English, of the great opening passage from Kant's *Grundlegung zur Metaphysik der Sitten* on the unconditional good that is the "good will."[49] Pleasure and happiness are "good," of course, but they do not exhaust the things that are good.

This pluralistic spirit Coleridge brings to his own analysis of pleasure and happiness. He provides us with a schema, albeit somewhat academic, based mostly on classical sources. There are, he says, four kinds of pleasure or happiness; they are physical pleasure, happiness in response to good fortune, intellectual pleasure, and moral pleasure. But he thinks Socrates and Plato have not quite succeeded in making proper distinctions among them. With Hobbes he fears that "from mistakes in words men fall into mistakes in the most important things."[50] Socrates' very slight laxity here produces confusion in disciples such as Antisthenes and Aristippus, who think that happiness is the absence of pain or that pleasure is purely quantitative. Eudaemonism, Epicureanism, Stoicism, hedonism, utilitarianism all have weaknesses in their analyses of pleasure and happiness.

The first state, *hedone*, is described correctly by the quantitative hedonists as a matter solely of "how much." Their error is to extend quantification to other kinds of pleasure and to moral judgment generally. *Hedone* is "the sum of agreeable sensations, the congeniality and commensurateness

49. OM, B$_2$, ff. 62–63.
50. PL, pp. 140–141.

of the exciting causes to the excitability."[51] Such pleasure offers in itself an insufficient basis for moral judgment, and Bentham's quantification of it is futile and myopic. Here Coleridge anticipates Mill's critique of Bentham's exclusively quantitative analysis of pleasure, though Aristotle anticipates everybody, of course, in *Nicomachean Ethics*, Book X. Of *hedone*, Coleridge writes that "considered . . . exclusively in and for itself, the only question is, quantum? not, quale? *How much on the whole?* the contrary, *i.e.* the painful and disagreeable, having been subtracted. The quality is a matter of *taste:* et de *gustibus* non est disputandum."[52] It is absurd to make a principle of action that which is "a necessary and essential instinct of our very nature." One cannot jump directly from psychological hedonism, which is an assertion about what human beings naturally desire, to ethical hedonism, which is an assertion about what human beings *ought* to desire. Of course we all desire a preponderance of pleasure over pain, and of course we all desire happiness. "But *what* happiness? That is the question." One person might say, "I delight in Milton and Shakespeare more than turtle or venison," and another might reply, "That is not my case. For myself, I think a good dish of turtle and a good bottle of port afterwards give me much more delight than I receive from Milton and Shakespeare."[53] We need moral criteria more comprehensive and discriminating than this one, obviously.

51. *N*, III, 4422.
52. *AR*, p. 41. See *N*, III, 3558, where this idea is in part attributed to Kant; also Kathleen Coburn's extensive note on this entry.
53. *PL*, p. 142. His thinking on this matter comes partially from Kant, as he says, but also, I would suggest, from his discussions with Hazlitt. In his *Essay on Human Action* (1805) Hazlitt writes that he cannot persuade himself that "our sensations differ only as to more, or less; or that the pleasure derived from seeing a fine picture, or hearing a fine piece of music, that the gratification derived from doing a good action and that which accompanies the swallowing of an oyster are in reality and at bottom the same pleasure" (Scholars' Facsimile & Reprints, 1969, p. 39n).

Coleridge notes, however, that Bentham himself might have to agree, because his analysis of pleasure in terms of intensity, duration, certainty, propinquity, fecundity, and purity itself presupposes "the intervention and union both of powers and motives which do not result from the relations between the animal life and the stimulants organic or external that call it into sensibility."[54] The mediation of intelligence and will in the process of selection of one pleasure over another presupposes human powers not included in Bentham's meager inventory of human nature, powers not satisfied by "agreeable sensations." Bentham's analysis is therefore self-contradictory from the start.

Coleridge would like to confine use of the word "happiness," the second state, to the sense of its etymological root. "Hap originally designated not mere chance, but a ⟨fortunate⟩ chance, even as the very word, fortune, fortunate, from fors, fortis, a chance—and our own Saxon Teutonic, Luck." Happiness was called by the Greeks "εὐτυχία, *i.e.* good-hap, or more religiously εὐδαιμονία, *i.e.* favourable providence."[55] This kind of happiness results not from our own efforts but from the "aggregate of fortunate chances," the circumstances ("whatever *stands round* us") of life. Epictetus reminds us we must exclude from "happiness" any feeling resulting from our own efforts. We are "happy" in having good parents, but morally "blest" in having good children whom we have properly brought up.[56]

Those pleasures that may be regarded as moral, the third and fourth states, are *eunoia* and *eupraxia*, though Coleridge thinks the word "pleasure" is not really applicable. Aristotle, commenting on Eudoxus' doctrine of the supremacy of happiness, says that pleasures and happiness are among the things to

54. OM, B₂, f. 48.
55. *AR*, p. 41.
56. *N*, III, 3558.

be "prized," not "praised." While Coleridge may appear to be moralizing pleasures, his account of *eunoia* and *eupraxia* is Aristotelian in approach. He is careful to describe these states of feeling as reflexes of the pursuit of intellectual and moral virtue, and not themselves moral values to be pursued as ends in themselves. *Eunoia* is a "certain joyousness" ("Gladness? Laetitia, εὐφροσύνη"), which is "the immediate consequent or accompaniment of the intellectual energies."[57] It was demonstrated when "Pythagoras [*sic*] discovered the proposition that made him cry out 'Eureka.' "[58] Coleridge may have in mind Spinoza's belief that in passing from confused to distinct conceptions we experience "active pleasure" as the mind's vitality is increased.

The highest pleasure is Socrates' *eupraxia* ("bliss," the "blessedness of a calm approving conscience"). It is a "spiritual sensation i.e. a sensation which is no sensation at all."[59] Socrates' *eupraxia* results from the exclusion of all "hap" or "chance." Coleridge thinks the German historian of philosophy Wilhelm Gottlieb Tennemann (1761–1819), in translating *eupraxia* as "*Glückseligkeit*," suggests an element of luck foreign to the concept.[60] Socrates is right to separate *eutuchia*, the pleasure attendant on good fortune, from *eupraxia*, or delight in moral virtue. "Bliss, not Happiness, is the true Summum Bonum, he asserted: but Bliss, or perfect Well-*being* is one and the same with well-*doing*, and Eupraxia accurately ⟨expresses⟩ this identity."[61]

The gulf between moral pleasure, *eupraxia*, and intellectual pleasure, *eunoia*, is not so wide, however. Coleridge, never one to underestimate the moral import of intellectual investigation, argues that *eunoia* should be classed more with

57. OM, B$_2$, f. 79; *N*, III, 4422.
58. *PL*, p. 141. He meant, of course, Archimedes.
59. OM, B$_2$, f. 78.
60. *N*, III, 4422n.
61. *PL*, p. 409n34.

eupraxia than with the physical pleasure *hedone*. *Eunoia* is "not indeed spiritual in the highest & most proper sense of that term," but it may be likened to an energizing "body celestial," not "terrestrial," of the soul. It is an active, not passive, "spontaneity." "I think therefore that both the philosopher of Königsberg, and his first disciple and rival Fichte, have erred, and verged towards enthusiasm in the confusion of . . . the Eunöya with the Hedone, the desirable of the intellect with the desirable of the body."[62] Intellectual pleasures are too intimately linked with reason and will to be termed "pathological" in Coleridge's estimation.

Psychological hedonism is attacked in the Opus Maximum with reference to this schema. The psychological hedonist, who thinks only pleasure is ever desired as an end, might claim as Bernard Mandeville does that we undertake virtuous action only for the pleasure of a good conscience.[63] But according to Coleridge this moral pleasure, *eupraxia*, cannot itself be an object of desire. The psychological hedonist begs the question: "For the conscience must be good in order to [have] this pleasure but a good conscience can only result from, or subsist in the consciousness of having done our duty because it is our duty." If we do our duty merely as a means to this pleasure, we would not have a "good conscience," and therefore not have the pleasure—our conscience would be "suspended by an usurping counterfeit."[64] Aristotle has much the same complaint, but it is really Kant who develops the argument in *Die Metaphysik der Sitten* (1797), probably Coleridge's source for this argument. Kant writes that the "eudaemonist's *etiology* involves him in a vicious circle: he can hope to be *happy* (or inwardly blissful) only if he is

62. OM, B₂, ff. 82, 84. The comment on Kant and Fichte is dubious. See N, III, 3558n for Kathleen Coburn's speculation as to the Fichtean doctrine Coleridge may have in mind.
63. *An Enquiry into the Origin of Moral Virtue* (1714), in *British Moralists*, I, 235.
64. OM, B₂, f. 76.

conscious of having done his duty, but he can be moved to do his duty only if he foresees that it will make him happy."[65]

One cannot without self-contradiction pursue the "pleasure of a good conscience," but Coleridge admits that a good conscience may occasionally enhance pleasure. It may add refinement and intensity even to "grosser" pleasures such as lovemaking, as is seen in "the smirk & indifferentism of the Sensualist immediately after, compared with the deep feeling of the Lover/This is one of the earthly rewards of being what we ought to be—but which would be annihilated, if we attempted to be it for the sake of this increased Enjoyment—."[66] Kathleen Coburn points out that Coleridge reverses Schiller's argument that "free delight" leads to a "finer morality." Instead, as she says, "a finer morality will lead to a finer delight." But Kant, Schiller, and Coleridge are agreed, she adds, that the pursuit of pleasure must be by indirection.[67]

In addition to its formal problems, Coleridge finds the hedonist's argument, whether psychological or ethical, counter to the entire weight of his experience. With Samuel Johnson he sees a futility in *seeking* happiness. The ultimate goal could only be a kind of sad satiety. He would agree with Johnson that mankind is not equipped for continuous happiness and that to bear down so hard on happiness is to extinguish its possibility through too corrosive a sense of expectation. Breaking with Johnson, who could not consider the question of happiness apart from that of duration, he wonders whether happiness in its purest form is not "total as long as it is?"[68] Perhaps duration is an inadequate gauge. The fear of expiration does, to be sure, pervade Coleridge's life in so many ways—the expiration of imaginative powers, of love, and especially of joy, the total vitality of the organism

65. *The Doctrine of Virtue*, p. 34.
66. *N*, III, 3584.
67. *N*, III, 3584n.
68. *N*, III, 3558.

that diminishes with age and disappointment. But though transitoriness is the bleak truth underlying so much of his later poetry, perhaps moments of happiness are not deprived of meaning because they do not last.

His personal agony, however, is not only that happiness eludes him when it is sought or that the moments of intensity pass, but that he cannot even in moments give himself over to them; they are never "total" for him. "I write melancholy, always melancholy: You will suspect that it is the fault of my natural Temper. Alas! no.—This is the great [Cross in] that my Nature is made for Joy—impelling me to Joyance—& I never, never can yield to it.—I am a genuine Tantalus—."[69] He is surely a modern Tantalus, one who cooperates to place out of reach the fruit and water he seeks. Coleridge cannot conceive of himself as the one chosen: chosen to write the great philosophic poem, for this is Wordsworth's privilege, chosen to receive love and return it, chosen to have the joy described in "Dejection: An Ode," which is not for him but for the "Lady." As an uninvited guest on the perimeter of life's feast, he feels he must pay in suffering for any happiness that may have been his. "Virtue & Happiness [are] incommensurate quantities—how much Virtue must I have before I have paid off the old debt of my happiness in Infancy and Childhood—."[70] Such perplexities as these make him think the hedonist foists a silly oversimplification on us if he asserts that we naturally desire happiness or that we ought to. Coleridge thinks the simple formula of what nature on an elementary level prompts one to do does not account for his own experience. The joy his nature impels him to is incommensurate with the enlarged concept of self that is the real moral desideratum, a self that should seek realization even when this means suffering, alienation, and leaving off from the pursuit of happiness.

69. *N*, I, 1609. See 1609n for discussion of a variant reading.
70. *N*, III, 4292.

This enlarged concept of self is more explicitly the basis of his critique of the menacing psychological egoism of Hobbes. Since scores of British moral philosophers from Cudworth to Shaftesbury to Hutcheson busy themselves with answering Hobbes, Coleridge is joining a community action more than a century and a half old. Psychological egoism is the theory that the only motive by which a person can ever act is self-interest. Coleridge attacks both the premises and the internal consistency of the theory. The unnamed immediate opponent in the Opus Maximum is William Paley, a "doctor of self-love," whose account of moral obligation in *The Principles of Moral and Political Philosophy* (1785) equates obligation with strong inducement. Paley asks why we are obliged to keep promises. We are obliged when we are "urged by a violent motive resulting from the command of another," but "we can be obliged to nothing, but what we ourselves are to gain or lose something by." Paley's psychological egoism merges with ethical egoism, the theory that one *ought* or has the right to act in his own interest. Is there anything in it for us when we keep promises? Not necessarily in this life, but God (for whatever reason) would like us to keep promises and will reward us in the life to come. The difference between "prudence" and "duty," says Paley, is simply that "in the one case we consider what we shall gain or lose in the present world; in the other case, we consider also what we shall gain or lose in the world to come." Both prudence and duty, then, are forms of self-interest based on different degrees of inducement. "Morality" is simply prudence directed toward God. Without God's sanction, we would have no reason to keep promises, unless someone "can shew that virtue conducts the possessor to certain happiness in this life," a dubious proposition, thinks Paley.[71]

This kind of twaddle rankles Coleridge, who pursues many

71. *The Principles of Moral and Political Philosophy*, 7th ed., I (London: R. Faulder, 1790), 57–62.

avenues of attack against what he thinks is the predominant
mentality of his day. He writes that the psychological egoist
in discussing motivation distinguishes between "selfishness, or
the unconsidered obedience to an immediate appetite or restlessness," and "self-interest," which is simply the same selfishness extended and modified "by an imagination of the future
as the present." In either case the egoist asserts that we necessarily act according to what we think our own best interest
is. Coleridge thinks the egoist is mistakenly presupposing
"the plenary causative or determining power [to reside] in
these motives or impulses so that both the one and the other
do not at all differ from physical impact, as far as the relation of cause and effect is concerned."[72] This conception of
human behavior comes, of course, from Hobbes. Coleridge
probably too loosely groups his malignant enemies—from
Hobbes and Mandeville to Locke, Bentham, and Paley—
under the rubric "mechanico-corpuscular philosophers," and
like Blake does not adequately sort out different strains of
the disease.

In any event, this conception of behavior is simply mistaken, he says, because it refuses to ask the more basic question of "what determined the mind to permit this determining
power to these motives and impulses?" As we saw in Chapter
1, his own answer is the acquiescence of consciousness to
will. But the Hobbesian would place will "in the same class
with the bullet or the billiard-ball." Anyone "who upholds
this scheme of universal selfishness or self-interest not from
any corruption but from the original necessity of our nature
implies the denial of a responsible Will."[73] (Hobbes might
reply, "That is exactly what I said!")

The Hobbesian conception of mind could not begin to
shed light on Shakespearean characters, and Coleridge thinks
a psychology that could not begin to explain the profoundest

72. OM, B₂, ff. 38–39.
73. OM, B₂, ff. 38–41.

and most accurate representations of human character would have to be found inadequate. That Iago is "represented as now assigning one & now another & again a third motive for his conduct" is no reason for concluding, as the Hobbesian would have to, that his fundamental orientation changes from one moment to the next. Iago's character, his evil will and "love of exerting power," have remained the same. He is simply "motive-mongering" to save face in his own eyes. Overnight character transformations are rare, says Coleridge, but they would be frequent indeed if we were as subject to the relentless laws of causation as Hobbes and his followers say we are. Now and then "a violent motive [Paley's phrase] may revolutionize a man's opinions and professions," but the more basic power of will makes this rare.[74] We turn into hypocrites not from violent motives but through imperceptible transformations as will and reason gradually give way. All human experience, imaginary and real, proves the inadequacy of the Hobbesian model of mind.

If we do assume the existence of a self deeper than the empirical, the psychological egoist's argument that the only motive by which we can ever act is self-interest or "self-love" is dubious. Strictly speaking, self-love is "impossible for a finite being in the absolute meaning of the term Self for if by the 'Self' we mean the principle of individuation [,] the band or copula, which gives a real unity to all the complex products[,] functions and faculties of an animal," and not simply the representative image, it is clear that the "Self in this sense must be anterior to all our sensations &c and to all the objects, toward which they may be directed."[75] The self cannot entirely become its own object, and therefore its actions cannot be entirely self-reflexive.

Beyond this, Coleridge argues that the representative image in itself is not altogether subject to physical causation, as the

74. OM, B$_2$, ff. 56–59.
75. OM, B$_2$, ff. 48–51; cf. *IS*, p. 68.

Hobbesian would argue. It is "by no means unalterably fixed in human nature by nature itself; but on the contrary varies with the growth bodily, moral and intellectual of each individual." One is free, in a way that a proponent of the billiard ball model of mind could not allow, to shape the image and to decide how to administer to it. The body, with its tendency to self-preservation, does not have to comprise the totality of the image, nor must one's own image be the sole recipient of the interior self's actions. Indeed one's image is not the first object, since "in the earlier periods of infancy, the mother or the nurse is the Self of the child. And who has not experienced in dreams the attachment of our personal identity to forms the most remote from our own." If we weakly permit our body to become our self, "when the reflections on our sensations[,] desires & objects have been habitually appropriated to it in too great a proportion," then we are indeed selfish. We are too closely identified with the bodily aspect of our nature and have suffered a "comparative narrowness of our moral view." But this is "not a necessity of our nature," as the Hobbesian would have it. Just as we are free to administer to our own objectified self and change it at will, literally to alter our "image," so can we say, "my Self loves A or B," as another object of our will. Instead of manifesting self-love, we become the "self that loves."[76]

To refute Hobbes, Coleridge does not have to say mankind is naturally loving; he says in fact the opposite. All he must demonstrate is that there is the *possibility* of acting on a principle other than that of self-interest. In this respect he differs from Hazlitt, who sets out in his *Essay on Human Action* to prove the "natural disinterestedness of the human mind." Although Coleridge hardly believes in natural disinterestedness, he agrees with Hazlitt on some other points. He even gets around to acknowledging Hazlitt's contribution

76. OM, B₂, ff. 49–51.

to the debate in a footnote to his *Second Lay Sermon* (1817), where he writes that the "fallacious sophistry" of Paley's theory of "enlightened self-love" has been detected by "Des Cartes, and Bishop Butler: and of late years, with great ability and originality, by MR. W.ᵉ HAZLITT."[77]

This is remarkable praise to bestow on his archenemy. It is one of those cheap ironies that these two, so often full of mutual loathing, should get together on the idea that benevolence is not to be written off. Hazlitt argues that while memory and sensation, the faculties concerned with past and present, do indeed feed self-love, the "imagination," which addresses itself to the future, fixes on that which has no subjective reference. The future, after all, is not yet part of our "personal identity." Attempting to reconcile what several moralists since Butler had already reconciled in other ways, Hazlitt writes that self-love and benevolence are identical, because the same imagination that takes us out of the self into the not-yet-self of the future enables us to sympathize with other selves.[78]

I think this work may be a source of Coleridge's comments in an 1810 notebook and in the Opus Maximum on our capacity to regard our future self disinterestedly. It is also likely that some of Hazlitt's ideas developed from discussions he had with Coleridge. Coleridge writes, "Grossness of Self love is no less diminished by distance in time than by distance in space." Someone who deliberately sacrifices an immediate gratification "to a greater good of that which his reason enables him to look forward to as a Self fifty years hence . . . exhibits as unselfish a love[,] as compleat a transfer of the idea Self from his visual form and the feelings and impulses connected with it as if the distance had been in

77. *Lay Sermons*, p. 187*n*.

78. For discussions of Hazlitt's *Essay on Human Action*, see Herschel Baker, *William Hazlitt* (Cambridge, Mass.: Harvard University Press, 1962), pp. 140–152; Walter Jackson Bate, *John Keats* (Cambridge, Mass.: Harvard University Press, 1963), pp. 255–259.

space and the transfer had been made towards a contemporary." The self is "generalized," and self and neighbor become "virtual synonymes."[79] Paley's talk about heavenly reward as an inducement to self-interest is wrong because "my self in eternity, as the *object* of my contemplation, differs unimaginably from my present Self." The anguish we might feel would differ immeasurably from "immediate self-suffering," one's hope and fear would be "too vast to admit of an outline—."[80]

In his arguments thus far, Coleridge is essentially saying that the egoist tries to limit the self to the puny dimensions of an unimaginative fiction. The fiction is that the self is comprised of matter in motion and that will and reason have no control over the pressing maneuvers of psychological mechanism. Coleridge has replied that these maneuvers actually spring from a deeper principle of will, that they can to a degree be guided by reason, and that the structure of consciousness—the psychic distance between the self as subject and the self as object—provides the possibility of genuine sympathy toward others and of disinterested action. The egoist denies the existence of powers the human being in fact has. Coleridge is perhaps too confident of the reality of these powers—and also for the sake of argument hides his own doubts about human sympathy—but until the egoist verifies his own model of mind, Coleridge would say the burden of proof is on the egoist. "Facts of immediate [benevolent] impulses" imply that we do act, if only on rare occasions, with sympathy for others and with self-sacrifice. The egoist has not proved these feelings to be illusory.

In addition to these arguments based on the power of reason and will to control psychological process from above and below, as it were, Coleridge argues, with Joseph Butler,

79. OM, B₂, ff. 53–54.

80. *N*, III, 4007. Kathleen Coburn detects the influence of Robert South's *Sermons* (1737) in this passage.

that the psychological egoist does not prove anything on the level of psychology itself. Butler's famous argument in his *Fifteen Sermons* is based on his pluralistic conception of self. The various impulses and appetites, to be distinguished from the "principles" of self-love and benevolence, do not seek out their ends for the sake of self-love, and indeed often injure the self. Rather, "particular affections tend towards particular external things: these are their objects: having these is their end: in this consists their gratification: no matter whether it be, or be not, upon the whole, our interest or happiness."[81] We do not seek out objects of desire for the sake of pleasure or self-love. The object of hunger is food and the gratification of hunger is the having of food, not the incidental pleasure that may result. Hunger, not necessarily self-love, is satisfied by eating, and may often prompt one to eat more than self-love would counsel. One would reply boldly to Hobbes, therefore, that human beings do not act with *enough* self-love.

Coleridge similarly argues, "It is not true that nature prompts a man to benefit himself. Nature only prompts him to gratify himself and that too often even to his foreknown injury." We are impelled "only to remove the pain of craving, whether it be the pain inflicted by positive want or the restlessness and uneasiness produced by the fancy from the remembrance of a prior gratification."[82] If someone objects that all impulses and actions must still derive from the self, and that egoism remains true since the self is still the source of all, Coleridge replies that this is "but a disguised way" of saying "that the agent is the agent or that every action supposes its own agent."[83]

He is here attempting not to prove the existence of altruistic impulses but to undo the egoist's simplistic theory of

81. *Fifteen Sermons,* in *British Moralists,* I, 366
82. OM, B$_2$, ff. 116–119.
83. OM, B$_2$, ff. 122; cf. Hazlitt, *Essay on Human Action,* p. 242.

human behavior. Not everything we do is necessarily based on what we conceive to be our best interest. Coleridge for one knows his own inexpedient actions prove otherwise. The unitary hypothesis of the egoist destroyed, there is no logical exclusion of altruistic impulses.[84] Both Coleridge and Butler can now claim it is simply a matter of empirical fact that these impulses do exist, just as it is true that one often acts against self-interest. Coleridge's example: we might assist a sick friend who is no longer in a position to benefit us.[85]

The psychological egoist sometimes makes an invalid leap to utilitarianism. Paley thinks it possible to base a social ethics on an ethics of self-love. Coleridge tries to undermine this kind of thinking with another attack on "naturalism." (The random development of his argument, which he makes two separate stabs at on two parallel columns of the Opus Maximum manuscript, certainly clinches the case that Coleridge, whatever his logical acumen, is no expositor.) He sets up some syllogisms with which he agrees: "It is my duty to love all persons[;] I am myself a person[;] Therefore it is my duty to love myself." And, "It is my duty to love all persons[;] My neighbor is a person[;] Therefore it is my duty to love my neighbor." From these he says we can correctly conclude, "It is my duty to love myself as my neighbor, and my neighbor as myself."[86]

If we begin our argument not with what duty prescribes but instead with what human nature *on a minimal level* prompts, we run into several problems, both factual and, of greater importance here, logical. The point at issue is whether one can guarantee from a position of "Amour de moi-même mais bien calculé" that the good of all will be served. He sets up syllogisms that might make such a case. These are reduc-

84. See Richard Garner and Bernard Rosen, *Moral Philosophy* (New York: Macmillan, 1967), pp. 43–45; and Frankena, *Ethics*, pp. 19–21.

85. OM, B$_2$, f. 41.

86. OM, B$_2$, ff. 115–122.

tions of Paley's implicit argument. "Nature prompts me to benefit myself[;] But in benefitting others I benefit myself[;] Therefore nature prompts me to benefit others as myself." The first premise is wrong, says Coleridge echoing Butler, because human nature on this minimal level does not prompt us to benefit, but only to gratify, ourselves. The minor premise is but a "gratis dictum," perhaps true in some cases. But more important, Coleridge writes that something is lacking in the syllogism without which it is "as lifeless as the assertion that there are trees in China or that Mary reigned before Elizabeth. Where is the obligation?"[87] In contesting a similar syllogism, he writes, "Add the words [']I ought['] to the ergo of the syllogism, and the non sequitur[,] the chasm[,] becomes obvious, and the logical salto of more than Rhodian temerity."[88]

Whether or not he gets it from Hume, he thus knows the logical difficulty of deriving "ought" from "is" statements. If we are naturally "compelled" to benefit ourselves, nothing can be more absurd than for the moralist to subject us to commands, "as if I should force a man's hand into the fire, and command him to feel pain." No exhortation can be derived from complacent descriptions of how nature behaves. But, ironically, license to behave in whatever manner one likes *can* be so derived. The good and prudent Paley would have to see the merit in the out-and-out sensualist's statement to the "philosophic Epicurean" that the "gratification of your pity or of a fine taste in the order or proportion of things, or a mere absence of pain with a long continuance of an indifferent state may be the prompting of your nature, and you may gratify yourself,—but my nature prompts me to a merry life though short one."[89]

Bentham commits a similar error and seems to Coleridge

87. OM, B$_2$, ff. 118–120.
88. OM, B$_2$, ff. 125, 127.
89. OM, B$_2$, f. 120.

to leave himself open to the grossest reductio ad absurdum: "The American savage, in scalping his fallen enemy, pursues *his* happiness naturally and adequately. A Chickasaw or Pawnee Bentham . . . would necessarily hope for the most frequent opportunities possible of scalping the greatest possible number of savages, for the longest possible time."[90] Bentham might object that this is more an attack on a narrow hedonistic egoism than on his own universalistic utilitarian theory, which advocates promoting the greatest happiness for the greatest number of people. But Bentham, too, does not make clear how or why one who acts on the basis of computation of his own pleasure and pain, can or should consult the pleasure and pain of others.

Paley and Bentham have tried to base a social theory on egoism; but that social theory in itself, irrespective of any improbable links it may have with egoism, has weaknesses even more fundamental. In the most rigorous moral treatise he published in his lifetime, an essay on Paley in *The Friend*, Coleridge criticizes the utilitarian theory of "general consequences." Paley's is an early form, I should explain, of rule-utilitarianism: one ought to act in accordance with those moral rules that, if followed by everyone in the community, would bring about the greatest good for members of the community. This is to be distinguished from act-utilitarianism: one should do those acts that, in any particular situation, would bring about the greatest good for the greatest number of people. Paley and Butler both see a problem in act-utilitarianism. How within its terms can we prohibit any act such as lying or forgery, in itself obviously wrong, when the particular act in question might result in widespread benefits?[91] Paley thinks general rules must be formulated based on what "would be the consequence, if the same sort of actions were

90. *Table Talk*, p. 369.

91. Paley, *The Principles of Moral and Political Philosophy*, I, 71; Butler, "Of the Nature of Virtue," in *The Analogy of Religion*, pp. 326–328.

generally permitted." The "particular consequence" of passing a counterfeit coin may be trifling, but the "general consequence" of everyone's doing it would "abolish the use of money."[92] That this theory does propose "principles" might make it attractive to Coleridge in some of his moods, since rule-utilitarianism is just as "principled" as Kantian formalism.

It is ironic that the founder of nineteenth-century idealism in England should attack utilitarian theory (which, so the story goes, derives from Lockean empiricism) because it is too "ideal" and "imaginary." But in many ways Coleridge is closely aligned with that empirical tradition. The thrust of what we have seen so far is his intolerance of any theory or attitude or act not firmly anchored in human experience. Paley's theory is

no less *ideal* than that of any former system: that is, it is no less incapable of receiving any external experimental proof, compulsory on the understandings of all men, such as the criteria exhibited in chemistry. Yet, unlike the elder Systems of Morality, it remains in the world of the senses, without deriving any evidence therefrom. The agent's mind is compelled to go out of itself in order to bring back *conjectures*, the probability of which will vary with the shrewdness of the Individual.[93]

One necessarily comes up with mere "conjectures" because the "individual is to *imagine* what the general consequences *would* be, all other things remaining the same, if all men were to act as he is about to act."[94]

This is a superfluous and dangerous policy. It is superfluous because one could not "form a notion of the nature of an action considered as indefinitely multiplied, unless [one] has previously a distinct notion of the nature of the single action itself, which is the multiplicand." But if we already understand the single act well enough to be able to multiply it

92. Paley, I, 78–79.
93. *F*, I, 317.
94. *F*, I, 318.

"generally," why multiply it at all? We have already answered
our question about the act, and elucidating it further by
"general consequences" is, he says, like trying to add light to
the sun or looking at our fingers through a telescope. The
theory would be dangerous in practice because it in no way
encourages a sense of obligation. It places the emphasis not
on the "real" particular and immediate consequence of the
act, but on the "imaginary" consequence of everybody's doing
it. Since one could easily and correctly reason that everyone
will *not* so act, and since the immediate good consequences
seem more real than the merely hypothetical bad consequences, one could justify by means of the theory almost any
act on an ad hoc basis. Paley's theory, when it attempts to
shed light on the brighter by the dimmer perspective, for-
sakes the real perceived contexts of human experience. "The
nature of every action is determined by all its circumstances:
alter the circumstances and a similar set of *motions* may be
repeated, but they are no longer the same or similar action."
It would be absurd if a surgeon had to ask himself, preparatory to removing a diseased limb, what would happen if
everyone removed other people's limbs.[95]

Coleridge's critique therefore points out the self-contradictory nature of Paley's doctrine. It "confounds morality
with law" because it "draws away the attention from the
will, that is, from the inward motives and impulses which
constitute the essence of *morality*, to the outward act."[96] If a
utilitarian asserts that he wishes to judge only the act, not the
agent, Coleridge replies that "the distinction itself is merely

95. Ibid. A rule-utilitarian could object that exceptions can be built into
every rule, though these cannot be stated in full for every contingency. As
John Rawls says, "some reliance on people's good sense and some concession to hard cases is necessary." Garner and Rosen comment that one
would have no way beforehand of knowing whether a particular case
would qualify as exceptional (*Moral Philosophy*, p. 77). Coleridge's objection is at least sensibly raised.

96. *F*, I, 314.

logical, not real and vital," because "the character of the agent is determined by his view of the action," and, in any event, morality must not be self-divisive.[97] Concentration on the outward act in no way lends concreteness or certainty to theory and practical decision-making. It results instead in a divorce of the agent from his own act. There is no necessity for coordination between them, if all that matters is the act itself. With no necessary personal commitment to it, the agent is encouraged to perform the act at arm's length. This schism between agent and act is disorienting and cuts the agent off from reality. To focus so much on the outward act is to lose one's sense of self and in turn of the *tangibility* of the external world. A notebook entry of 1810 argues that conscience "knits us to earth, to the flesh and blood of our human nature with all its food and fuel of Affections, local attachments, predilections of Language & Country," while expediency "inevitably unloosens the Soul from its centripetal Instincts, makes man a thing of generalities and ideal abstractions, Shadows in which no life is, no power. . . . [L]ike a spherical Balloon we float between earth & heaven without belonging to either/."[98]

What is unexpected in Coleridge's critique of British moralists is his down-to-earth practicality. His position derives less from the Kantian haze-world than from this very practicality that is sometimes said to be the cornerstone of the British moralism he is attacking. He distrusts schemes that are too confident, as Godwin's is, in the power of reason to guide us; too complacent about human nature, as is Shaftesbury's; too optimistic about our ability to set proper goals and attain them, as is utilitarianism. This is not a conservative attack on liberalism; it is simply a kind of analytic stubbornness not often recognized in Coleridge. The Hobbesian idea that "self-interest in a more or less gross form is the true Spring . . . of

97. *F*, I, 325.
98. *N*, III, 3875.

human Actions" is today one of the "accredited facts, almost universally considered as universal Experience, which yet neither or ever were actually experienced/." We accept such "facts" when we rely too much on received opinion and the "habit of referring to notions formed from books . . . instead of trying them by our experience & actual Observation—."[99]

John Stuart Mill thinks the Benthamite and Coleridgean schools of thought could profitably listen more to each other. The degree of deafness, he notes in passing, is unequal in the two schools. The Coleridgean philosophy "denies less of what is true in the doctrine it wars against, than had been the case in any previous philosophic reaction." Coleridge had been infatuated with the empiricism of Hartley, and that he should have passed through this "highest form" of Lockean empiricism "without stopping at it is itself a strong presumption that there were more difficulties in the question than Hartley had solved." The Coleridgean school was the first to inquire into "the inductive laws of the existence and growth of human society," and this it did "in the spirit of Baconian investigation."[100] Coleridge does, Mill recognizes, write against the theory of general consequences and he does agree with Kant that one should obey "the simple unconditional commandment of eschewing every act that implies a self-contradiction." But Mill adds, quoting from *Aids to Reflection*, "Even a utilitarian can have little complaint to make of a philosopher who lays it down that 'the *outward* object of virtue' is 'the greatest producible sum of happiness of all men,' and that 'happiness in its proper sense is but the continuity and sum-total of the pleasure which is allotted or happens to a man.' "[101]

99. *N*, III, 3556.

100. "Coleridge," in *Dissertations and Discussions*, II (New York: Henry Holt, 1874), 15–25.

101. Ibid., 70.

Though Mill had to base his estimate on such published writings as *Biographia Literaria* and *Aids to Reflection*, and did not read the Opus Maximum and notebooks, he has adumbrated a truth, I think, which is still not completely accepted. Coleridge does not altogether reject in spirit the British traditions of empiricism and utilitarianism. It is certainly true that there are few closer observers of external phenomena and their interaction with the human observer than Coleridge. His notebooks reveal an attentiveness to bodily process and sensory response, especially sight and touch. If we use the term loosely, this habit could be called "empirical." We might recall Pater's comment on his "physical voluptuousness." There are few prose styles more sensuous, more crammed with image and metaphor, more insistent on giving color to abstraction. And in moral concerns we have seen how his talk of duty and universals gives way to that of situation, consequences, and psychological health. Coleridge questions not so much the values of the utilitarians as the self-defeating strategy of setting up pleasure and happiness as ends in themselves. While he does not promise happiness as an offshoot of the moral life, he believes any happiness not morally sound is banal and illusory.

Coleridge's most provocative and original criticism of utilitarianism has been directed against its impracticality, its judgment of an act in terms of its nebulous consequences. He criticizes its dislocating neglect of the agent's inner life. The utilitarians are right to insist that the well-being of the agent, his pleasure and happiness, must be written into moral formulae, but they would ironically separate the agent from his own act in such a way that he could no longer be the act's beneficiary. The happiness sought is thus imperiled by the character of the approach to it.

Indeed the utilitarian formula lends a certain banal, unimaginative character to the pursuit of happiness. Its usual habit of quantifying pleasure and its limited idea of what answers to man's deepest needs, its lack of tragic perspective, are everywhere apparent in the writings of Bentham, Paley, and James Mill. Coleridge's rejection of it comes less from its nonconformity with Kantian categories than from its failure on its own terms to prescribe a plausible formula for the end of happiness. He tackles it with its own presumed interest in staying within the realm of observed human experience.

Coleridge himself effects something of the reconciliation of Coleridgean and Benthamite perspectives John Stuart Mill thinks is so needed. Human well-being is a significant moral concern, as the utilitarians say, but Coleridge with his enlarged conception of self thinks the utilitarian formula of what constitutes well-being is absurdly limited. The utilitarian commitment to practicality is also attractive to him, but it is precisely its latent impracticality that he attacks. Coleridge, then, has outflanked Bentham by subscribing to his major concerns while rendering them, he thinks, more plausible and more consistent with a greater estimate of human possibility.

5 | Theory and Contexts

Postulates of Humanity

Coleridge is suspicious of the very enterprise of moral philosophy. The moral life is a "principle without a system," he writes. "Systems of morality are in truth nothing more than old books of casuistry generalized," and casuistry often promotes the thing it would prohibit when it treats of "particular actions, minute case-of-conscience hair-splitting directions & decision. O how illustrated by the detestable character of most of the Roman Casuists of Diana de digito in maritali fruitione!!" A moralist should describe only those actions that "tend to awaken the Heart to efficient Feelings, whether of Fear or of Love, actions that falling back on the Fountain, ⟨keep it full,⟩ or clear out the mud from its pipes."[1]

Some desynonymizations are relevant here. "Ethics are not Morals—any more than the Science of Geometry is the Art of Carpentry or Architecture. We make maps by strait lines, and celestial observations, determining distances as the Crow would fly; but we must travel by *Roads*."[2] With contempt

1. *F*, I, 445; *N*, II, 2435.
2. MS Notebook 49 (1830), f. 36ᵛ.

he speaks of "our idealess schemes & systems of//Morals—or Moral Science—as if Morality were, like geometrical Lines & Circles, an abstraction."[3] The very word "ethics" suggests an aridity, and it might have been better "if 'ethic' instead of clinging to Titlepages and literary Nomenclature a lame Semisynonime of 'Moral' had been adopted to express 'manner[l]y.' "[4] When he rejects utilitarianism he does not object to its attempt at "travel by *Roads*"; morality he insists is the sphere of the practical, of "practical reason," after all. What he does criticize in most forms of prudentialism is, as we have seen, their impracticality, their inability to achieve their own ends.

Throughout this study we have been pursuing what Coleridge thinks one should do and be, but we have not asked him how one justifies moral judgments in theory, nor have we asked him what the nature of moral judgments is. He does not really separate metaethical from normative discussion; that is, he does not see much point in separating talk *about* morality from moral recommendation. Although there has been of late something of a return to normative ethics, a strong tendency in twentieth-century moral philosophy has been to back off from the imposing, even embarrassing task of moral recommendation, and instead to focus on such problems as the nature and justification of moral judgments, and the meaning of basic moral terms such as "good" and "right." We have already seen Coleridge undertake some of these problems, but his more academic discussions always have normative content and purpose; and it should be added that a divorce of metaethical from normative discussion is always difficult to maintain.

My interest here is in his thinking that the nature, meaning, and justification of a moral judgment are functions of one's practical commitment to it. As he expounds it, the "science of

3. MS Notebook 50 (1831), ff. 14–14ᵛ.
4. *N*, II, 2431.

morality" turns out to be not separate from human commitment, not laid out in geometric patterns. A seemingly stuffy discussion of moral judgments in the Opus Maximum becomes, on closer inspection, an argument for strong moral commitment even though one has no ultimate guarantee of truth. What emerges is the drama of humanity holding tenuously to moral judgments against encroachments from all sides. Discursive reason may encroach by insisting that moral judgments are imaginary. Religious doctrine may encroach by treating moral judgments as insufficient, prideful, and even superfluous. Political theory may encroach by insisting that morality give way to expediency. Most important for Coleridge personally, the self may encroach on its own moral commitments through the maneuvers of bad faith. He gives in to all these threats at various times in his career; his humanism remains precarious.

In *Aids to Reflection* Coleridge calls, inconsistently with some of the remarks quoted above, for a "moral science." "Ethics, or the *Science* of Morality, does indeed in no wise exclude the consideration of *Action;* but it contemplates the same in its originating spiritual Source, without reference to Space or Time or Sensible existence." Instead of burying the idea of a moral science, he wishes here to rejuvenate it:

For this is no Compost, Collectorium or Inventory of Single Duties: nor does it seek in the "multitudinous Sea," in the predetermined waves, tides and currents of Nature that freedom, which is exclusively an attribute of Spirit. Like all other pure Sciences, whatever it enunciates, and whatever it concludes, it enunciates and concludes *absolutely.* Strictness is its essential Character: and its first Proposition is, "Whosoever shall keep the whole law, and yet offend in one point, he is guilty of all."[5]

Although the passage is declamatory, it has a concealed personal note. He has quoted James ii.10 earlier in a letter de-

5. *AR*, p. 289.

scribing his opium habit. He had thought the verse very harsh, "but my own sad experience has taught me it's aweful, dreadful Truth.—What crime is there scarcely which has not been included in or followed from the one guilt of taking opium?"[6] The "strictness" in the passage above refers confusedly both to the elaboration of moral science and to the conduct of life. The lingering Cartesianism, which would seem to set moral science apart in a world of "strict" theoretical certainty, is already compromised by the implicit connection between strict theory and strictness in the moral life.

We might expect from what we already know of him that Coleridge, having enunciated such a portentous format for a moral science, would summarily abandon the whole topic. And in *Aids to Reflection* this is precisely what he does. Such failures of exposition might understandably have led F. J. A. Hort to conclude that "Coleridge's moral philosophy need not detain us long. Perhaps the most striking fact, considering the universal supremacy which moral considerations held in his mind, is that there is so little to say about it."[7] But *Aids to Reflection* is not his only forum for moral theory. Hort did not have access to most of the materials used in this book, and he might have changed his mind if he had read the Opus Maximum alone, especially "Chapter III," which discusses the nature of moral judgments and suggests a more promising line of inquiry than does this call for a "moral science." This chapter explains why there can finally be no moral *science* at all.[8]

6. *CL*, III, 490.

7. *Cambridge Essays* (1856), pp. 335–336.

8. OM, B_2, ff. 1–14. B_2 begins with the heading "Chapter III," but it is unclear what might have constituted the first two chapters, if they were ever written. A brief monograph by Elio Chinol, *Il Pensiero di S. T. Coleridge*, pp. 99–122, looks at some of the material in "Chapter III." One finds similar arguments, though not with the same intent, in the various versions of Fichte's *Wissenschaftslehre* that were in Coleridge's possession. See *The Science of Knowledge*, trans. A. E. Kroeger (Philadelphia: J. B. Lippincott, 1868), pp. 11–60.

Coleridge attempts in it to define moral judgments as distinct both from statements of empirical fact and from analytic truths. He is disagreeing with the claims of both rationalists and empiricists that moral judgments belong exclusively to their camp. Rather than conceiving a compromise, however, he works toward a conception of moral judgment as a unique category. On the one hand, he is probably thinking of Cartesian rationalists such as Clarke, Cumberland, and Wollaston. Clarke writes that moral judgments are of the same order as mathematical or geometrical truths. Anyone who would assert that there is no unalterable difference between right and wrong would be making as much sense as a "geometer who would seriously and in good earnest lay it down as a first principle, that a crooked line is as straight as a right one."[9] Coleridge is no doubt thinking, on the other hand, of the "naturalists" such as Bentham and Paley, who define good in terms of psychological facts, thereby effectively eliminating the need for a special moral vocabulary. A naturalistic "definist" is one who thinks all moral terms—such as "good" and "bad," "right" and "wrong"—can be replaced by nonmoral terms—such as "productive of happiness" or "pleasurable"—without changing the meaning of the statement in which they occur. Coleridge's critique of "pleasure" and "good," we recall, was directed against this kind of definism.

In this same chapter, he describes more precisely what he means by rational truths and empirical facts, so as to clarify in what way moral judgments differ from both. A rational science, such as geometry, a superstructure of the "pure intellect in which the speculative necessity reigns throughout," consists of propositions to which we must assent. The proposition that the shortest distance between two points is a straight line cannot be disputed; the only element of will involved in the proposition is the decision to engage in reasoning in the first place. The lack of a strong element of

9. *A Discourse of Natural Religion*, in *British Moralists*, I, 194.

will means that purely rational a priori statements are true but lacking in what he calls "realizing power"—the real world may or may not correspond to them.

A proposed empirical "fact," Coleridge continues, is "nothing more than an assertion respecting particulars or individuals," which may or may not be the case. We can concoct valid syllogisms ("all stones think; but men are stones; therefore men think") with true conclusions but based on a "fact" which happens to be a "notorious absurdity." The hypothetical nature of "fact" is further demonstrated in the way we use the term. We do not say, "it is a fact that two straight lines cannot enclose a space," though we would say "it is a fact that this position is to be found in Euclid's axioms." Any premise of fact such as "all stones think" must be prefaced by an "if" that would be inappropriate to the more dignified Euclidian axiom.

If a moral judgment were merely an assertion of "fact," as the empiricists say, it would be every bit as hypothetical and idle as the assertion that "all stones think." Coleridge thinks moral judgments must instead "maintain an equality of rank" with and "superior dignity" to purely rational truths, without at the same time *being* them. To define the exact nature of moral judgments it is necessary to "discover an opposite to the hypothetical positions no less than to the unconditionally necessary." A moral judgment must be "in some sense necessary," like geometrical truths, but without being, like them, "unconditional."

Again in its relation to hypothetical positions, or those grounded on facts, [the moral judgment] must be contingent and yet contingent in a different manner which can only be, that as in the hypothetical affirmations the contingency remains for the mind when it is removed by the establishment of the fact, so here the necessity must remain in the mind while the contingency is retained in the fact.

(One would enjoy the facial expression of Coleridge's amanuensis through all this.) The truth of the baroque argument is demonstrated by "the usage in all languages." If we say to someone, "I, or you, must do this or that," must, for example, go to aid a "deserving and afflicted parent," the import contained in the word "must" would remain even if that person were to reply, "There is no 'must' in the matter, for who shall make me[?] If you threw me out of the window I must go but while you are no stronger than I believe you to be I know & feel that I can & shall stay where I am."

Coleridge makes an important and difficult distinction here between the contingency involved in turning rational truths into empirical realities and that involved in deciding whether or not to obey moral commands. The properties of the mathematical arch remain intact, he says, even though one can build a bridge that only approximates these properties. The construction of the bridge is therefore "contingent," but this contingency is "wholly divided" from the a priori mathematical arch itself, which retains its unquestionable authority. The possibility of challenging the authority of moral judgment, however, is very real. The "denial of the position must be itself a reality and a realizing act," and each of us has the power to undermine the authority of moral judgment. The first premise of morality is the idea of responsibility, but rationally one need not accept the premise: "as to your 'ought' so you and the parson say, but I deny it and believe that nature tells me more than all the priests in creation, and all the herd of ninnies that are duped by them." Both the affirmation and the denial of moral responsibility require an "act of mind," an appropriation of the position, not mechanical acquiescence. The act of dissociation from morality is not absurd, as the rationalists would have us believe, nor does it go against undeniable empirical evidence. There can indeed be no argument against one who denies that moral judgments can be made, because he has simply separated himself from the entire grammar of morality.

He may not lose the argument, but he loses something far more important—his humanity! Moral judgments are, Coleridge writes, "postulate[s] of humanity." They are not merely hypothetical, but they are contingent on our acceptance of them. Their "necessity arises out of and is commensurate with human nature itself[,] the sole condition being the retention of humanity, while that this is contingent i.e. that a human being may be dishumanized which it cannot be but by his own act." If we deny in our deeds the idea of moral responsibility altogether, we become the "fiend." The natural man, unlike the fiend, is still within the moral sphere; he accepts the idea but with insufficient ardor to realize it. To acknowledge the responsible will and yet transgress is the "mystery of the world."

Morality, then, has a "reality of its own." It is analogous to, though qualitatively different from, mathematical truths in that we can speak in a certain sense of its "necessity," and it has a kinship with "empirical positions" by its "reality & realizing power." Coleridge says elsewhere in the Opus Maximum that he is not talking abstractly. We should remember the "state of our consciousness, while we were following Euclid through the 37.th proposition, and then our state while we were perusing the pages of Tacitus or contemplating the creations of Milton." The sciential reason, potentially the same in all persons, does not lead us to ask what the purpose of a circle is. As a "verb impersonal" it produces no "excitement of the sense of our individuality."[10]

Thus the very nature of moral judgment implies a commitment's having been made. It is meaningless to speak of morality apart from an agent who makes the commitment and who takes the risk commitment must entail. The unrealized personality signifies a failure of imagination, because the "postulates of humanity" that excite the sense of our

10. OM, B$_3$, ff. 166–171. This argument, to be sure, contradicts what he says elsewhere about the self-knowledge entailed in learning Euclidian geometry, which is but a "History and graphic Exposition of the powers and processes of the Intuitive Faculty—" (*CL*, VI, 630; see also *N*, I, 1717).

individuality are accessible only through our own capacity to intuit and create.

Coleridge's theoretical explanation of the nature of moral judgments is in keeping with his view of human potentiality. We recall his image of the "shipwrecked man stunned, & for many weeks in a state of Ideotcy or utter loss of Thought & Memory—& then gradually awakened/." Agonizingly, he awakens to a lack of context. He gradually discovers it is his own resourcefulness that will shape a context and not the island on which he, not through his own choice, has landed. All that he affirms can be denied, but his task is to be most fully human, and for no *reason* other than that he has the inchoate capacity and feels the need to "declare his particular existence." This reading admittedly emphasizes an element in Coleridge's thought that never quite emerges into full theoretical articulation, but it is there in more than embryonic form. There is a theoretical continuity between the poet who writes *The Ancient Mariner* and the moralist who speaks of the postulates of humanity.

This account of the nature of moral judgments anticipates what Coleridge has to say about their justification. He seems flagrantly to have begged the questions of what the idea of humanity entails, and why, once we could agree on that, we should even choose to be human. But he admits to the circularity. "I *ought* because I ought i.e. because I see the act in question, inclusively in that law of conscience, by which this *ought* is the contradistinguishing ground & predicate of my humanity—."[11] The conscience, which invests us with this "ought," is both volitional and cognitive, and in this respect his conception of it differs from that of Kant. Though Frederick Copleston and others think Kant himself was reaching beyond epistemology and the limits of our knowing to a metaphysics based on moral consciousness, the usual

11. OM, B_2, ff. 131, 133; cf. *N*, III, 3583 and *AR*, pp. 88–89.

interpretation of Kant, and it is Coleridge's, is that Kant's "practical reason" is but a mode of volitional consciousness issuing "as if's" with no necessary cognitive content.[12] Coleridge does not wish to divorce moral judgments from cognition, and the close link between conscience and consciousness shows that he would break with Kant on this point.

"Knowing" or "intuiting" a moral judgment is not simply a matter of opening one's eyes. There is not a body of immediately comprehensible moral truths that one perceives with some innate moral sense. Coleridge is an intuitionist with a keen sense of the limits of intuition. Moral judgments must not simply be intuited, they must also be willed and constantly reaffirmed. And they are reaffirmed, Coleridge has said, only in the act of *being* human. The existential character of his thought permeates his view of intuition itself. It is closely aligned with imagination, which combines discovery and creation, which invests the "Ancient of Days" with the sense of wonder and novelty. The circularity of "I *ought* because I ought" perhaps best declares the plight of the shipwrecked person, who does not have the rationalist's assurance that it would be absurd not to go about the business of being human. The shipwrecked person suspects that there may indeed be an absurdity in being human, but that that is the risk he must take. Thomas McFarland quotes Ortega y Gasset in relation to existential shipwreck in Coleridge. The "ideas of the shipwrecked" are the only ones that are not mere rhetoric, writes Ortega, because "he who does not really feel himself lost, is lost without remission; that is to say, he never finds himself, never comes up against his own reality."[13]

12. Coleridge writes that Kant's proofs "are *moral*—and he himself expressly entitles the result, Vernunft-Glauben, i.e. a *belief* consistent with reason—expressly declares that even a *practische* Vernunft, or reason proceeding on a praeter rational Ground, demands only that we should act *as if* the proof were scientific" (*CL*, IV, 863).

13. *The Revolt of the Masses*, quoted in *Coleridge and the Pantheist Tradition*, pp. 314–316.

Coleridge's own moral discourse reveals a tendency to reification that betrays his own will to believe. One watches him nervously write the words "Will," "Conscience," "Principle," "Good" with big caps and underlining, as if hoping they will somehow become more real through emphasis and reiteration. He hopes to make language and concept contain the truth itself. This tendency, combined with a psychology that sometimes reverts, against his own views, to "faculties," makes for a vision of the human mind as a kind of metaphysical gearbox. We tote around these *things* called will, conscience, reason. It is easy, consequently, to forget about the unity of the self as we travel through the long list of the mind's properties. Coleridge's use of language here is itself related to his fear that one must will to believe. The "postulates of humanity" are as problematic as the human will that must affirm them; and I suggest it is his inability resolutely to affirm them that leads to the collapse of the ethical.

The Collapse of the Ethical

In an 1828 notebook Coleridge writes that he would readily adopt Spinoza's denial of personal immortality if he did not "necessarily link it to my individual *Despair*—."[14] The poem "Human Life" (1815) treats with nervous sarcasm the implications of such a denial:

> If the breath
> Be Life itself, and not its task and tent,
> If even a soul like Milton's can know death;
> O Man! thou vessel purposeless, unmeant,
> Yet drone-hive strange of phantom purposes!
> Surplus of Nature's dread activity,
> Which, as she gazed on some nigh-finished vase,
> Retreating slow, with meditative pause,
> She formed with restless hands unconsciously.
> Blank accident! nothing's anomaly!

14. MS Notebook 40 (1828), f. 10^v.

If there is not the substantiation to this life that immortality promises, then hope, fear, sadness, gladness—all human values—are pointless "counter-weights" one to another. If we are but an "Image of Image," the moral life is a fiction, and it would be absurd to rejoice "with hollow joy for hollow good."

A marginal note to Kant's *Träume eines Geistersehers* (1766) treats the problem of the relationship between morality and supernatural sanction. Kant asks, "Does the heart of man contain no direct moral prescripts? Must his moral nature derive motive power from another world?" Coleridge's comment indicates that, like Locke and Clarke before him, he wishes to have it both ways on the relationship of virtue, consequence, and supernatural sanction. Certainly "Vice . . . is hateful on its own account," and "True! What I do, I would fain do well. It is not any Hope of future Reward that impels me." But he feels that lack of a religious backdrop would turn this life into a dream. He is horrified at the thought that "all men and all things are but Dreams, that nothing is permanent." Then follows yet another qualification of Kantian ethics:

Away with Stoic Hypocrisy! I know that in order to [retain] the idea of Virtue we must suppose the pure good will or reverence for the Law as excellent in itself—but this very excellence supposes consequences, tho' not selfish ones. Let my maxim be capable of becoming the Law of all intelligent Being—well! but this supposes an *end* possessible by intelligent Beings. For if the Law be barren of all consequences, what is it but words? To obey the Law for its own sake is really a mere sophism in any other sense: you might as well put abracadabra in its place.[15]

Clarke comes to a similar conclusion when he writes, "Though virtue is unquestionably *worthy to be chosen for its own sake*, even without any expectation of reward; yet it does not follow that it is therefore entirely *self-sufficient*,

15. *IS*, p. 142.

and able to support a man under all kinds of sufferings, and even death itself, for its sake; without any prospect of future recompense."[16] Clarke and Coleridge both think it an intolerable prospect to die for virtue's sake when nobody could possibly profit from that dying; as Clarke recalls, Regulus died the cruelest death rather than break faith with an enemy. Kant himself, of course, thinks the disproportion of happiness to virtue in this life makes immortality a necessary hypothesis, as a kind of compensation that a sense of justice would insist upon. But what is a necessary hypothesis in Kant is an essential article of faith in Coleridge. He would "rather not have been" than find that his status is lower than animals, "for they enjoy a generic immortality having no individuation."[17]

Coleridge's humanism, I have emphasized, is vulnerable and unstable. The development of the self is the highest goal within the moral sphere, but this very development carries with it an element of presumption: it would indicate that one has set up "an independent base" on a purely human level. The presumption in such a humanism prompts Coleridge to warn that morality must not be separated from religion, nor must religion be turned into a mere "Code of Ethics."[18] D. G. James writes in *The Romantic Comedy* (1949) that Coleridge

beheld in the conscience and its law, first and foremost, certainly not something human by which we may be impressed to the point of reverence, but something divine, the indwelling of the Divine Reason which acts upon us, seeking to draw us to knowledge of itself, and which obtains from us not merely reverence but worship. In the philosophy of Coleridge the autonomy of the ethical is collapsed; the ethical occurs through the action of the Divine Reason on the creaturely and animal.[19]

16. *A Discourse of Natural Religion*, in *British Moralists*, I, 215.
17. *IS*, p. 142.
18. *CL*, III, 152–154.
19. *The Romantic Comedy* (New York: Oxford University Press, 1948), pp. 187–188. I might mention also in this context G. E. Moore's critique of

There is a partial reply to James consistent with Coleridge's philosophy of religion. Coleridge emphasizes that religion is based on morality, not vice versa. In this matter he follows Fichte, who deduces faith in spiritual reality from the prior dictates of conscience. Coleridge's best known, if loosely worded, statement of this idea is in the *Biographia Literaria*, where he writes that religion must have a *"moral* origin; so far at least, that the evidence of its doctrines could not, like the truths of abstract science, be wholly independent of the will. . . . The belief of a God and a future state . . . does not indeed always beget a good heart; but a good heart . . . naturally begets the belief."[20] He thinks the structure of morality that might be built up on its own foundation like a castle would have "religion for the ornaments & completion of it's roof & upper Stories—."[21] Adopting his favorite metaphor once again, he writes that one can speak of "Morality proceeding from the Root of obedience as the Stem, with its sprays and leaves, and Religion from the summit of the Stem, as the Crown and Flower of the Plant."[22] Both structurally and temporally, morality is prior to religion. The Opus Maximum describes the growth of religious faith from the development of strong family ties. The Hartleian idea of associative transfer of affection applies to religious feeling: love of parent leads to love of God.[23] It is through the "personality" of the human being that we come to know the "personëity" of God. Finally, we have seen throughout that the conscience puts us in touch with *human* reality, the

---

"Metaphysical Ethics," theories not supported by their own moral propositions but based on some prior, more encompassing conception of the universe. Whether this principle more fundamental than the ethical be God or a principle of rational order, the autonomy of ethics is compromised (*Principia Ethica*, pp. 110–141).

20. *BL*, I, 135–136.
21. *CL*, III, 313–314.
22. *IS*, p. 389.
23. OM, B₃, ff. 78–79.

reality and worth of other selves. Such comments would make dubious James's point that for Coleridge morality is but an offshoot of religious consciousness.

I would agree that the autonomy of the ethical frequently collapses in Coleridge, though the primary cause is not always his bump of reverence. His arguments above suggest not only the priority of morality to religion but also a harmony between them that much of his writing and his view of his own life simply do not bear out. *The Ancient Mariner* poses the problem implicitly. We have noticed that the Mariner may have an evil will but that he sometimes gives us glimpses of a humane consciousness as well. The many men for whose death he feels responsible are "so beautiful!" and the skylarks and little birds fill the sea and air with "sweet jargoning." He tries to pray whether or not he is able; his homeland fills him with joy. That he feels his loneliness so painfully implies his wish to be reunited with "the one Life within us and abroad." His very capacity for guilt indicates he is fighting the fiend within him. When he blesses the watersnakes "unaware" in a "spring of love," we think momentarily that the curse has been expiated. But this is the delusion of the moral perspective. Love of the creatures and humane concern for his crew prove to be insufficient propitiation. The Mariner's (and the reader's) sense of justice is offended by the seeming willfulness of the Polar Spirit, or of God himself, if this Spirit be his representative.

In *Aids to Reflection* Coleridge argues that rejection of religion most often results from those doctrines that jar one's "*moral* feelings," such as (and there are echoes of the Mariner's plight here) "Arbitrary Election and Reprobation; the Sentence to everlasting Torment by an eternal and necessitating Decree; vicarious Atonement, and the necessity of the Abasement, Agony and ignominious Death of a most holy and meritorious Person, to appease the Wrath of God."[24]

24. *AR*, pp. 151–152.

The metaphorical interpretation Coleridge gives in *Aids to Reflection* to much Christian dogma, and his development of the idea of a personal God who must "concern" us, are efforts to make religious doctrine coincide with our *"moral feelings." Aids to Reflection* is in effect an effort to argue away the terrifying import of *The Ancient Mariner*, which would lead us, since it jars our moral feelings, to hatred of God. The Mariner may not be "a most holy and meritorious Person," but he and, of course, his crew are afflicted beyond the limits of human justice. *Aids to Reflection* notwithstanding, the problem of unjust suffering in this life persists in Coleridge's notebooks, letters, and for that matter his epitaph, in which he tells the passer-by he was one who, for all his humility and contrition, "many a year with toil of breath / Found death in life." The cruel verdict of the tossing of dice aboard the deathship was for him never reversed.

The dramatic conflict between moral and religious spheres implicit in *The Ancient Mariner* is significant in the larger patterns of Coleridge's life and work. I do not mean to appear casually dismissive of his contribution to the philosophy of religion—in fact the conflict I am sketching is an element of it. We have seen that he develops, extraordinarily, a humanistic philosophy based on the depravity of the will. The precariousness of that humanism results from the barely submerged bestiality and demonism that lurk in us all; civilization is a fragile construction indeed. He writes that moral consciousness is the center of his system, but he does not well protect that center. Just as the Mariner finds that moral consciousness does not propitiate divine wrath, so Coleridge senses the inadequacy of the humanistic ideal to negotiate, finally, with the depraved will. To think it adequate would recapitulate in another key the prideful independence characterizing the depraved will itself.

Of course the "autonomy of the ethical" is collapsed in Coleridge, just as the man himself collapses again and again.

The idea of the fully realized self has in it the threat of heresy, and Coleridge, from "The Eolian Harp" on, has always been too infirm to sustain the heretic's role.

Political Apostasy

Coleridge's politics can be seen as sometimes manifesting a regressive dialectic that leads to the collapse of the ethical. The ethical or humanist perspective is subverted from within by the self's cooperation with enemies of its own freedom. One enemy, I have suggested, is God himself, whose will is inscrutable at the same time that the baffled soul scrambles to live in conformity with it. The politics of fear, which we occasionally encounter in Coleridge, originates in a similar usurpation of the self's center—here, by the state.

The political theory of Rousseau is seductive because of its moral cogency, but it is precisely its moral cogency that makes it dangerous as political directive. Emphasizing Rousseau's affinities with Kant, Coleridge writes that Rousseau's system is based on the sacred principle "that a person can never become a thing, nor be treated as such without wrong." Each person owes allegiance to his own conscience, which cannot be violated by the state. But to apply principles of morality to affairs of the state is inappropriate, he replies, for "with what shew of Reason can we pretend, from a principle by which we are to determine the purity of our motives, to deduce the form and matter of a rightful Government, the main office of which is to regulate the outward actions of particular bodies of men, according to their particular circumstances?"[25] Morality when misappropriated to the affairs of the state gives rise to Jacobinism and totalitarianism, to the "conscientious Persecutors" of the French Revolution, who, not admitting of prudence and compromise or any scruple

25. *F*, I, 194–195.

about means, pursue their vision of moral perfection ruthlessly.

Coleridge is self-contradictory here. We have seen that morality *itself* must prudently take into consideration all relevant circumstances and consequences. Hence there would be no necessary contradiction between such a morality and a political orientation that combines principle with prudence. But in *The Friend* he often seems to say that the affairs of state should proceed on the basis of prudence alone; the only thing the state must consider is the outward act. This muddles, of course, his position as a moral critic of social and political affairs. How can he continue to denounce the expediency he seems in these instances to be recommending? As John Colmer points out, he is himself guilty of what he accuses Burke: "If his opponents are Theorists, [writes Coleridge,] *then* every thing is to be founded on PRUDENCE, on mere calculations of EXPEDIENCY: and every man is represented as acting according to the state of his own immediate self-interest. Are his opponents calculators? *Then* calculation itself is represented as a sort of crime."[26]

In *Aids to Reflection* he writes emphatically, "It is most true (and a truth which cannot with safety be overlooked) that Morality, *as* Morality, has no existence for *a People*."[27] This position can, obviously, be held by the political left or right. On the left, for example, Fichte argues that the state does not concern itself with moral freedom but instead provides the control of external affairs that is prerequisite for individual moral freedom.[28] The more conservative Coleridge writes, in opposition to *"Legislative* Jacobinism," that the

26. *F*, I, 188. See John Colmer, *Coleridge: Critic of Society* (Oxford: Clarendon Press, 1959), pp. 99–103, for a judicious discussion of some of Coleridge's confusions here.

27. *AR*, p. 288.

28. Fichte develops this argument in *Grundlage des Naturrechtes* (1796), translated as *The Science of Rights* by A. E. Kroeger (London: Trübner, 1889; rpt. London: Routledge & Kegan Paul, 1970). This work is possibly a source of Coleridge's thinking on this subject, though Fichte does not argue that from the state's perspective people are its "property."

law should treat murder and robbery "not as *Guilt* of which God alone is presumed to be the Judge, but as *Crimes*, depriving the *King* of one of *his* Subjects, rendering dangerous and abating the value of the *King's High*-ways. . . . Jack, Tom, and Harry have no existence in the eye of Law, except as included in some form or other of the *permanent Property* of the Realm—." He thinks the "pretence of considering Persons not States, Happiness not Property," will bring in a regime "more oppressive than the former."[29] Morality should be something altogether irrelevant to the affairs of state: crime is redressed by law, guilt by religion. Coleridge's argument, which may begin as a defense of personal freedom from the state's inquisition, ultimately invites the state to treat its subjects as if they were property or things.

That he has not reconciled the claims of politics and morality is hardly surprising—few theorists have. But the form his particular failure takes is significant. If the state's proper role is the guardian of property, and if people are themselves its possessions, the state becomes analogous to the loveless observer, here writ large. It does not consider our worth as persons but only our value as things. If morality is so clinically separated from politics as Coleridge seems to recommend, the same blind judgments and authoritarian treatment he fears in human relationships may become the privilege of the state.

We know from many contexts involving the claims of authority that his guilt often prompts him to join the forces he fears seek to persecute him. We can see this in the way, for instance, that he seeks to placate his disapproving brother George, or in the all too ingratiating tone of his *Lay Sermons*, addressed to "the Higher Classes of Society" (the one addressed to the lower classes never got written). He feels guilty and embarrassed about his youthful support of the aims of the French Revolution, and he vigorously disputes Pitt's maxim, "Once a Jacobin, always a Jacobin." To be-

29. *CL*, III, 537–538.

come his own accuser is to preempt the scornful eye of the public. He makes apologies that one often wishes he would not make. Even the Pantisocrat who does not think highly of Godwin argues, "Wherever Men *can* be vicious, some *will* be. The leading Idea of Pantisocracy is to make men *necessarily* virtuous by removing all Motives to Evil—all possible Temptations."[30] This focus on the likelihood that man will sin if only given the chance reveals a suspicion of human nature present even in his "optimistic" period.

Coleridge in the course of his life has played all the roles in *The Ancient Mariner*. As one who knows his own evil potential, he is the Mariner who shoots the bird. More often he is the Albatross itself, who awkwardly tries to bring good cheer to others and is ruthlessly shot. Again he is the Mariner whose punishment seems disproportionate to his crime and who feels alone on a wide wide sea. And not infrequently, to be sure, he joins the persecuting forces themselves. As he says, "perhaps we never *hate* any opinion or can do so till we have *impersonated* it."[31]

It is not surprising that the change in political orientation between the young and the old Coleridge is not so drastic as used to be thought. His apostasy is not so much a falling away from youthful radicalism or liberalism to the conservatism of his old age, as it is a quality of his political character from the beginning. It is an apostasy from his own humanism, from his confidence in the power of the self's moral center and in its relevance to all varieties of human community.

The Phantom Plagiarist

Coleridge himself indirectly expounds the meaning of his habitual plagiarizing and untruthfulness. Within the context

30. *CL*, I, 114.
31. *N*, II, 2121.

of his own moral dialectic, it is his clearest illustration that the evolution of the self comprehends other moral ends. His failure here is the ultimate collapse of the ethical.

We recall that he often distinguishes between what he is and what he does. Though he has admitted that the distinction is merely logical, not vital or even healthy, he continues to find it convenient because it suggests that he can dissociate himself from his own actions or inaction. Since one of his habitual actions is plagiarism, it permits him *not to be* the plagiarist. At times he feels everything he presents to the world is a shadowy dramatization—and one presented in a self-defeating effort to protect what is real. This process is not the willful ironic manipulation of the persona we find in Swift or Carlyle; as I have said, Coleridge is no ironist. Rather it is the psychic splitting of a cripple, who, instead of using the play of imagination to create personality from his rich store of possibilities, attempts to dissociate himself from the many phantom selves he has weakly permitted himself to occupy. He does not distinguish between the portion of the "doer" as objective phantom self or representative image projected by his own mind, and the portion he borrows or steals. Neither is, after all, his true self. That self is the wiser and sturdier one behind the curtain. The phantom self, a patchwork both of his own making and of stolen properties, is a kind of facade for the true self, which thereby hopes to retain its integrity and freedom, its freedom from the loveless observers that surround it, its freedom also from self-scrutiny.

In putting together the *Biographia Literaria* or *Theory of Life* or "On Poesy or Art," he tries to be consistent with the representative image. If that image is defined as "genius," what better way to feed the phantom than with Schelling's "subjects" and "objects"? His plagiarisms are efforts to increase the felt sense of separation between self and representative image, to make that image even more a fiction and, in the end, a fraud. The entire effort to gain, in this way, greater freedom for the interior self is doomed. The phantom self is always there to haunt the interior self; it becomes, like conscience, an avenging demon. Instead of maintaining its freedom, the interior self begins to be depleted, farmed out altogether to the image, and thus the "unnatural outwardness" of which Coleridge complains in others threatens him too. He begins to become what he has attempted to project *beyond* his own consciousness. He begins to *be* the plagiarist.

In a famous letter to Southey he writes of his "sense of weakness—a haunting sense, that I was an herbaceous Plant, as large as a large Tree, with a Trunk of the same Girth, & Branches as large & shadowing—but with *pith within* the Trunk, not heart of Wood/—that I had *power* not *strength*— an involuntary Imposter—that I had no real Genius, no real Depth/—."[32] The clumsy plant is a parody of the thriving organism and of his own moral ideal. In these moments of self-doubt, he sees himself as a fraud. The depleted self confronts the phantom self, cringes from its parodic aspect, and then becomes all the more its captive.

Indeed his fear that he is an impostor makes him all the more compulsive about being so. The phantom self, for all its repugnance, offers a dangerous simulacrum of what Coleridge would like to think is his true self. It is the genius, after all; it is the moralist who issues exhortations on public platforms; it is the brilliant young poet who composes masterpieces off the cuff as mere psychological curiosities. When he looks inward he sees little that remains his own; there is no genius and no depth. He tries not to hear the phantom self telling him he is, in *essence*, derivative and untrustworthy. He is haunted by the fraud, but he cannot call himself, except on rare occasions, the liar that he is. Even in his notebooks, where he attempts to speak to himself and to hear his own voice, he cannot quite bring himself to admit what

32. *CL*, II, 959.

he knows is the truth about himself. There is a split in his consciousness, then, between what appears as the sphere of fraud (the phantom plagiarist) and what appears as the sphere of nonentity (the interior self or trunk filled with pith instead of wood). It is little wonder that he finally identifies his true self with neither, and turns introspection into a complex strategem of evasion. It is little wonder, too, that another tactic of evasion should be the habit, so psychologically naked to us now, of accusing others of plagiarizing from *him*.

Sartre would call the attempt to dissociate oneself from what on some level one knows oneself to be, an act of bad faith, a lie to oneself.[33] To publish another's work as one's own is to assert that one is something other than what one is. Coleridge is not Schelling and for him to write what Schelling writes, for almost an entire chapter of the *Biographia Literaria*, is a *self*-contradiction. One wonders what he would do if one were to confront him with parallel texts and ask him to explain himself. Sartre tries to establish that bad faith must exist wholly in consciousness and does not represent censorship and repression. A lie to oneself requires the selectivity that only consciousness can provide. Coleridge's thefts are so palpable that it is difficult to think he could have performed them unconsciously, so blatant that, once conscious of them, he could hardly have expected to get away with them.

And this may be the point: some part of him does not wish to get away, as Walter Jackson Bate has suggested. He leaves some pathetic clues just prior to that theft in Chapter XII of the *Biographia Literaria*. "But it is time to tell the truth," he writes. And a little later, "The postulate of philosophy and at the same time the test of philosophic capacity, is no other

33. *Existential Psychoanalysis*, trans. Hazel E. Barnes (Chicago: Henry Regnery, 1962), pp. 153–210. This volume is a translation of a portion of *L'Etre et le Néant*.

than the heaven-descended KNOW THYSELF!"[34] The
letter interrupting the plagiarized passages is itself a plagiarism, this time copped from himself and masquerading as another's. No one cops passages wholesale in a dream, surely.
Sartre might suggest that for him to confess he is a plagiarist
would be to constitute himself as thing, as one defined entirely by his representations. It would mean giving up the
illusory freedom to be what he wishes to be behind the
curtain.

It is not just that Coleridge is in bad faith. It is that he
makes such a *spectacle* of it and comes so close to articulating
it for us as a problem that infects all consciousness. His
plagiarisms constitute his desperate, insistent, and telling
statement to us that the most encompassing moral task is the
enrichment of personality.

Frost at Midnight

Amid so many threats to the humanist perspective, Coleridge unsteadily holds to his longing vision of the self who
with moral intelligence and love has mastered the chaotic
powers within and has found beyond alienation the promise
of community.

Both longing and vision receive their most memorable expression in "Frost at Midnight." This poem most perfectly
catches the unique temper of the man, representing in the
triumph of humane consciousness a hint of the alien, transcended by an act of imagination and love, but transcended
only briefly in a tenuous union of remembered past and
prophesied future. The alienation and sinister setting of *The
Ancient Mariner* undergo a transformation in "Frost at Midnight," but they are nonetheless present in it. The "secret
ministry" of the frost, "unhelped by any wind," suggests in

34. *BL*, I, 163, 173. Walter Jackson Bate notes that Coleridge puts us on
our guard in this work by his very insistence that he is not plagiarizing
(*Coleridge*, p. 136; see *BL*, I, 102–105).

the poem's opening lines a kind of magic—even perhaps a sinister magic. It recalls the ministry of the Polar Spirit, who moves the ghostship without wind and who is indeed sinister and uncanny. By the end of the poem the frost's ministry will be explained, and its agency identified as benign. This transformation in the poet's consciousness of a chill and alien power into a familiar, benevolent, and beautiful one is much of the poem's action.

The poet, like the Mariner, is alone, but his is a "solitude" that pressures consciousness into perplexity as his act of interpreting the scene begins. The "hush of nature" produces a sense of alienation in the poet, who is so aware of the silence that he focuses on the "sole unquiet thing," the "film," soot-flakes which flap on the grate of the fireplace. Its "motion" in contrast to the silence "gives it dim sympathies with me who live, / Making it a companionable form. . . ." The sense of dimness and perplexity, we remember, is associated with the delving into the self that Coleridge thinks necessary for all moral growth. The indistinct probings and associations, prompted by the "puny flaps and freaks" of the film, are a process of self-exploration. The growth of consciousness of self is linked, we have seen, with that of conscience, of one's sense of relatedness to others in a moral universe. Paradoxically, the more he delves into his own mind, the more the poet senses his participation in a human community.

The use of "stranger" to refer to the film above the grate is not gratuitous folklore. (Coleridge writes that "in all parts of the kingdom these films are called *strangers* and supposed to portend the arrival of some absent friend.") The word reconciles the opposites most expressive of Coleridge's life: the strange and the familiar. He would like to be, as it were, in the absolute midst of things, known and recognized by friends; but of course the friendship he so seeks has always contained alienation, which has been its dominant mode. His childhood eagerness for relationships with others is suggested in his excitement when the schoolroom door "half opened" in promise of "the *stranger's* face, / Townsman, or aunt, or sister more beloved." But the door never yielded the stranger.

At the exact center of the poem is the "stern preceptor," who holds the child in awe and forces him into "mock study on my swimming book." The preceptor (in both educational and moral senses) is the threat that forces the child into evasions while his imagination runs rampant. He tells the child what he *ought* to do, and the child resists the menacing imperatives with imagination and love, not with the crippled indolence of the poet's later years. We know from Coleridge's writings on education the destructiveness he found in such authoritarian masters. The poet's own son will have a different teacher, God speaking through nature: the "lovely shapes and sounds intelligible / Of that eternal language, which thy God / Utters." The "Great universal Teacher" will not punish or usurp or issue dogmatic imperatives; rather he will, through the ministry of natural beauty, encourage a reciprocity of unrepressive giving, a reciprocity the child's father can never know. The child's imaginative spirit will be "moulded," integrated into a scene that makes its meanings intelligible in a transcendence of alienation.

The blessing the poet bestows on the babe, the almost ritualistic blessing of "This Lime-tree Bower my Prison" and "Dejection: An Ode," parallels the Mariner's blessing of the water-snakes. But here the blessing has the added element of a prophecy. The Mariner's freedom from the Albatross is temporary—the only perpetuity is that of the curse. In "Frost at Midnight," however, the poet sees a continuity of growth in time. The child's future will redeem the poet's past, his having been "reared / In the great city, pent 'mid cloisters dim. . . ." The sadness of the Coleridgean perspective clings to this poem too. It is *"thou,* my Babe!" more than the poet himself, who will be so fulfilled. The poet's fulfillment is in his power of prophecy itself, as if the "secret ministry of frost" has given him some of its magic. The prophecy is an imaginative act that creates not a "dome in air" or work of art but a future, indeed a *life*. This imaginative act is a moral one freely made, an identification of I with Thou as intense as the poet ever achieves. Yet even here he knows he is more in symbol than in substance the inheritor of new earth and new heaven. Having ushered both babe and reader into the beautiful scene, he absents himself.

The poem's structure has revealed exactly the paradox of an increased sense of self that is identical with a sense of community. The poet's attention at the beginning is on the external setting and the slightly eerie frost; by the poem's end the frost is simply beautiful, and it belongs to the infant. The movement inward is from the initial solitude amid the external setting to the poet's memory of his schoolroom, and then yet deeper to his memory of his childhood dreams. Those dreams and the stern preceptor who challenges them are pivotal. The moment of deepest personal exploration reveals both the threat of perversion and the imaginative longing, and it prompts the poet to begin his movement outward, stronger for having made the exploration. From a memory of a dream his consciousness reemerges into a primary memory: once again he recalls his own youth, but this time with the promise of redemption through his son, who will know "far other lore" than the great city that had trapped the poet. And finally his eye fastens once again on the external setting, the ministry of frost, now viewed, in the poet's imagination, by the son in some future moment. The Romantics' preoccupation with private ego has its well-known tendency toward claustrophobia and pride, but it contains as well this contrary promise. Only the self in possession of its own powers can give itself, the poet seems to say.

Appendix: A Note on Coleridge's Plagiarisms

The plagiarism issue does not rest with the interpretation I have made in Chapter 5 of its significance in the context of Coleridge's own moral thought. The question still remains whether Coleridge is so addicted to sources that his position in intellectual history is wholly compromised. Norman Fruman, in *Coleridge, The Damaged Archangel* (1971), presents an impressive consolidation of his plagiarisms. Though Fruman concentrates on many of those works in which plagiarisms have already been found out—*Biographia Literaria, Theory of Life, Shakespearean Criticism*—he extends disturbingly the range and implications of Coleridge's potentially most damning habit. It is the bulk of the evidence presented that makes this a book to contend with. Fruman thinks the academic profession, wishing not to disturb the literary hierarchy on which it relies, duly acknowledges evidence of plagiarisms and then brushes it aside. He ties the plagiarism problem to a larger portrait of the man—a man whose sense of his own inadequacies, from the intellectual to the sexual, is so strong that intellectual dependency is inveterate. His wish to be thought a *Wunderkind* combines with his fear that he is an impostor to produce a pattern of chronic intellectual theft and frequent accusations of theft brought against others.

Yet Fruman seems to back off from altogether dismissing Coleridge as thinker or poet, and he does not really bring up the question of what remains after the plagiarisms have been hacked out of the canon. Perhaps he thinks it so riddled with derivative material that such surgery would simply murder the patient. I suggest, though, that the question of what remains is an essential one.

Perhaps it is significant that I did not find the book very useful in a purely practical sense in my own study; the materials that I have presented here are not treated at any length by Fruman. He does not dwell on my main sources, the notebooks, letters, and MS B₂ of the Opus Maximum. And whatever Coleridge's dependency on Wordsworth for poetic material (a dependency that certainly works both ways), Fruman has not argued outright that *The Ancient Mariner, Christabel,* "Kubla Khan," and the conversation poems could be taken away from him. Apart from the poetry, the notebooks constitute the most exciting portion of the Coleridge canon. Kathleen Coburn's commentary is helpful in avoiding use of wholly derivative material, and one knows, with the help of her commentary, that the notebooks are made up of intense and, yes, often original reflection. Fruman presents a cogent discussion of the early Gutch Memorandum Notebook, which John Livingston Lowes had used in *The Road to Xanadu* (1927), in part to demonstrate the brilliance of Coleridge's associative powers. The jottings in this notebook are probably not free associations coming from the imaginative energies of the young poet, but are rather a mechanical copying down of passages from the Bible and elsewhere to be exploited later for purposes of poetry. But the great bulk of the notebooks, while much concerned with comment on other literary and philosophical works, is not of this order. One can agree in one respect with Fruman that Coleridge's canon has been shrinking continuously since the 1830s; but, paradoxically, with the publication still in progress of the notebooks, the Opus Maximum, and the marginalia (which alone will run to five volumes), the canon is expanding in another way even more rapidly. (See Thomas McFarland, "Coleridge's Plagiarisms Once More: A Review Essay," *Yale Review*, 63 [1974], 252–286, for an extensive look at the Fruman book; and by the same author, "The Originality Paradox," *New Literary History*, 5 [1974], 447–76. Walter Jackson Bate's *The Burden of the Past and the English Poet* [1970] and Harold Bloom's *The Anxiety of Influence* [1973] have already become classic texts on the ways the individual talent comes to terms with predecessors.)

It would be idle and dangerous to assume that none of the Coleridge material I have used in this book is lifted from sources that I have not yet identified. One can assume that some of it is so lifted or paraphrased. But we have seen so much material with the recognizable Coleridgean accent, writing that obviously comes from the pressure of intellectual perplexity and not from the intellectual insecurity of the would-be prodigy. One feels when reading Coleridge that discoveries are being made *through the act of* speaking and writing; he reveals to us the exploratory possibilities of language. I should think that any material exhibiting this intellectual and verbal excitement would qualify as "Coleridgean," even when the abstract content is reducible to some other system.

We have seen more, however, than rhetorical energy; there has also been close and comprehensive argument. Thomas McFarland begins his book, *Coleridge and the Pantheist Tradition* (1969), with an examination of the plagiarism problem. He presents a good history of the controversy from De Quincey's charge of plagiarism in *Tait's Edinburgh Magazine* of September, 1834, to just before publication of *The Damaged Archangel*. His argument, in brief, is that Coleridge as thinker is being taken to task for lack of originality, but that originality in philosophy is not something we demand when reading other philosophers. Coleridge may get his talk of "potence" from Schelling, but Schelling himself gets it from Bruno. A truly original idea is a rarity, McFarland reminds us. The more serious charge to be brought against Coleridge would be that of René Wellek, who accuses him of limp eclecticism, or, as McFarland puts it, a "failure of the reticulative function." Wellek charges that Coleridge does not distinguish between incompatible modes of thought. His "structure has here a storey from Kant, there a part of a room from Schelling, there a roof from Anglican theology and so on. The architect did not feel the clash of the styles, the subtle and irreconcilable differences between the Kantian first floor and the Anglican roof" (*Immanuel Kant in England*, 1931). McFarland demonstrates that Coleridge does make distinctions, and comes to see, for example, that Schelling's philosophy is in a radical way opposed to his own, in part because of what he sees to be its pantheistic implications.

Coleridge never creates a coherent philosophical structure or system, and to that extent Wellek's argument must retain its force; but he does exhibit in his moral thought sharp critical discrimination. We have seen him emerge as something more than a Kantian postscript, though Wellek dismisses his moral thought as not much more than a reiteration of Kantian categories. There is never such an outright rejection of Kantian moral philosophy that Coleridge, having fully absorbed the implications of his rejection, *then* applies himself to the task of shaping his own system. Indeed he is not a moral *philosopher* in that sense. Rather we find him thinking in some *direction* or other. He is always testing, reformulating, or rejecting the premises of both Kantian formalism and the rival British egoism, hedonism, and utilitarianism, in such a way that the moral orientation that results is his own. The heavy emphasis on self-realization makes up for what he sees to be the deficiencies of both systems; and while this emphasis certainly owes something to such other sources as Schiller, Fichte, and Schelling, it introduces into Britain a kind of moral thinking that is not seen again in the nineteenth century until Bradley, if then. The content of his self-realization theory remains challenging and even contemporary. Perhaps the word "original" still does not apply (it might not be honorific in any event), but a serious and discriminating mind has been at work here—one certainly damaged but able, even because of its receptiveness to other minds, to do its own thinking.

Index

Literary and philosophical works except Coleridge's own are listed under their authors' names.

Coleridge the Moralist

Designed by R. E. Rosenbaum.
Composed by York Composition Company, Inc.,
in 11 point Linotype Janson, 2 points leaded,
with display lines in Weiss Roman and Italic.
Printed letterpress from type by York Composition Company
on Warren's Number 66 text, 50 pound basis.
Bound by John H. Dekker & Sons, Inc.
in Joanna book cloth
and stamped in All Purpose foil.

Library of Congress Cataloging in Publication Data
(For library cataloging purposes only)

Lockridge, Laurence S   1942–
   Coleridge the moralist.

   Includes bibliographical references and index.
   1. Coleridge, Samuel Taylor, 1772–1834—Religion and ethics. I. Title.
PR4487.E8L6   821'.7   77–3120
ISBN 0-8014-1065-7